What
do you
say to a
hungry
world?

What do you say to a hungry world?

by W. Stanley Mooneyham

WORD BOOKS, Publisher
Waco, Texas

WHAT DO YOU SAY TO A HUNGRY WORLD?

Library of Congress catalog card number: 75–10086
Printed in the United States of America

Photographic credits:
Joost Guntenaar—Preface, Introduction,
            Chapters 2, 3, 4, 5, 7, 10, 12, 13,
            Notes
Eric Mooneyham—Part Titles,
            Chapters 1, 6, 11
    Dan Stearns—Chapter 9
Eric L. Wheater—Chapter 8

Scripture quotations from the Revised Standard Version (RSV) are copyright 1946 (renewed 1973), 1956 and © 1971 by the Division of Christian Education of the National Council of the Churches of Christ in the U.S.A., and are used by permission.

Quotations from *The New English Bible* (NEB), © The Delegates of The Oxford University Press and The Syndics of The Cambridge University Press, 1961, 1970, are used by permission.

Quotations from *The Living Bible, Paraphrased* (LB), published by Tyndale House Publishers, Wheaton, Illinois, 1971, are used by permission.

Quotations marked Phillips are from J. B. Phillips, *The New Testament in Modern English,* copyright 1958, 1960, 1972 by J. B. Phillips, published by The Macmillan Company.

The quotation from The New International Version of the New Testament is copyright © 1973 by the New York Bible Society International.

Quotations marked KJV are from The King James Version of the Bible.

A few portions of this book appeared previously in *World Vision* magazine.

To
Dushkal, Kallello, Jobeda
and so many more
whose lives are,
in the words of
Mahatma Gandhi,
an
"eternal compulsory fast"

Contents

7

CONTENTS

Acknowledgments

THIS BOOK, I think, is quite a bit like Topsy, the little slave girl in *Uncle Tom's Cabin*. When asked about her parents she maintained that she had neither father nor mother. Her solution to her existence was:

"I 'spect I grow'd."

What I mean is I can't remember the genesis of this book. Oh, I know the day I started writing and the day I finished—how well I know that one!—but it hardly seems right to name either of those as the birthdate since so much had already transpired before then. I think the seminal idea for the book was dropped into my consciousness about six years ago when I lived in Asia, and it's been growing ever since.

At any rate, I can remember vividly the final labor pains which lasted several months. They were real enough. To a team of fantastic people who gave invaluable help at that agonizing stage, I owe an enormous debt of gratitude which I shall try now partially to repay.

Notable in that list is William Needham, a colleague at World Vision who heads the Research and Information Department. Not only did he coordinate the work of the research team, but made significant suggestions about the subjects which should be treated and was my almost daily counselor and advisor. In any birth announcement, he certainly would

9

have to be listed as the attending physician. And mention should be made of three very helpful young ladies in his department, Ellen Gilbert, Susan Bauer and Donna Burns.

Another colleague, Robert Larson, agreed to stop China-watching from Hong Kong long enough to travel with me and write and record hundreds of pages of notes and interviews. All he got for it was writer's cramp and mention here, but his contribution was vastly more valuable than any note like this can ever indicate.

The library research—involving incalculable hours—which must go into a volume like this was handled by Mary Tregenza, a truly dedicated craftsman (craftsperson?), whose ability to sort out the irrelevant and keep the nuggets made the final job a lot easier. Being a competent writer herself, she knew what would be maximally helpful.

How could I have done it without the assistance of the genial Scotsman, scholar and author, and my long-time friend, Dr. J. D. Douglas? The answer is I couldn't—although Jim will blush with characteristic modesty when I say it. Nonetheless, his biblical and historical research have provided a dimension too often missing in books on this subject.

The enriching photographs are the talented work of two very creative people who traveled around the hunger belt with me. One is Joost Guntenaar, a smiling Hollander whom I first met in Amsterdam. I call him "young Rembrandt with a camera," and his work has appeared in *Time* magazine as well as numerous European journals. The other is my son, Eric, whose sensitive heart frequently sees more through the camera's lens than I see with my two eyes.

Finally, I am warmly grateful to my two secretaries who tied off the umbilical cord with typewriter ribbon and presented the publisher with a polished manuscript. Nancy Moyer and Cynthia Chance are not only God-gifted, but also God's gifts.

I thank them all. I am sure that without them the book—whether it was born or just "grow'd"—would never have seen life.

Preface

TELEVISION COMMENTATOR John Chancellor said not long ago at the conclusion of an NBC White Paper on the world food problem, "If the world is not fed, it will be a different and more dangerous world."

Daily headlines chronicle the deteriorating situation:

National Observer, March 30, 1974: "The Next Crisis: Universal Famine."

New York Times, August 21, 1974: "Expert Says World has 27 Days' Food."

Honolulu Advertiser, October 24, 1974: "On The Road to Famine."

Times of India, October 8, 1974: "FAO Chief Warns of Big Human Disaster."

Ethiopian Herald, October 2, 1974: "Drought, Famine Will Overtake the World."

Los Angeles Times, October 9, 1974: "One Billion Face Not Deprivation but Death."

The doomsayers are not wild-eyed, hair-shirted prophets. They are responsible, respected scientists. The principal architect of the "green revolution" and president emeritus of the Rockefeller Foundation, Dr. J. George Harrar, soberly admits: "I'm scared. We could have a lot of starvation by 1980. It is unrealistic to think that this could not happen."

11

Newsweek quotes a worried U.N. official: "The food problem today is probably the most serious one in the world's history. It now quite literally threatens the survival of hundreds of millions of human beings around the world." [1]

An assessment of the world food situation by the U.S. State Department, a sober bureaucracy not given to exaggerated statements, concludes: "it is doubtful whether such a critical food situation has ever been so worldwide."

But the food crisis does not stand in isolation from the rest of the world's problems. If we were dealing with just an agricultural shortfall, the solution would be relatively simple. But add changing climatic conditions and you complicate the problem. Link it with an uncontrolled world population—as you certainly must—and you further intensify the dilemma.

Now compound it by introducing ecological factors plus deficiency of medical services, inadequate educational programs, discriminatory distribution systems, global economic inequity and repressive political regimes—add these and you've got an apocalyptic situation.

Which is right where we are.

And some of my friends would suggest—even insist—that I stop right there. Their reasoning is something like this: Since the situation seems obviously beyond solution, and since the apocalyptic nature of our times indicates that the return of Jesus Christ is near, and since the wrongs of this world can be made right only by the establishment of his kingdom, there is no need to do anything about the human crisis, so let's concentrate on "eternal" things.

I suggest—rather, insist—this is a cop-out and differs from the "lifeboat ethic" espoused by some secularists only in approach. (It is called an ethic, but to me it sounds like callous elitism.) It goes something like this: The function of a lifeboat is to save lives in case of a disaster. Each country is like a lifeboat and some of them have their support systems taxed almost to capacity. When the boat is full, the fortunate ones on board are faced with the terrible task of pushing away the others, who are doomed to drown.

The end result of both views is the same—millions of human beings are consigned to die. Of course, the Christian might do something which the secularist wouldn't. He would likely put a tract in each outstretched hand.

I reject both approaches. The first because I am a humanitarian; the second because I am a Christian.

I have accepted my dual citizenship—earthly and heavenly. The earthly was not negated when I took on the heavenly. Rather, for me, the second enhanced the first. The nearer I come to the true person of Jesus Christ, the closer I feel to suffering humanity. Or is it vice versa? I haven't got that part sorted out yet. I only know that one day I saw people as whole persons, not just disembodied souls, and my view of man was perceptibly heightened.

Believing that God is for man (does that make God a humanitarian, too?), I know I must care about man in his hungry suffering and oppressed physical condition as well as his alienated and lost spiritual state. That makes it impossible for me to limit my concern to man's spiritual needs while ignoring his other problems.

At the same time, my Christian conscience will not permit me to accept as a viable alternative the "full lifeboat" theory. I am not a Pollyanna about the situation. I know the hard choices which face us all. I just happen to believe that if those in the lifeboat adopt a policy which cynically denies a place to those who are unfortunate enough to be born too late, it will no longer be a lifeboat but a floating insane asylum in which I would not feel very much at home.

I refuse to opt out without a struggle.

Even though one man is not required to do everything, I firmly believe each of us is responsible to do what he can. I know I cannot feed the whole world, heal every sick child, liberate every oppressed person. I accept this as my human limitation even though it frustrates me. But I know I can help some people as I tackle the problems common to all. I know others can do the same, and I am optimistic that if enough of us act responsibly and decisively we can make a difference, and the difference might be just enough to turn the tide.

This book is one man's attempt to grapple with some of the problems. If this effort has any unique contribution to make on a subject about which a great deal is being written, it will be

its moral and ethical approach to the use and misuse of resources, to our view of persons, and to the problems of food
production, distribution and consumption.

Most authors whom I have read generally agree that the
basic issues of hunger are moral and ethical. But many of them
seem to have no apparent belief in absolute values, so they
avoid or ignore answers which suggest moral and ethical
absolutes. While they brilliantly diagnose and analyze the
crisis, their prescriptions are, for the most part, sociological
placebos which cannot reach the root of the problem—man's
alienation from God and his resulting alienation from his fellow man and his environment.

I do not mean to suggest that this volume will provide total
answers or easy answers. There are no easy answers and the
total answer is beyond the scope of any one person's effort. It
would be egotism and folly to think otherwise. Rather, I hope
we may point a direction which leads around and beyond Pil-
grim's "Slough of Despond" where so many contemporary
thinkers on the subject seem to wind up.

Let me introduce you to this book and its objectives. There
are some things I hope it will achieve as one man's contribution
to the total answer.

First, I hope it will help demythologize the hunger issue. I
am amazed at the number of popular myths which, so recently
arisen, are so authoritatively repeated. I heard one again just
the other night around a dinner table. I was eating with a
group of well-read, informed and distinguished friends.
Leaders all.

Just that day I had returned from an in-depth survey trip
around the hunger belt, gathering data for this book. It had
taken me to eighteen of the hardest-hit countries in Asia, Africa
and Latin America. Everything I had heard, seen and experienced had convinced me the world can be fed. Yet one of my
friends stated a popularly held misconception with such finality
that it almost defied challenge:

"It is impossible to produce enough food to feed the present
world population, much less any increase!"

Just as I was about to protest, jet lag hit me and I let the
statement pass simply because I didn't feel like refuting it.

But let me do so now. That is a myth.

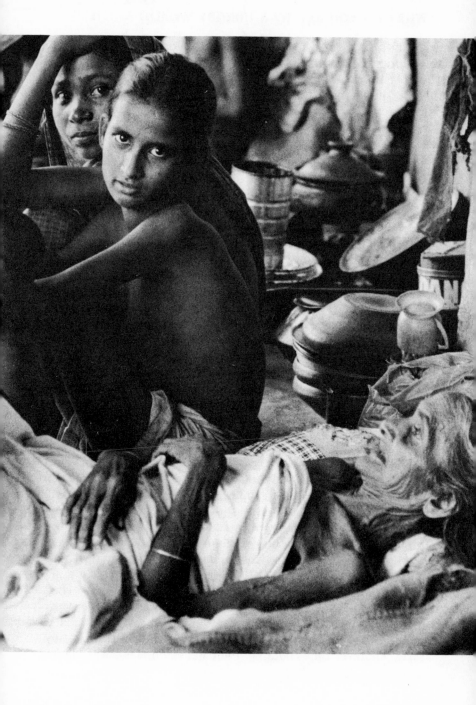

And it is a very convenient myth because it allows us to do nothing and still have a clear conscience. I am not saying it will be an easy thing to feed the world. I am only saying that it is not impossible. And I am not alone in that view. A British agronomist says that on existing diets worldwide the world could feed about 40 billion people—ten times the present population—if it really put its mind to it.

It would mean no golf courses, and I for one would deplore that loss. But it can be done. That is my point.

Roger Revelle, a director of the Center for Population Studies at Harvard University and president of the American Association for the Advancement of Science, argues persuasively for an even higher figure with an even better diet. He says 50 to 60 billion people, and up to twice that number if the diet is reduced to subsistence levels.

More about that later.

You ask what is missing? The will—and the money. But the money is there if we had the will. It was there when we decided to go to the moon. That, too, was "impossible." The job took us ten or twelve years and some $50 billion, but we did it because the will was there.

And in the doing of it, incidentally, developed a whole new technology which we are presently enjoying as spin-off benefits in everything from medicine to food preservation.

We don't need a drastic new technology to feed the world. We have virtually everything we need except the determination to apply it. The solution to the problem is far more political than it is technological. It could require the changing of some of our systems and the scrapping of others, but I view that as no great tragedy. There is nothing sacrosanct about the systems. Indeed, some of them are so deeply at the heart of the problem that they *must* go if humanity is to be served.

Myth number two: "The starving masses are going to revolt!"

Don't you believe it. They should—but they won't. They can't. How do you mount a revolution when you are too weak to get off your cot? I used to have waking nightmares of emaciated, hunger-mad creatures crawling over the earth taking by force whatever they could lay their hands on. That was before

I saw them in the refugee camps and at the feeding stations. Now I know it won't happen. Not that way.

I am not saying that it won't happen at all. Not for one moment do I rule out a revolution by the have-nots. And the Communists won't have to organize it. But if it comes, it will be led by deprived workers, students and farmers in the lesser-developed countries who have just begun to taste the firstfruits of affluence and want the rest of the harvest immediately.

That's one thing television does for us. It not only brings the hungry masses into our living rooms—it takes our living rooms and our dining rooms to them. This is the way it was when America's ghettos rioted in the late sixties. Deny the hopes and dreams of a people when their expectations have reached a fever high, and you've got a pressure cooker that inevitably will blow a gasket.

Latin America is such a pressure cooker. A student in Colombia told me: "This government is our country's last chance. If it does not deal with the social problems of the people, we will have anarchy. I do not want it, but that is what we will have."

What a different thing I found in the huts and camps of the starving. I remember Jobéda who was sitting in the shade of a tattered lean-to in a refugee camp in Dacca. A small withered form lying close beside her whimpered and stirred. Instinctively, she reached down to brush away the flies. Her hand carefully wiped the fevered face of her child. At six years of age, acute malnutrition had crippled his legs, left him dumb, and robbed him of his hearing. All that was left was the shallow, labored breathing of life itself—that, too, would soon be gone.

But death is no stranger to Jobeda. She has seen starvation take away her husband and five of her seven children. And now, with her sixth child near death, there was still no anger, no bitterness. As long as I live I will never forget her calm resignation as she said, "Look at the parents who have no children at all. I, at least, have two of mine. How can I be bitter?"

I wanted her to scream out against the misfortunes of her sad life, to blame nature, God, or even me for the famine which had robbed her of family and hope. I somehow thought the agony of listening to her cries might help expiate my own feelings of guilt. But I have seen a universal phenomenon which haunts me day and night, and it is this: The hungry and starving go to their graves in eerie silence. With no strength left for living, they cannot utter even a feeble protest over the inequities and injustices in our world, much less start a revolution.

They can only die.

A third myth—one which I wish were true—is that the United States is a generous country. Don't misunderstand me. We do have many generous people in our country. I know that better than most, because every day our organization gets letters and contributions from people who are making sacrifices to help the rest of the world—retired people on social security, children who give their allowances, college students who send their spending money, young families who do without conveniences and even necessities to share with the hungry. Many times I am overwhelmed by the generosity of such people.

Because the heart of America is still large and generous, most Americans would be surprised to find out how little goes from our government in actual grant assistance to the poor countries.

"But," someone protests, "what about all those millions that Congress appropriates for foreign aid?"

Foreign aid may be the biggest misnomer since an unnamed general had his army "advance to the rear" instead of retreating.

Let's look at the record. It has not always been as shabby as it is today.

In 1949, during the Marshall Plan period, $8 billion was approved for economic aid. This represented 2.8 percent of the gross national product for that year. In 1975 economic aid totals $1.4 billion—down from $1.7 billion in 1973—and this represents .25 percent of our gross national product!

Not only have the totals and ratios been drastically revised downward, but—even more critically—what they represent has also been changed. We have kept the same terminology

but changed the content of the words. This is why so many
Americans are fooled about "foreign aid."

The term is applied to any form of capital invested outside
the country, whether grants, loans, goods, services or whatever.

Gunnar Myrdal quotes a former head of the Agency for International Development (AID) who told a presidential committee: "The biggest single misconception about the foreign
aid program is that we send money abroad. We don't. Foreign
aid consists of American equipment, raw materials, expert
services, and food—all provided for specific development projects. . . . Ninety-three percent of AID funds are spent directly
in the United States to pay for these things. Just last year
[1967] some 4,000 American firms in 50 states received $1.3
billion in AID funds for products supplied as part of the foreign
aid program." [2]

Much of the money appropriated by Congress for foreign aid
is used to buy and ship American goods which many countries
do not need, to pay for American-exported expertise which
many countries do not want, and to make available to the poor
countries American industrial technology which most of them
cannot absorb.

If you subtract loans and military hardware from the total,
there isn't much left which fits the term. That may be why
foreign aid has fallen into such disrepute with both Congress
and the people. It is, in large part, self-interest flying under the
false colors of generosity and altruism.

I find myself agreeing with Julius Nyerere, president of
Tanzania, who said in a speech in New Zealand in 1974: "I
believe the term 'Aid' should only be used when there is a real
transfer of resources to the poor, for the purpose of raising
living standards and narrowing the gap between the poor and
rich nations." [3]

If this volume can help demythologize our popular understanding of both hunger and assistance, maybe then as a
nation and a people we can begin to deal with the issues as
they really are, not as we romanticize them to be.

There is something else I hope this book will do—emotional-
ize the hunger issue for you. I know that has dangers. A
bleeding heart's credibility can suffer from dramatizing issues

about which we prefer to read tables of statistics. It is a lot easier emotionally to handle the fact that millions of people are starving if we don't see them as individuals. If we can consign them to be a part of a gigantic, impersonal, global problem, then we don't have to feel the hurt and pain of their condition.

One person said, "When I think of hunger it's like when I think of death. I detach myself from it. I use picture words, not feeling words, because I haven't been in that situation." Another commented: "We don't use feeling words because it might hurt too bad to feel." [4]

But until we feel we are not going to act, and I am, quite frankly, hoping to move you to action.

While this book was in preparation, the Central Committee of the World Council of Churches met in Berlin. A staff member was telling me about one of the sessions in which the world food crisis was presented. It was a depressing and pessimistic report. There seemed to be no human answers to the problem. Human inadequacy and the need for God's help were keenly felt.

The chairman called for a time of prayer. It was a moving moment. However, my friend said that some of his German colleagues complained to him that the whole experience was "too emotional" for them.

Why, in the name of heaven, shouldn't we be emotional about suffering and death? Hunger and starvation are not only physiological experiences which cause the bodily functions to cease. Starvation is emotional!

I am still pained when I remember little Dushkal. She was born in a mission hospital in India. The mother died in childbirth; the father had died from typhoid a week earlier. The nurses called her Dushkal, which means "famine."

Her mother, who was nineteen, did not starve to death because, the doctor says with a trace of sarcasm, "starvation" is not a medical term. She died because she couldn't resist tetanus which infected her while she squatted in the heat, her hands lacerated from breaking stones with her crude little hammer for about twenty-one cents a day.

Dushkal has a fifty-fifty chance of surviving, according to a doctor, but it probably won't be much of a life for her, even if she does.

"The problem is," the doctor says, "she grew from a fetus in a sick, exhausted, starved body and we cannot predict the effects of that."

In "The Cry of the Children," Elizabeth Barrett Browning writes movingly.

> Do ye hear the children weeping, O my brothers . . . ?
> .   .   .   .
> . . . the young, young children, O my brothers,
>   They are weeping bitterly!
> They are weeping in the playtime of the others. [5]

I have heard them. Sometimes now I can still hear their cries.

I have looked into the face of hunger and out of the data bank of my memory my mind can still retrieve some of those faces. And when it does, I do not sleep well. Or eat comfortably. In this book I want you to see some of the faces which have emotionalized the issue for me.

Don't be afraid of emotion so long as it's honest.

Colin Morris has something very important to say about the impersonality of our world: "I saw a starving man and there was no gnawing pain in my belly. I saw a hunchback and my own back did not ache. I watched a pathetic procession of refugees, being herded back and forth sleeplessly, and I slept well that night. The theologians call it Identification and it is worth fifty pages in a reputable text book. It is easier to read the fifty pages than to feel one pang." [6]

Both for your sake and the world's, I hope you will allow yourself to feel as you read. Feeling will lead to identification and it is here that creative compassion begins.

There is a third objective toward which I hope this volume will make a contribution. We all need to be sensitized to the huge economic gap separating "us" from the "rest of the world," to the crisis nature of the situation, and to the necessity of re-evaluating our own life styles.

Television and newspapers are already making a contribution toward sensitizing the American conscience to waste and overconsumption. It is hard to get up from watching the evening news where you have seen the desperate need in famine areas, go to your dinner table and gorge yourself. Possible, but hard.

Our family is becoming a sensitized family, each reminding and admonishing the others about unnecessary consumption and especially waste. That growing sensitivity is largely the result of a continuing exposure to world need.

Just after I returned from a recent trip around the hunger belt, I was speaking in the San Francisco area and had to eat out for Sunday lunch. I ordered chicken and dressing, and the waitress brought me a plate heaped with the entrée plus all the trimmings. It was at least twice as much as I could comfortably eat. As I looked at it for a moment, remembering how many were slowly starving in the areas from which I had just come and realizing how much food would be thrown away from that one plate, my appetite vanished. Sensing that something wasn't right, the waitress asked me what was wrong.

I tried to explain, but I couldn't blame her for not being able to understand. She offered me a doggie bag!

Our luxury diets are not only wasteful, but downright unhealthy. If we can become sensitive enough about a calorie-deficient world to bring our average 3,300 calorie intake down to a healthy 2,400 calories a day, we will find that in addition to gaining an easier conscience, we will be healthier, feel better and live longer.

But we do have a choice. It is this: Change our life styles a little or watch millions die of starvation on our living room television sets.

And if that choice doesn't increase our sensitivity by several degrees, let's remember this warning from Father Theodore Hesburgh of Notre Dame: "One of these days, they [the 900 million poorest] are going to start walking west, saying, 'You've got a house and we're going to help you live in it; you've got food and we're going to help you eat it.' " [7]

I don't think the Western world has yet realized the seriousness of the situation. Either that or we are deceiving ourselves like the party-goers on the *Titanic* who kept telling each other the ship could not possibly sink.

Reflect on this bit of cop-out copy which was printed in the program of a style show given by the Chicago Wash Dress and Apparel Association in the spring of 1958:

While the world is still in turmoil, while the possibility of a third world war still gnaws at the roots of peace, there is a swing to gayety. Most people feel that they are helpless as individuals to influence or alter the course of the world events. In their helplessness they have decided to let the statesmen worry over world problems and have turned for escape to personal enjoyment, for one last fling, perhaps, before the dark curtain comes down again. Let us hope they are wrong. In the meantime, let's sell them wash apparel.

Unbelievable! The world may be on the brink of catastrophe, but let's keep on pretending! We are far past the business-as-usual stage. This much is for sure: our life styles will change. Either we voluntarily alter them to fit the world's realities or they will be changed by violence or drastic legislation. If we are sensitive to the inequities which exist in our world and not merely to the danger but also to the sin of perpetuating them, we can make a start toward righting the wrongs before it is too late.

Finally, it is my hope that this book may help tens of thousands get mobilized for action. Individual response is good and necessary; collective response is better and more productive. The problem is of such magnitude that it will require the mobilization of communities, churches, Scout troops, business associations, women's societies, civic clubs, student groups, trade unions, national and international bodies. Our efforts must indicate how seriously we view the task. We must act as if we are preparing for war, for that is what it is—not to destroy mankind, but to save it.

Surely for that noble effort we can all become allies.

Writing in the August 1967 issue of *Pace* magazine, Robin Hoar correctly says: "The war on hunger may offer the new brand of social involvement this generation will take to heart as its own. The truth is, this crisis demands far closer cooperation among all people than anything in history, even the fear of atomic war. . . . It may compel us to live greater than we otherwise would."

The picture is not all dark. I personally know of scores of successful programs to help the world feed itself. Thousands of people are already committed not only to make changes in their own life styles, but to become agents of change in their organizations, their churches, their communities and the world. Taken singly, their efforts may seem small and insignificant. But it is the weight of collective efforts of individuals impacting on the problem that produces most substantive change.

If some of our suggested courses of action seem useless and futile before the immensity of the task, I hope you will remember that.

I am under no illusions about what it will take to solve the hunger problem. I just happen to believe with Arnold Toynbee that this generation has the chance to be remembered as "the first . . . since the dawn of history in which mankind dared to believe it is practical to make the benefits of civilization available to the whole human race."

There is no question that it is practical. If 6 percent of the world's people in a place called North America can have these benefits, why not the rest?

I like what Dr. Georg A. Borgstrom, professor of food science and geography at Michigan State University and author of *The Hungry Planet,* said not long ago in an address: "I would argue that the hunger crisis reflects man's inability to imagine what he already knows. We are participating in a grand-scale evasion of reality which bears all the signs of insanity. In order to bring health and restore vitality to the whole human species, *nothing less* is required than a global will to act, simple justice, true population control, worldwide food planning, effective execution . . . and a massive commitment of funds." [8]

And may I remind Dr. Borgstrom and us all: *Nothing more* than that is required, either. All that is needed is available to us.

President John F. Kennedy echoed those words in his own cogent way: "We have the ability, we have the means, and we have the capacity to eliminate hunger from the face of the earth. We need only the will."

If this volume contributes in even the smallest way to a strengthening of that will, to putting muscle into our resolve, I will feel amply rewarded.

And, more importantly, the world will be fed.

Introduction
ON BEGINNING A CRUSADE

IT ISN'T ONE WORLD ANYMORE.

Probably it never was, except in fantasy.

From certain perspectives it may look like one world. Remember your reaction to that spectacular first television picture of the world beamed from the Apollo spacecraft two hundred thousand miles away? Suspended in the inky blackness was our Earth, painted in azure and overlaid with brush-strokes of clouds, dazzling our eyes with what seemed to be its pristine beauty.

It was almost too pretty, and you probably said, "It looks unreal."

You were right. It is.

From that distance the world looked whole. The fractures didn't show. From the moon it's hard to see the world's broken and hurting realities.

But it is also possible to ignore them from a lesser distance. Just an ocean away. Or a city block. Especially if you live in an affluent global subdivision which has been psychologically fenced and screened against the disturbing sight of starved, emaciated bodies and lulled with Muzak to cover the cries of hungry children. Thus snug in our cocoon of self-imposed and unreal isolation we can pretend that it is still "one world"—if, indeed, it ever was.

The truth is our world is divided, and all the divisions are not geographical. Man has learned to handle separation by space. Challenged always to explore what he could not see, he made machines to cross oceans, span inhospitable deserts and conquer mountain ranges. He made the world into a global village.

But we have not dealt with the real divisions. Those that are not geographical. Those that have created on this planet two worlds so different—so totally different—that until you have seen them you find it hard to believe they can exist among a race of people who were made from "one forefather . . . to live over the face of the whole earth." [1]

Two worlds? At the very least, two. Simply stated, they are the worlds of the rich and the poor. The haves and the have-nots. The world of need and the world of plenty. The hungry and the full. In some places these worlds exist side by side on the same continents. In other places they may be—literally and figuratively—a world away.

Some people say there are three worlds. The free world. The Communist world. And the more-or-less nonaligned nations— generally referred to as "the developing countries"—the Third World. Let us agree that, with all their imprecision, these categories do make for convenient designations.

(It should be noted here that "developing" is generally used as a euphemism for "underdeveloped" since it is a less offensive term. On the other hand, those in the LDCs [lesser-developed countries] could—and do—argue with no little validity that they are not as much *underdeveloped* as Western nations are *overdeveloped*. An interesting thought which we will pursue later.)

There are others, however, who insist there are four worlds —the three described above, but with the Third World being further divided into Third and Fourth Worlds. In some ways this is more precise and definitive because it allows us to recognize that the LDCs are in differing stages of development. Venezuela and Colombia, for example, would both qualify for the Third World designation, but with Venezuela's new oil millions, that country would be several rungs above Colombia on the economic ladder.

The Fourth World has been defined by British economist Barbara Ward as "the one that is about to fall off the edge of the global economy." It is composed of about forty nations. It contains about one-fourth of the world's population. And those one billion people are trying to exist on an average of twenty-seven cents a day.

Compare that with your own economic situation at this moment. Even if you are so poor that you are reading a borrowed copy of this book, you are not *that* poor. Poverty is relative but total poverty is absolute, and total poverty is the only term that adequately describes masses of people in the Fourth World.

But it isn't crucial whether the figure is two, three or four. What is important for us to know—really know—is that racial, ethnic and geographical divisions take second place to the gulf that separates our world of plenty from their world of need.

And it is important—no, vital—that we care. Caring is the crux of the matter. Knowledge will not produce change. It won't make any difference for you to know that ten thousand people die every day from starvation and diseases related to malnourishment unless you care. And it is scant comfort to the world's children for you to know that malnourishment in the early years of their lives is likely to produce irreversible brain damage, unless you care enough to do something about it.

Knowledge can motivate, but action is born out of caring. And there are some strong reasons why you and I should care.

Some are selfish reasons. If we care about future generations we had better consider how long the rest of the world will sit quietly by and allow their hunger to support our wasteful life styles. Hunger, in its prestarvation stages, is a powerful stimulus and motivator. It produces violence in the nonviolent.

In 1970, hungry peasants in Northeast Brazil organized Robin Hood-type gangs to attack trucks and trains in search of food. A thirty-nine-year-old hunter and sharecropper, Ze Bezerra, tells how it was: "No one in my house had eaten for three days. Others were in even worse condition. Everyone knew that the trucks passing on the road and the freight trains that passed at night were carrying food. Finally it was the only thing we could do. We might die of disgrace but not of hunger. If somebody dies of hunger, it is because he doesn't want to eat." [2]

You don't have to agree with his philosophy, but you'll do yourself no favor to ignore his feelings. Seneca once said, "A hungry people listens not to reason, nor cares for justice, nor is bent by any prayers."

And Virgil, in a Latin proverb (*Malesuada famēs*), speaks of "hunger that persuades to evil." Which reminds me of a long and stimulating conversation one rainy night in Bogotá with Father Gerard Rosier, professor of social psychology at Colombia's National University. In speaking of the desperate need in the *barrios* surrounding the city, Father Rosier said that the streets of Bogotá would never be safe as long as there were hungry people in those barrios. He called this kind of crime *delincuencia provocada,* or provoked delinquency.

Obviously there are other kinds of crime and obviously not all crime is caused by hunger. But the point I want to make is that hunger sometimes causes people to do things they would never consider if their stomachs didn't ache, and that our continued national well-being is one good reason for caring about hungry people.

There are other reasons, too, and some of them are better. At least the motivation is higher. Like compassion.

While it is not exclusively a Christian virtue, I believe it finds its highest expression in the Judaeo-Christian ethic. Ancient Israel had a great tradition of concern for the underprivileged and needy. In fact, so much was the practice of charity considered a bounden duty that one of Job's friends suggested that Job's sufferings were due to his failure just there: "You must have refused water to the thirsty, and bread to the starving." [3]

In his stout defense Job invites God's judgment upon himself if he practiced inequality, failed to provide for the poor and the widow, if he did not share his food with the fatherless, if he did not clothe the destitute, or if he put his trust in riches. [4]

Jews were exhorted not to live in any city which had no alms box, for almsgiving was of paramount importance—so much so, that "righteousness" and "almsgiving" came to be interchangeable terms. Blessedness meant sharing actively in the misfortunes of others.

But where else does one find both teaching and example of compassion so perfectly combined than in the person of Jesus Christ? His very coming was the highest demonstration of love that acts, and those who would truly follow him will find his ways frequently lead into situations where the only appropriate response will be compassionate acts done in his name. This was the hallmark of the early Christians.

During his three-year reign as emperor in the fourth century, Julian the Apostate tried to restore the polytheism of Rome's earlier days and to undermine the position of Christianity, but he was unable to ignore the Christians' works of love. Indeed, in urging his government officials to charitable works, he said: "We ought to be ashamed. Not a beggar is to be found among the Jews, and those godless Galileans [the Christians] feed not only their own people but ours as well, whereas our people receive no assistance whatever from us."

Now perhaps it is the Christians who ought to be ashamed. The church which bears the name of the Man who lived for others is more and more living for itself. In 1971–72, sixty-three church denominations in the United States and Canada reported contributions in excess of $4.5 billion. About $1 billion of that was spent on new church buildings, while less than half of that amount was invested in foreign missions and all overseas ministries. There is no way to know how little of that went into programs that would relieve the sufferings of humanity.

There is something unbelievably immoral about Christians who still demand to be convinced of the biblical mandate for what is called "active involvement in the world hunger crisis" (our own convenient euphemism for millions of individuals who are starving to death one by one). Their question was put and answered long ago: "Lord, when did we ever see you hungry or thirsty or a stranger or naked or sick or in prison, and not help you?"

Jesus doesn't beat around the bush: "When you refused to help the least of these my brothers, you were refusing help to me." [5]

While the world goes through its greatest food crisis in

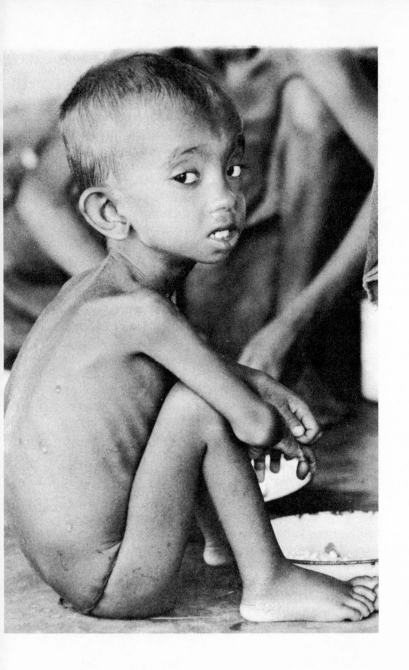

history, the church shows a great capacity for diversion and
not a little for self-deception. It is reported that on the eve
of the Bolshevik Revolution two conferences were held in
hotels on the same Moscow street. One was sponsored by the
Orthodox Church: the principal item on the agenda was vestments for the clergy. In the other meeting, Lenin and his
friends drew up final plans to overthrow the czarist regime.
Let the church take care! A church preoccupied with triviali-
ties soon becomes blind to the basic needs of the age.

I think you might like to read something written by Colin
Morris. He is general secretary of the Methodist Missionary
Society in London, formerly a missionary in Zambia. Like
many of us he was in a comfortable rut, finding the status
quo eminently satisfying. Then one day he was slapped so
hard by reality that it turned his whole value system upside
down and inside out.

Let him take up his own story in his pungent little book,
Include Me Out!:

The other day a Zambian dropped dead not a hundred yards
from my front door. The pathologist said he'd died of hunger.
In his shrunken stomach were a few leaves and what appeared
to be a ball of grass. And nothing else.

That same day saw the arrival of my *Methodist Recorder*, an
issue whose columns were electric with indignation, consternation, fever and fret at the postponement of the final Report of
the Anglican-Methodist Unity Commission. . . .

It took an ugly little man with a shrunken belly, whose total
possessions, according to the police, were a pair of shorts, a
ragged shirt and an empty Biro pen, to show me that this whole
Union affair is the great Non-Event of recent British Church
history.

For the first time I was able to see out of another's eyes. And
through that pair of dead eyes all our organization of ecclesiastical structures had the aspect of a man spending ten years of
his life building a model of Blackpool Tower from a million
matchsticks. . . .

That magnificent grotesque structure has value for him. He
has gone on, through hail and sun and snow and sleet, sticking
those little bits of wood together. It is both a genuine labour of
love and a classical example of Marxist economics—its sole
value lies in the labour that has been invested in it. But it is

not worth a fiver at the nearest pawn shop, because the world doesn't happen to be perishing for lack of matchstick models of the Blackpool Tower.[6]

But the world is perishing for bread, and we mount a multitude of crusades against less crucial issues—school textbooks, X-rated movies, fluoridation of water, the Revised Standard Version, mini-skirts and *Jesus Christ Superstar*. You might note these require an expenditure of energy which only the well-fed can afford.

Somehow I can't imagine my Ethiopian friend, Kallello Nugusu, feeling very strongly about any of those things. Not long ago we were sitting outside his little stick-and-mud shack ten miles from the nearest road. The previous year an estimated hundred thousand people in his country had died from the famine. Kallello and his family survived, but it was very rough. He had to sell his two oxen to buy food to keep his wife and six children alive. Without oxen he could not plow his fields or plant his crops, and now his food was gone.

I asked him what he would do. He didn't know, but I can still feel the depth of that moment when he dropped his head into his hands and told me, "When my children cry because they are hungry, then it is very hard to be a father."

I think I know a little bit about what Colin Morris is saying. After talking with people who expect to be dead from starvation within a few weeks, some things just aren't important anymore. So I hope you'll excuse me from the other crusades. I just can't seem to get worked up over the issues.

But I would like to join a crusade. Or start one.

It would be on behalf of those who cannot mount their own. Those whom the Bengali poet, Rabindranath Tagore, described as "eternal tenants in an extortionate world, having nothing of their own." Those to whom, if I may speak a pun to make a point, hunger is the gut issue.

It is a crusade on behalf of the voiceless millions for whom . . .

. . . life is short
. . . hunger is daily
. . . disease is rampant
. . . infant mortality is outrageous

. . . life expectancy is low
. . . illiteracy is widespread
. . . unemployment is endemic
. . . economy is subsistence
. . . opportunity is restricted
. . . hope is in short supply.

It is a crusade for earth's starving and malnourished who, facing the end without ever knowing a beginning, pose this searching question: "Is there life before death?"

It is a crusade which arises out of my deepest Christian convictions, although for humanity's sake I am not going to quibble over motivation. Personally, I embrace this view of Dietrich Bonhoeffer: "To allow the hungry man to remain hungry would be blasphemy against God and one's neighbour, for what is nearest to God is precisely the need of one's neighbour. It is for the love of Christ, which belongs as much to the hungry man as to myself, that I share my bread with him and that I share my dwelling with the homeless. If the hungry man does not attain to faith, then the fault falls on those who refused him bread. To provide the hungry man with bread is to prepare the way for the coming of grace." [7]

I cannot separate proclamation and presence in Christian witness. While they are not the same, they are like the two wings of a bird—one without the other is so impotent as to be virtually useless.

Or, as Rabelais so succinctly put it: "Hungry bellies have no ears."

So if you believe, as the Chinese say, "Of all the precious things, human life is the most precious," then come and join my crusade.

Or, if you can show me that it will do more to feed a hungry world, I'll join yours.

Whichever it is, I've got to get started.

PART ONE

CONTEXTS
OF HUNGER

Chapter 1
Poverty: Hunger at the Edge of Hell

$\mathbf{A}$LL THE TIME I WAS TALKING with Mrs. Epefania Alarin, I kept wishing that the editorial writer for Manila's *Bulletin Today* were with me. In that day's issue he had written about "Nations in Need." Admitting that the Philippines had the same kind of serious economic problems which afflicted all developing nations, he went on to say rightly that "here, starvation has not become a threat."

But then he added: "There is malnutrition, to be sure, but this is, to our mind, largely a matter of making the people aware of what constitutes a good diet."

On the first count, he was right. Malnutrition, especially among children, is endemic, with government surveys showing an incidence as high as 80 percent in many areas. On the second count, he was dead wrong. Mrs. Alarin could have told him. For tens of thousands of families in the Philippines and for millions all over the world, the right diet is not a matter of awareness, but of cold, hard cash.

Or as the U.N. "Assessment of the World Food Situation" puts it, "the causes of inadequate nutrition are many and closely interrelated; including ecological, sanitary and cultural constraints, but the principal cause is poverty."

Poverty is the knockout punch in an uneven encounter. It

leaves them flat on their backs—or, at the very least, too demoralized to fight back.

If World Bank President Robert McNamara had met Mrs. Alarin, she would have undoubtedly been in his mind when he said: "two-thirds of mankind—two billion individuals—remain entrapped in a cruel web of circumstances that severely limits their right to the necessities of life. They . . . are caught in the grip of hunger and malnutrition, high illiteracy, inadequate education, shrinking opportunity, and corrosive poverty." [1]

Yolanda Marbela, the pretty but very professional Filipina social worker who was our guide through one of Manila's many slums, sees every day the human implications of Mr. McNamara's words. In the area where she works many fathers are sidewalk vendors whose monthly earnings are around fifty pesos—about eight dollars. Many families are broken because one of the first things which "corrosive poverty" corrodes is the husband-wife relationship. This was one of the commonalities of poverty which I observed around the world.

But Mrs. Alarin has managed to hold her family together. We met her when Yolanda led us into a kind of slum cul-de-sac at the end of a driveway not thirty feet off one of Manila's busy streets. I confess I would have missed it without a guide. From the street it looked all too normal.

But once inside this other world it was like having the lights turned on. Suddenly things not visible from the street began to take shape. For one thing, our presence brought the families out of their hovels. They were shy, but very friendly. A dozen or more families shared the cramped facilities which had been thrown up around the driveway. We were invited by a number of them to inspect their living quarters. Three families shared the crawl space under one of the houses. It couldn't have been more than thirty-six inches from ground to top.

Mrs. Alarin's family, numbering seven, lived in an eight-by-ten foot room. The ceiling was higher than the crawl space I had seen earlier, but it wouldn't accommodate my six-foot height. The room was bare of furniture except for a few cooking utensils.

She looked older than her forty-two years. That's another commonality I have noticed about poverty—the poor age early. Tears washed her dark, sunken eye sockets as she spoke:

"I feel so sad when my children cry at night because they have no food. I know my life will never change. What can I do to solve my problems? I am so worried about the future of my children. I want them to go to school, but how can we afford it? I am sick most of the time, but I can't go to the doctor because each visit costs two pesos [twenty-eight cents] and the medicine is extra. What can I do?"

She broke down into quiet sobbing. I admit without shame that I wept with her. There is something excruciatingly sad about despair that knows no hope.

Mr. Alarin is an ice vendor, but it is not regular work and on a good day he makes only about five pesos (seventy cents). She tries to supplement this, but she cannot work away from home because the youngest of her five boys is only two years old and the oldest is eight. So she stays up at night making a kind of coconut candy which she sells on the street near the school in the neighborhood. She can do this only a couple of times a month, however, and for all her work she nets not more than forty cents a day.

She knows what her family needs to eat in order to be healthy, but she can't remember the last time they could afford such a meal. Meat was on the table about a month ago she thinks.

Such is the life of poverty. What can you and I know about it—about a life where each day is a nightmare because it puts you further behind and each night is only an empty link connecting emptier days? Growing up as the son of a Mississippi sharecropper during the Depression, I knew privation and temporary hunger, but I never have known total despair. I have only read about it and talked to people who live in an intimate relationship with it.

One of the most gripping and poignant descriptions of poverty and despair I have ever read was by an anonymous welfare mother in the hills of southern Tennessee. She gave it as a statement to a case worker for the Office of Economic Opportunity, and after the language, colloquialisms and syn-

tax were edited for polite society, it was carried as an article by C. E. Jackson in *Christian Herald* magazine from which I have excerpted it with permission.

I suggest you read it with your emotions wide open and allow yourself to feel everything the words suggest to you, from sadness to revulsion to anger. The words are honest and they are powerful:

"You say you want to know what it's like to be poor? Well, you've come to the right person. But you won't enjoy my definition . . . I'm dirty. I'm smelly. And I have no proper underwear beneath this rotting dress. I don't know about you, but the stench of my teeth makes me half sick. They're decaying but they'll never be fixed. That takes money.

"Listen to me without pity. . . . Listen with understanding, if you can. What is poverty? Poverty is getting up every morning from a dirty and illness-stained mattress—a hard, lumpy mattress. Sheets? They have long since been used for diapers, for there are no real diapers here, either.

"That smell? That *other* smell? You know what it is—that, plus sour milk and spoiled food. Sometimes it's mixed with the stench of onions cooked too often. Onions are cheap. We're like dogs in that we live in a world of smells and we've learned to identify most of them without searching them out. . . .

"Poverty is being tired—dog tired all the time. I can't remember when I wasn't tired. When my last baby came, they told me at the hospital that I had chronic anemia caused by a poor diet, a bad case of worms, and the need for a corrective operation. When they told me about my condition I listened politely. The poor are always polite, you know. We can't afford to offend those who might decide to be big and give us something. . . . What good would it do to say there is no money for iron pills, better food, or necessary medicine?

"Poverty is dirt. You may say, in your clean clothes and coming from your clean house, 'Anybody can be clean.' Let me explain housekeeping with no money. For breakfast, I give my children grits with no margarine, or cornbread made without eggs or oleo. For one thing, that kind of food doesn't use up many dishes. What dishes there are, I wash in cold water. No soap. Even the cheapest soap has to be saved for washing the old sheets I use for the baby's diapers.

"Look at these cracked red hands. Once I saved up for two months to buy a jar of Vaseline for my hands and for the baby's diaper rash. When I had the money and went to buy the Vaseline, the price had gone up two cents, and I didn't have another two cents. Every day I have to decide whether I can bear to put these cracked, sore hands into that cold water and strong soap. Why don't I use hot water? It takes money to get something with which to heat it. Hot water is a luxury. We don't have luxuries.

"You would be surprised if I told you my age. I look 20 years older than I am; my back has been bent over tubs so long I can't stand up straight any more. I can't remember when I did anything but wash, but we're still dirty. I just can't seem to keep up with all the washing. Every night I wash every stitch my school-age child had on and just hope the clothes will be dry enough to wear when morning comes.

"Poverty is asking for help. Have you ever had to swallow what pride you had left and ask for help, knowing your children will suffer more if you don't get it? . . . I'll tell you how asking for help feels: You find out where the office is, the one from which paupers are supposed to get help. When you find it, you circle that block four or five times trying to get up nerve enough to go in and beg. Finally, the thought of your children's needs and suffering pushes you through the door. Everybody is very busy and official. After an eternity, a woman comes out to you and you tell her you need help, and you force yourself to look at her.

"She isn't the one you need to see. The first one never is. She sends you to someone else and after spilling your poverty and shame all over the desk you find out this isn't the right office. Then you repeat the procedure. It doesn't get any easier.

"You ask for help in two or three places, until you're sick of the whole procedure, but you're always told to wait. You are told why you have to wait, but you don't really hear because the dark heavy cloud of shame and despair deafens you with its roar of recrimination.

"Poverty is looking into a future devoid of hope. Your children wouldn't play with my children; you wouldn't allow it. My boys will someday turn to boys who steal to get what they need. I can already see them behind prison bars. . . . My daughter? She'll have a life just like mine, unless she's pretty enough to become a prostitute. I'd be smart to wish her dead already.

"You say there are schools? Sure there are, but my children have no paper, no pencils, no crayons, clothes, no anything worthwhile or useful. All they have is worms, pink-eye, infections of all sorts all the time. They aren't hungry, but they are undernourished. There are surplus commodity programs some places, I hear, but not here. Our county said it would cost too much. There is a school lunch program, but I have two children who are already too damaged for that to do them any good.

"Yes, I know there are health clinics. They are in the towns, and I live eight miles from any town. I can walk that far, but my little children can't, and I can't carry them.

"Poverty is an acid that eats into pride until pride is burned out. It is a chisel that chips at honor until honor is pulverized. You might do something if you were in my situation—for a week or a month. Would you do it year after year, getting nowhere, going nowhere? . . . I did not come from another place, and I did not come from another time. I'm here now, and there are others like me all around you." [2]

She is right. Although there are many more hungry and poor overseas—and it could well be argued that their plight is more desperate—there is an appalling amount of real poverty in the United States, particularly in the South. In his book, *The American People*, E. J. Kahn makes the point that the world's sixth largest underdeveloped nation is contained within the borders of the United States. With 25 percent of the nation's population, the South has 38 percent of its poor, some ten million people.[3]

And while there are relative degrees of poverty, some of it in the United States is at a shocking level for a developed country. The Southern Regional Council, which is trying to raise the standard of living for blacks in the South, reports that even today the eating of clay and starch is still common among the low income population and that almost one-third of the patients who come to urban clinics are found to be suffering from malnutrition.

This is borne out by Dr. Raymond Wheeler, a member of the medical team that helped "discover" hunger in the South, who testified in 1970 before a Congressional committee: "We stopped and examined children at random and almost every child had some preventable physical defect. We saw tiny youngsters drinking rice water . . . because their mothers had no milk to give them. . . . rickets is supposed to be a rare disease today . . . but we saw one child after another with deformed ribs and legs and thickened wrists, classical landmarks of the disease."

So poverty bears her sick and sad children here in the United States and all over the world. Their presence among us in such numbers is one of the shameful blots on the record of affluent nations. And it cannot be simply dismissed with one of our glib clichés like Kipling's Englishman who, with an easy wave of his hand, spoke what he thought was both a classic observation and the final word: "The natives are bloody lazy, you know."

It was neither classic nor final. Merely stupid.

Similar words spoken with colonial condescension got me into one of the most heated arguments I think I have ever had. It happened on a plane between Manila and Hong Kong when my seat companion asked me my line of work and then marshalled all his inaccurate stereotypes to prove I was wasting my time trying to help the poor. His mouth spewed venom: "If the lazy bastards in India would get off their butts . . . ," "The Filipinos in the Tondo slums are perfectly happy with what they have . . . ," "Why don't the Africans quit asking . . . ?" and so on ad nauseum.

The Irish in me flashed—my mother was a Sullivan—and the debate was on. I simply refuse to let such spurious and uninformed judgments pass as unchallenged truth.

Poverty is not a single "thing." It is a net woven of many strands which surrounds and traps the poor. It is a chain forged of many links which binds the poor to their circumstances. It is a prison from which the rare escape is even more rarely an "inside job." Escape is not simply a matter of desire or will. Would to God that it were! The prison would be empty tomorrow. But outside help is required to release the net, break the shackles, spring the door. Jesus' reminder that the poor are always with us is no excuse for inaction and resignation. It should rather be a challenge to break out as many as possible from the prison, knowing that when we have done our very best many will still remain.

Understanding the nature of the problem is the place to begin. The causes of poverty are numerous, they are inter-related and they are complex. You can blame lack of re-sources, overpopulation, colonial oppression, insufficient capi-tal, inverted value systems, and class exploitation—and be both right and wrong. That is, all contribute to the problem; no single factor is solely responsible.

Robert Heilbroner uses the phrase "vicious circles" when he talks about the causes of poverty: "It is not just a lack of capital, or just backward ways, or just a population problem or even just a political problem which weighs upon the poorer nations. It is a combination of all these, each aggravating the other. The troubles of underdevelopment feed upon them-selves." [4]

Ignorance could be cited as another cause of poverty, but if it is spawned by ignorance, the imbalance of wealth is an even more fertile father of the poor. You don't have to be a Communist or socialist to know that the world's wealth and resources are all askew. It just seems they are the ones who point out the inequity most often, but does that very fact say something about *us* which we ought to hear? Who gives at least the appearance of caring? Our strange silence may itself be deafening to the world's poor.

Did you ever wonder why communism finds a fertile seed-bed among the workers and students in Latin America?

Consider some facts. Of the continent's three hundred mil-lion people, 60 percent have incomes of less than $50 a year. Another 30 percent earn up to $190 a year, making 90 per-cent of the people with incomes far below the subsistence level. Of the rest, 9.9 percent earn over $500, but there is an elite strata of .1 percent with incomes of more than $27,000 a year!

Or look at it this way. In Brazil in the last decade, with a real GNP growth of 2.5 percent, the share of the national income received by the poorest 40 percent of the population declined from 10 percent to 8 percent, while the richest 5 percent of the population increased its share from 29 to 38 percent. It was a similar story in Mexico. While the economy was growing, the richest 10 percent of the population increased its share of the total national income from 49 to 51 percent, while the share of the poorest 40 percent of the people decreased from 14 to 11 percent.

Who, by any stretch of his conscience, can justify such growing disparity in the face of such growing need?

Dom Helder Camara, archbishop of Olinda and Recife in Brazil, says sadly: "In Latin America rich Christians are holding onto their wealth and power at the expense of the misery of their compatriots."

Never mind that communism can't deliver on its promises. Never mind that in Russia, after more than half a century, some are still more equal than others. I simply ask you who is more believable to the Latin American *campesinos* as their friend and champion?

A friend isn't indifferent. A friend speaks up for you. A friend cares—cares about the family disintegration which is so often a bitter fruit of poverty, about the frustrated hopes, blighted dreams and crushed spirits of the totally poor.

During the height of the bombing of London during World War II, Prime Minister Winston Churchill visited a section of the East End which had been devastated the previous night. Greatly moved by the plight of those made homeless, he wept.

"You see," exclaimed one of the victims, "he cares, he really cares!"

Who cares for the poor of our world and the degrading rituals through which they must daily go in their desperate attempt to survive?

"The study of the causes of poverty," said Alfred Marshall in *Principles of Economics*, "is the study of the causes of the degradation of a large part of mankind." [5] Perhaps nothing short of physical or psychological torture degrades and dehumanizes as much as poverty. I have known poverty in the rural South where I was born and reared. I have seen it in Appalachia where I have spent extended periods. I have felt it in the shantytowns of Africa and the *favelas* of Brazil where I have tried to understand the distress of the poor.

My conclusion is that poverty is like a bleeding wound which never heals, hemorrhaging strength and life out of the body and contributing to the chronic sickness of society. Nowhere have I seen the despair of poverty more movingly described than in the writings of a child of Brazil's *favelas*. Actually, she was a woman and her name was Carolina Maria de Jesus. She recorded her feelings on scraps of paper picked from gutters. Discovered and published under the title *Child of the Dark*, it is a raw, primitive journal of a street scavenger who fought daily for survival for herself and her three children in a squalid São Paulo *favela*—a human garbage dump, home of the poor, the hungry, the desperate.

Try to feel the world of Carolina Maria de Jesus. One entry in her diary may help you!

"Today I'm sad. I'm nervous. I don't know if I should start crying or start running until I fall unconscious. At dawn it was raining. I couldn't go out to get any money. I spent the day writing. I cooked the macaroni and I'll warm it up again for the children. I cooked the potatoes and they ate them. I have a few tin cans and a little scrap that I'm going to sell to Senhor Manuel. When João came home from school I sent him to sell the scrap. He got 13 cruzeiros. He bought a glass of mineral water: two cruzeiros. I was furious with him. Where had he seen a *favelado* with such high-born tastes?

"The children eat a lot of bread. They like soft bread but when they don't have it, they eat hard bread.

"Hard is the bread that we eat. Hard is the bed on which we sleep. Hard is the life of the *favelado*.

"Oh, São Paulo! A queen that vainly shows her skyscrapers that are her crown of gold. All dressed up in velvet and silk but with cheap stockings underneath—the *favela*.

"The money didn't stretch far enough to buy meat, so I cooked macaroni with a carrot. I didn't have any grease, it was horrible. Vera was the only one who complained yet asked for more.

" 'Mama, sell me to Dona Julita, because she has delicious food.'

"I know that there exist Brazilians here inside São Paulo

who suffer more than I do. So as not to see my children hungry I asked for help from the famous Social Service. It was there that I saw the tears slipping from the eyes of the poor. How painful it is to see the dramas that are played out there." [6]

Dramas indeed—and painful because the last act has a real life-or-death ending. One can never be sure how it will turn out.

In Natal, about 1,400 miles north of São Paulo, I sat on the dirt floor of a hovel and shared one of those dramas. In the cast were Sebastian and Maria Nascimento and their nine children. The stage was a one-room thatched lean-to, more or less divided into living and sleeping areas by a torn piece of rubber sheeting. The floor was sand. The stage props were minimal—one stool, a charcoal hibachi, four cots covered with gunny sacks filled with a thin layer of straw.

My emotions could scarcely take in what I saw and heard. The three-year-old twins, lying naked and unmoving on a small cot, were into the last act of their personal drama. Mercifully, the curtain was coming down on their brief appearance. Malnutrition was the villain. The two-year-old played a silent role, his brain already vegetating from marasmus, a severe form of malnourishment.

The father is without work. Both he and Maria are anguished over their existence, but they are too proud to beg. He tries to shine shoes. Maria cannot talk about their condition. She tries, but words just will not come. Her mother's love is deep and tender, and the daily deterioration of her children is more than she can bear. Tears must be the vocabulary of the anguished soul, for, like Carolina Maria de Jesus, I have noticed that the poor cry a lot. At such an intimate moment, my own words sound empty and hollow so I, too, choose not to speak. The drama has reached its most intense moment as it moves from words to feelings.

I have entered into the edge of their hell, but I can go no further.

As I walk out slowly through an opening in the thatch wall —there is no door—I am met by the most incongruous sight I can imagine, and I suddenly realize that what I have left is reality and what I have stepped into is fantasy. Stretched out before me is one of the most beautiful expanses of beach in Brazil. The Atlantic Ocean which washes the sand is shaded from pale green out to deep blue. It is a holiday and the beach is thronged with swimmers and surfers. The nerve ends of my emotions are still raw and hurting from my encounter with the Nascimentos, so I am shocked at the gaiety and frivolity going on below me while a struggle with death is taking place behind me.

It takes me a little while to remember that what I have seen is the story of all humanity and that most of the time I, too, am figuratively "at the beach" while the poor fight their daily survival battles. When I remember, I am ashamed.

I notice an interesting thing about Brazil's *favelas*. Most of them are built on the sides of hills around the cities. The thought struck me that the poor have the best view in town.

The one question I forgot to ask the Nascimentos was how they enjoyed it.

If poverty is a social cancer, our world can never be whole until we attack it with all our vigor and all our resources. Robert S. McNamara, whom I have quoted before, lists three broad categories of poverty in the developing world:

(1) The poverty of too few resources which affects entire nations. The United Nations has listed twenty-five rather small nations in this category. Haiti, in our own hemisphere, heads the list as the poorest.

(2) Impoverished regions within larger developing countries. Northeast Brazil where the Nascimentos live is such an area, as are northeast Thailand and southern Yugoslavia.

(3) Finally, says the World Bank president, the most extensive poverty is that of the low income strata—roughly 40 percent of all the people in the developing world. It is these, he says, who "remain trapped in conditions of deprivation that fall below any rational definition of human decency." [7]

As distressing as is this fact of pervasive and persistent poverty, it is further compounded by the certainty that the percentage is not decreasing and the gap is not narrowing. On the contrary, the per capita income disparity between rich and poor nations has continued to widen in the past twenty years. It now approaches the magnitude of a chasm as the rich get richer and the poor get poorer. Just one example: in one year the increase in the per capita gross national product of the United States is equal to the increase that India may be able to manage in one hundred years!

In the developed Western nations today, our average per capita income is $2,400. In the developing world it is $180. The $2,220 differential is hardly a mere gap. But by 1980 it is expected to widen by another $1,100, and there is no evidence that the trend will ever be reversed if present economic policies are perpetuated.

The question which the whole world must face is whether or not those policies can be allowed to continue in the face of the widening and explosive poverty chasm.

Richard J. Barnet, director of the Institute for Policy Studies, thinks not. He categorically states:

> The best contribution the U.S. can make to the problem of world poverty is to abandon or revise many policies it is currently pursuing in the name of development that have the effect of perpetuating misery in the undeveloping world. It is much more exciting and far less "sacrificial" to conceive and fund imaginative "projects" than to change policies that preserve American wealth and power at the expense of poor countries. Any serious commitment to development by the United States, however, would begin by confronting instead of hiding the deep conflicts of interests between Americans, struggling to maintain and increase an unparalleled level of prosperity, and the people of the undeveloping world who are struggling for survival and dignity. We need to find out what it would cost the United States in comfort, convenience and prosperity to change policies that keep poor countries poor.[8]

If this reassessment does not take place voluntarily—and soon—we are going to face an increasingly hostile and resentful world. If we just understood a little more, cared a little more, none of this would seem so strange. Personally, I am amazed at the patience and forbearance of the poverty-affected world. They have suffered long with "aid" that isn't, with discriminatory trade policies, with the rape of their resources, with our clumsy attempts to buy friends. I can tell you this much—if the roles were reversed, we would have repeated long ago on a worldwide scale the revolution of 1776.

Listen to a Third World leader: "the developing countries should organize their 'poor power' to wring major concessions from the rich nations and to arrange for a genuine transfer of resources. Since the rich nations are going to shrink in the next few decades to less than 10 percent of the total world population with over 70 percent of the world income, the poor will be numerous enough to organize such an effort." [9]

You may not like to read his words, but I can assure you he speaks for far more people than just himself. That is why our opportunity to take positive action cannot be dragged out interminably. Grasping the nettle may seem to be a courageous act, but it will be dictated as much by the desire for self-preservation as courage.

Instead of approaching the problem gingerly and fearfully, we should boldly thank God that the possibility of remedial and equalizing action is even an option. Such a glorious and satisfying opportunity has come only at this point in human history, as Mr. McNamara points out: "There is no cause for despair. There is every reason for hope. In the past few generations the world has created a productive machine capable of abolishing poverty from the face of the earth." [10]

This generation can do what no previous one would have found possible. We can, simply by willing to do it, change the face of a poverty-cursed world.

"Why is there this great blanket of poverty stretched across the face of the globe?" economist Barbara Ward asks, and then comments insightfully: "We should, I think, remember that ours is the first century in which such a question can even be put. Poverty has been the universal lot of man until our own day. No one asked fundamental questions about a state of affairs which everyone took for granted. The idea that a majority could have access to a little modest affluence is wholly new." [11]

In another of her books, Miss Ward writes: "As we read the portents—the cold statistics, the burning realities—it is hard to believe that a great deal of time is left in which to reverse the world's drift via indifference to destruction. But Christians do not only need portents. They make them. They are called . . . to give the sign that all this wealth, all this power, all this technology can be made to work for life, not death.

And with faith that miracles are not beyond God's will for us, we can 'work while it is day.' " [12]

And that work must include not only acts of charity to the poor, but bold efforts to change the structures which keep them poor.

The words of Ambrose of Milan may be even more apropos today than when he spoke them in the fifth century: "How far, O rich, do you extend your senseless avarice? Do you intend to be the sole inhabitants of the earth? Why do you drive out the fellow sharers of nature, and claim it all for yourselves? The earth was made for all, the rich and the poor, in common. Why do you rich men claim it as your exclusive right? . . . The earth is the Lord's, and we are his offspring."

Chapter 2
Ignorance: The Curse of Not Knowing

A STONE AGE PEOPLE WITHOUT STONES."

Robb McLaughlin didn't mean his description of the Nuer tribespeople as a putdown. Not this sensitive man. It was simply another fact out of his vast store of knowledge about these dwellers on the tall grass plains of Sudan and Ethiopia. Knowledge gained over more than twenty years of working with them.

Numbering some fifty thousand, the Nuer are one of the most primitive tribal groups remaining in Africa. That bit about their being without stones is literally true. Living in the dust and mud of Africa's savannahs, they must import from the high plateau even the stones they need for grinding their grain.

With a literacy rate of about 1 percent, they live a numbing existence in the twilight world of ignorance. Robb leads a small, elite team of Presbyterian missionaries which is trying to help the Nuer move a rung or two up the ladder of self-development without Westernizing them and obliterating their culture.

It is a noble experiment, and one in which I am pleased to have a very small part.

I got my first glimpse of the Nuer when Denny Hoekstra banked the little Cessna 185 to check out the grass landing

strip at Adura, Ethiopia. Even from our altitude I could see
their tall, angular bodies, silhouettes in ebony against the
high green grass which lined the runway alongside the Baro
River.

It was the start of the rainy season when everything becomes mud—the ground, the houses, the simple furniture,
pots and pans, and even the toys of the children. Since stones
and wood aren't available, the ever-present mud becomes the
substance from which all is made. It may sound like planned
obsolescence, but at least the replacements don't cost anything.

The torrential rains end after six months and the choking
dust returns for the rest of the year.

When it is wet they grow corn, but like their neighbors,
the Dinkas and the Annuak, they are primarily a cattle society.
Their cows provide milk to mix with their corn mush and
dried dung for cooking the mush.

So it has always been, generations without number.

Why should anyone want to change it?

The answer isn't hard if you have seen their struggles.
Each successive generation has had not a life, but an existence. With all its simplicity and unsophistication, their life
hardly could be called idyllic, and it certainly is not to be
envied. The Nuer are victims of the curse of not knowing.
Wise in the lore of their ancestors, they know nothing about
diet and disease, hygiene and health. This has caused endemic
malnutrition, chronic illnesses and early death.

Robb and his team faced tough questions. How do you in-
struct a people who do not know they don't know? How do
primitives learn? How should materials be designed for teaching? With wise patience, they waited about three years until
some answers began to evolve before they started actual programs.

Finally, it was decided that the first problem to tackle was
teaching the value of pure water. Until this time the boiling of
water was an unknown practice. Water was simply dipped
from the nearest stream with no thought that it might not be
fit for human consumption. Even if there had been signs warning of the danger, who could have read them?

Robb and a nurse developed a mimeographed flip chart

showing in pictures the steps in purifying water. A Nuer woman agreed to be the model for the simple photographs illustrating the steps. The chart was designed like a kindergarten primer, with all but the essential elements of the pictures eliminated. They showed in progression the mother going to the river for water, dipping it up with her clay pot, boiling it until it steams, covering the boiled water and allowing it to cool in the same vessel, then giving her child a drink of the water.

The charts were presented in village after village and the people were catechized in their use. Robb explained that diseases can be spread by contaminated water, but he struggled with how to explain germs. He wound up calling them "seeds of sickness." The people understood. In one area where forty-eight deaths had occurred from what was later diagnosed as hepatitis, the villagers listened with special interest.

After leaving charts with six village leaders who accepted the responsibility of spreading the word to the rest of the community, the team went back to Addis Ababa to await the coming of the dry season when they could once again trek back to the villages and measure the results. The suspense was high.

Just recently I received a letter from Robb. "I wish you could have seen the faces of some of the people who have been boiling or treating their water for some months when I asked them about it," he wrote. "They really lit up and said they feel much better than they ever did before they started drinking pure water. You can believe that helps make a lot of rough trekking worthwhile."

Next he proposes to take on the fly, of which there are millions around the Nuer's cattle. When I talked to Robb, however, he was having trouble finding as willing and photogenic a model as he had for the boiling water flip chart. Something on diet and agriculture is also being planned. As the Nuer take each small step out of the dark night of ignorance, it becomes a giant step toward a happier and healthier life.

I remember something written by Julius Nyerere, president of Tanzania: "People tell me the Masai [tribe] are completely happy. I tell them it's not a question of whether they are happy. That is a philosophical question. I'm not trying to make them happy. But there is a difference between clean water and dirty water. My problem is to get that [Masai] woman clean water. My problem is to get her a healthy child. Happy! I'm not involved in that. The question is, what kind of water are the Masai drinking?" [1]

For both the Masai and the Nuer, what is needed is not money nor advanced technology nor Western culture. What is needed is knowledge, the simple "how-tos" which more advanced civilizations have long taken for granted. This is why I personally believe the Peace Corps and similar programs have made a greater impact for good on the developing world than all the investment capital poured into industrial projects. It is the pragmatic expression of a saying which I have heard scores of times all over the world, each version slightly different, allowing for cultural variation. In its most common form, however, which is attributed to the Chinese, it goes: "Give a man a fish and you feed him for a day; teach him to fish and he will feed himself for a lifetime."

In his book *Small is Beautiful*, E. F. Schumacher underscores this with a pertinent statement: "The best aid to give is intellectual aid, a gift of useful knowledge. A gift of knowledge is infinitely preferable to a gift of material things. . . . The gift of material goods makes people dependent, but the gift of knowledge makes them free—provided it is the right kind of knowledge, of course." [2]

Out in Wollo province of Ethiopia, one of the hardest hit areas in the 1973–74 drought, an Australian named Bob Buttenshaw showed a remarkable understanding of this concept. The need in scores of villages was for water. Deep wells were the answer, but he knew that Western machines and technology were not the answer because the comprehension level of the average villager of these pumps was zero. I never met Mr. Buttenshaw, I am sorry to say, for I'm sure I would have immediately liked him. A friend told me about him and about the simple indigenous pump he invented for these dry villages.

It was constructed entirely of pipe available on the local market. It embodied a simple concept which any villager could grasp. Washers for the plunger were cut from discarded in-

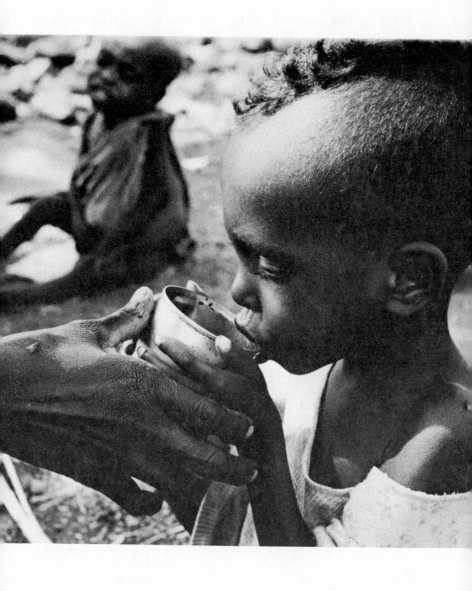

nertubes. The pump could be maintained and repaired with minimum effort. And it cost only about $50.

But Buttenshaw didn't stop even there. He trained a team of men to manufacture them and to go around repairing them.

Now you know why I would have liked him. Any man who operates on the premise that the answers for the Third World are not wrapped up in Western gadgetry is a friend of mine. The world needs more like him—givers of the gift of knowledge.

Listen again to Julius Nyerere:

"I've been telling my own people, 'We've got to change, we must mechanize, we must have better tools.' But what better tools? Not the combine harvester. If I were given enough combine harvesters for every family in Tanzania, what would I do with them? No mechanics, no spare parts. . . . It would be a very serious problem—unless, of course, I could sell them for hard cash. But we still have to give the people better tools, tools they can handle, and can pay for. Americans, when they speak of better tools, are talking about something quite different. We are using hoes. If two million farmers in Tanzania could jump from the hoe to the oxen plough, it would be a revolution. It would double our living standard, triple our product." [3]

We need to listen to this man. He is pleading for something basic and urgent. Far too many of our development schemes are impractically sophisticated and grandiose. I have seen the skeletons of many such projects littering the landscape of Third World countries because they were planned and engineered in Washington or Paris or Tokyo, far over the heads and skills of the people they were intended to help.

On a recent trip to Niger, I was discussing this problem with my friend Oumarou Youssoufou, whom I regard as one of the most brilliant, sensitive and dynamic young leaders of Africa. He had just been appointed his country's ambassador to Nigeria after serving as an advisor to the president and a diplomat in Washington. Educated in a mission school and a committed Christian, he brings an ethical and moral perspective to world problems which I do not find often enough among statesmen.

He told me that virtually all the drought relief and development programs for Niger had been planned abroad.

"Why is it," he asked in genuine puzzlement, "that when a country wants to help us with an agricultural program, they send an expert who knows nothing about the land or traditional practices of my country? Asian experts brought rice here, but Africans don't like that kind of rice. These experts are good people; they don't dislike Niger, but they don't have enough elements from our country in the program to make it successful. They transfer inappropriate experience from some other part of the world which just can't be applied here. We are not children. A village man doesn't need a degree from MIT to know what will work and what will not work, and he should not be ignored when the plans are made."

Can we hear what this man and other Third World leaders are saying? The needs of the poor are simple and the help they plead for has to do with the basic problem of survival. They have not yet progressed to gourmet diets. They are still praying, "Give us this day our daily bread."

Frequently, I have found, people are hungry or malnourished because they do not have the most elemental knowledge or information which will help them improve their situation. If a man needs to be taught only to fish, we do him no favor to buy him a trawler with nets so huge they must be lifted by power winches. We have only compounded his problem because we have now forced him to find a crew to man it, diesel fuel to run it, and markets for his surplus catch.

Exaggerated? Not at all. There are more than a few places in our world where simple needs have been oversupplied because our bigger-and-better philosophy couldn't be scaled down to fit a people barely emerging from the seventeenth or eighteenth centuries. Or maybe it was the result of our cold war politics. After all, if the Russians gave them a dam, how could we possibly think about anything less than a nuclear reactor—only for peaceful purposes, of course.

The most basic and fundamental of all human needs—the one which underlies all others—is the need to be literate. There is absolutely no way a country can move ahead socially and economically until a majority of its people are able to read and write. Illiteracy is a millstone around a nation's neck.

"The problem of illiteracy cannot be isolated from the problems of community underdevelopment," says a study issued by the Committee on World Literacy and Christian Literature. "It accompanies and has a bearing upon undernourishment, disease, and all kinds of economic and cultural problems. We hear that half the world is hungry, and we may be sure that it is the same half of the world that is illiterate. It is not a simple case of cause and effect; all these problems are interlocked." [4]

Nothing dispels the darkness of this twilight world of ignorance as surely and firmly and dramatically as the ability to read and write. Two of the truly great and liberating revolutions of human history were the leap from oral to written language—generally credited to the Sumerians about 3000 B.C.—and the leap from the written to the printed word, made possible by Gutenberg's moveable type printing press about A.D. 1450.

Yet still today, over 30 percent of the world's adults are illiterate. Five centuries after Gutenberg, in the midst of an age of space exploration, global electronic communication, and a vast outpouring of printed pages, more than eight hundred million people cannot read! In Africa alone, almost 74 percent of adults are in that category, while for African women the figure is almost 84 percent. This latter figure is particularly tragic because women are the teachers in the family and could, if they were able to read, break the vicious cycle of illiteracy at the family level.

While the *percentage* of adults who are illiterate has declined, UNESCO figures confirm that the *number* of adult illiterates actually has increased because of rapid population growth.

For the 810 million who are functional illiterates, it is a personal tragedy of monstrous proportions. In an article in *Africa* magazine, M. N. Smart calculates a part of the price which the individual pays: "The fact of their illiteracy cripples them physically and mentally, it cancels out nearly all their opportunities for self-training, and it disqualifies them for participating in democratic government at the national level."

He goes on to say, "The debilitating effects of illiteracy are confirmed quickly by a UNESCO atlas: it is no coincidence

that the belt of illiteracy, stretching across Africa, the Middle
East, Southeast Asia and Latin America, is also the belt of
poverty and hunger. It is no coincidence that the map's cross-
hatching that marks areas of illiteracy also marks areas
plagued by high disease incidence, malnutrition and blindness." [5]

Have you ever tried to imagine what it would be like to
live in the belt of poverty, illiteracy and hunger? In his book,
The Great Ascent, Robert Heilbroner takes the reader through
an exercise which—at least on paper—reduces his life style
to that which is the daily existence for at least a billion souls.
It is an illuminating and frightening exercise.

He starts with a typical Canadian-American family, with
an income of $6000–$7000 per year, in a small suburban
home. Then he refashions this home, and the life of its inhabitants, into a typical scene in the vast "under $200" areas
of the world:

1. Take out the furniture, except a few old blankets, a
kitchen table and one chair.

2. Take away all the clothing, except for the oldest dress
or suit for each member of the family, and a shirt or blouse.
Leave one pair of shoes for the head of the family.

3. Empty the pantry and refrigerator except for a small
bag of flour, some sugar and salt, a few moldy potatoes for
tonight's dinner, a handful of onions and a dish of dried
beans.

4. Dismantle the bathroom, shut off the water, remove
the electric wiring.

5. Take away the house itself, and move the family into a
toolshed.

6. Remove all the other houses in the neighborhood, and
set up in this place a shantytown.

7. Cancel all subscriptions to newspapers, magazines and
book clubs. This is no great loss, as our family is now illiterate.

8. Leave one small radio for the whole shantytown.

9. Move the nearest clinic or hospital ten miles away and
put a midwife in charge instead of a doctor.

10. Throw out the bankbooks, stock certificates, pension
plans and insurance policies, and leave the family a cash
hoard of $5.

11. Give the head of the family three tenant acres to cultivate. On this he can raise $300 in cash crops, of which one-
third will go to the landlord and one-tenth to the local moneylender.

12. Lop off twenty-five to thirty years in life expectancy.

"And so we have brought our typical American family down
to the very bottom of the human scale." [6]

Multiply the above by a billion and you begin to have some
idea of the consequences of the twin tragedies of poverty
and ignorance.

But if illiteracy is a great personal tragedy, it is also an
enormous national calamity. No nation has so much greatness
that it can afford to lose the leadership potential, literary
achievement, economic contribution, and spiritual and moral
dynamic of a single one of its citizens. Yet that is exactly
what is happening with disastrous consequences across the
globe. These qualities are being subtracted from the GNW
(gross national well-being) of dozens of countries in almost
the exact ratio of the number of illiterates in each.

Literacy has three principal effects in a typical underdeveloped village: (1) It brings forth a new kind of leadership
from the middle and lower classes, ones who know how to
read and think more effectively. (2) The organization of literacy campaigns creates the framework of an organization that
enables a community to work as a community. It also has
a direct relationship on the thinking processes of individuals,
allowing them perhaps for the first time to think in a logical
way. (3) It allows a village access to a fund of new information which can bring new ideas into the community and encourage its development.

There's more. It lays the groundwork for acquiring higher
skills in all areas of work, including agriculture. It strengthens
the cooperative processes of government. It makes possible
mature dialogue for building all human relationships.

It is, in short, the essential skill.

Knowing this, and with tried and proven solutions at hand,
there is no way we can "tut-tut" our way to an easy conscience
over the magnitude of illiteracy as if it were a problem without solutions. In fact, no other single problem contributing

to a hungry world has the same surefire answers which can be immediately applied. There are a variety of completely successful techniques for conquering illiteracy.

Not all of them are related to formal education. In fact, Gunnar Myrdal boldly states that "much education in these [underdeveloped] countries is now even plain miseducation and apt to raise the impediments for development." [7]

As with so many of these problems which impact on hunger, we need creative and fresh approaches. Too much formal education in developing countries is designed to produce educated professionals rather than skilled literate people who can help with development. At a time when "dirty hands" are needed in hard development tasks, secondary and tertiary education in developing countries tends to produce a "clean hands" syndrome which causes the graduates to shun anything but a white collar job.

To overcome some of these problems growing out of the formal education processes, more and more countries are experimenting with nonformal schooling at the village level. Working through a curriculum which will help each person to acquire the amount of education that enables him to be a productive, contributing citizen, this kind of nonformal education can be geared to all ages and levels.

Working with a semitrained nucleus of the Nuer tribal leadership, Robb McLaughlin is using this approach to take the first step in rolling back the darkness of ignorance accumulated over many generations.

Across the globe in Haiti, health teachers of the Methodist Church are using a similar technique to teach a balanced diet to the village women. The teachers point out that the women use three stones to hold their cooking pots. They explain that these stones are analagous to fats, proteins and carbohydrates —the three main foods that are necessary for a balanced diet. To remove one stone, they tell the women, would be sheer disaster.

The analogy communicates. The light comes on. One more bit of helpful knowledge is imparted. And as a result, families will eat better, be healthier, live longer.

What does ignorance mean?

It means not knowing that a better way exists.

It means going hungry because you don't know how to grow more food or higher yield crops.

It means not being able to read the instructions on a bag of fertilizer or understand how to use a piece of simple farm machinery.

It means not knowing how to think about a problem so that it may be solved.

It means continual hunger and poverty for tens of millions.

What does it mean to conquer ignorance?

It means to give the most precious gift of all—the gift of knowledge.

That is not beyond the ability—nor, hopefully, the desire—of any of us.

Chapter 3

Climate: The Calamities of Nature

Each year we could see our pastures growing drier and drier. We had to drive the animals for twenty kilometers to find food for them. Then it was thirty kilometers and then forty, and then all the animals but the camels began to die.

"The camels? They were sold for almost nothing to traders from Dahomey, for I could see they would not last long, either. Now I have nothing."

The Tuareg chief had spoken quietly. When he finished, he lowered his head so the stranger would not see the tears in his eyes. The eloquent silence was interrupted only by the soft bleating of the little kid goat I held in my lap.

In a few moments, other desert sounds which filtered into the tent gently pulled us back into reality. The tent—skins stretched over a rough frame of acacia branches—couldn't have been more than three feet off the scorching sand at its highest point. It was typically Tuareg, unchanged over the centuries.

I looked at my host. He still wore the famed indigo robes of his unique culture. The dye, which rubbed off on their faces as they held the robe there to keep the blowing sand away, earned them the name "blue men." But the robes are about all that remain from his past. Once he was wealthy, at least by Tuareg standards. He owned no land, but he didn't need to. For millennia the whole Sahara had belonged to him and his ancestors. He went whenever and wherever he pleased, taking with him his family and his large herd of camels, goats and cattle. These were his bank account, his stocks and bonds. This herd was his inheritance from his father and one day would be his legacy to his son.

He was a prince on the desert. Caravans paid him tribute to cross his territory. If he needed more than the tribute and his cattle would provide, he collected salt from the flats near Timbuktu and bartered it in the distant towns for life's other necessities.

A descendent of proud Berbers, he was fiercely and ruggedly independent, debtor to no man and servant of none.

But that was before. Now he is a refugee from drought and death. Around him in this one camp outside Niamey, Niger, are sixteen thousand more, some from as far away as Mali. They sit in their little round tents and wait for the daily distribution of grain and powdered milk.

It is a sad camp. Day after day there is the grinding monotony of waiting for nothing. The children study the Koran, learning it by rote. It is the only education they will ever get. The women wander far on the desert to find a few sticks of wood for cooking. The men think about the past.

Epidemics sweep through the camp. Dysentery. Measles. The very young and the very old die. More sadness. Each tent has its heartache.

Over three cups of sugary green tea, prepared and downed ceremoniously, the chief and I talked about his heartache and the disappearing way of life of his people.

It started about 1968, he remembers. The occasional rains which made the desert blossom came with less frequency and then not at all. The oases dried up. Grazing land became scarce and then nonexistent. Desperate herdsmen cut too much of the brush to get leaves for their animals, allowing the hot Sahara sand to cover and choke the roots. Finally, beaten by nature and his own unknowing misuse of land and water, he wandered south, watching his emaciated cattle drop one at a time under the relentless desert sun.

When he arrived in Niamey, only a single camel remained. I had ridden it earlier—an adventure undertaken at the urging

of my friends and to the whooping delight of the local tribes-
men.

The death of his animals was a bitter loss for the chief. He
tells me sadly that almost every night he wakes himself calling
over the names of his favorite cattle in his sleep, and when he
realizes they are dead, he cries for them.

He tries to think about the future, but it is so empty and
uncertain that mostly he just lives today, doing what he
thought a proud Tuareg would never do—begging for food
to stay alive.

He is just one of hundreds of thousands of victims of
drought in Africa's Sahel, a term derived from the Arabic word
for border. Stretching across West Africa, it is the barely
arable zone where grass and shrub struggle against the desert
to stay alive. In recent years the Sahara has been winning—
helped unwittingly by the nomads—as it moves southward at
an estimated four to thirty miles a year.

To tell this Tuareg tribesman that he is just one victim of
the most serious drought in the Sahel in living memory is
scant comfort to him. He cannot grasp the geography beyond
his desert haunts well enough to comprehend the magnitude
of the disaster. It means almost nothing to tell him that from
Ethiopia on the east to Senegal and Mauritania on the west,
no African country between the 10th and 20th parallels of
latitude has escaped.

He only knows that landmarks once familiar to him have
disappeared. Pastures are denuded. Oases have dried up.
Rivers have become trickles and some have vanished altogether. Lake Chad, which once covered 9,000 square miles,
now covers about a third of that and is actually three small
lakes instead of one.

His personal losses—cattle, family, way of life—are even
more shattering. Wrenching social and economic changes to
a man whose culture has been static for centuries further contribute to his disorientation.

Although he knows the weather signs on the desert and can
predict with uncanny accuracy the coming of the *soudura*, or
dry season, it is too much to expect him to understand the
fiendishly complex weather systems which have contributed
to his tragedy.

Even meteorologists who study them and chart them barely understand them. They know this much, however: the African drought is part of a widespread dry-weather pattern which stretches all the way to North China and includes parts of the Middle East, India, and South Asia. Central America has also been affected as was part of North America in 1974.

It is also known that some fairly drastic climate changes are going on, although once that much is said, the picture tends to get confused. Scientists and meteorologists do not agree on just what those changes mean for the future.

One man who thinks he knows and who doesn't hesitate to speak of climatological disaster is Reid Bryson, director of the Institute for Environmental Studies at the University of Wisconsin.

"There is very important climatic change going on right now," Bryson says. "And it's not merely something of academic interest. It is something that, if it continues, will affect the whole human occupation of the earth—like a billion people starving. The effects are already showing up in rather drastic ways." [1]

Bryson contends, with convincing documentation, that the period from 1890 to 1945 was one of the most abnormally favorable periods for weather in the past thousand years. And he believes the present cooling trend indicates that this brief fifty-five year span will be bracketed on this side, as it was on the other, by what some scientists call the "little ice age." The earlier frigid interlude, covering roughly the sixteenth through the nineteenth centuries, produced significant changes in the world.

The Viking colonies on Greenland, established as early as the tenth century, were wiped out or driven out by cold and hunger as an ice cap now measuring hundreds of feet in depth descended on the once lush fields. England's grape vineyards ceased to be a threat to the French wine industry. The great "potato famine" in Ireland was only one of several agricultural disasters to strike during that period. Although India had experienced famines before, her worst time was in 1769–70 when it was estimated that one-third of the population of Bengal—ten million people—perished. Another five million died in

India in 1876–78, and some nine and one-half million Chinese were wiped out when famine struck there in 1877–78. Before the end of the century, Russia had also been seriously affected.

By the beginning of the twentieth century, according to Bryson's theory, the warming trend was already contributing to a climatic "golden age." Bryson's data clearly show, for example, that droughts in northern India declined in frequency during the period when the earth was getting warmer. He believes it was the availability of more food plus improved medical care which allowed India and other comparable regions to more than double their populations in this century.

And to what does Bryson attribute this "heating up" of the earth? The Industrial Revolution, for one thing. Other climatologists agree that the increased burning of fossil fuels in the industrial furnaces helped produce what they call the "greenhouse effect" as more carbon dioxide was released into the air. These molecules, while not impeding the sun's radiation, do trap that energy once the earth has converted it into heat by preventing the infrared wavelengths from being reradiated into space.

So the earth became, with only slight exaggeration, a solar-heated hothouse.

Enter earth's climatic "golden age."

And if Bryson's theory is right, that golden age, after a brief but beneficent tenure, is now exiting.

What is responsible for its early and lamented departure? Partly, and paradoxically, the Industrial Revolution! The same furnaces that release carbon dioxide into the air also generate pollution, and the detrimental effects of increasing pollution are overriding the positive values of the CO_2. Bryson believes, however, this is just one contributing factor to the present cooling trend. He says there are more guilty culprits which produce the tiny stratospheric dust particles that filter and reflect the sun's radiation.

Volcanoes, for one. Eruptions spew enormous quantities of dust into the air and much of it rises too high to be washed out by precipitation. Just as I am writing this, the *Los Angeles Times* reports that stratospheric dust from a volcanic eruption in Mexico has produced some of the most spectacular sunsets we have seen in Southern California. Having just read Bryson, I feel a reflexive chill shudder go through my body even while I am enjoying the beauty.

An interesting corollary between periods of lower temperatures and volcanic activity has been noted by scientists drilling through layers of the icepacks covering Greenland and the Antarctic. Similarly, it has been noted that volcanoes were generally quiet during the first half of this century, but that activity has accelerated considerably since 1955 with a resulting increase in particle fallout.

It is also confirmed that since that time the atmosphere has become less transparent.

Bryson blames other things as well. Smoke from slash-and-burn farming which is so popular in primitive areas of the tropics. Dust generated by mechanized agricultural methods and arid lands which have been overgrazed. Salt particles from evaporated ocean spray.

Both nature and man must share the guilt.

While not all meteorologists accept Bryson's hypothesis as the reason for the gradual cooling which has been going on, none dispute the fact that the earth is keeping its cool too literally. It may sound insignificant to say that the average surface temperature has fallen only about 2.7° Fahrenheit since the peak high in 1945, but *Time* magazine says that "even this small drop has trimmed a week to ten days from the growing season in the middle latitudes that are the earth's breadbasket." [2] England has had two weeks lopped off its pre-1950 growing season.

Warning that a continuation of the trend could bring about agricultural disasters, *Time* points out that the so-called "miracle" strains of wheat and rice which brought about the Green Revolution are highly vulnerable to weather uncertainties, having been developed for maximum yields under the highly favorable weather conditions of recent years.

Robert Heilbroner, socioeconomist and writer, is concerned about the climate too, but from 180 degrees in the other direction. He thinks the heat added to the atmosphere by energy spent in industrial production could ultimately—say in two hundred fifty years—make the earth so hot it would be unsuitable for human habitation. He is no doomsday prophet, for he

admits that present industrial heat emission is adding to the
natural flow of solar and planetary heat only in insignificant
amounts. And he thinks there is plenty of time for us to find
solutions before we have to shut down the furnaces for good.

But he does warn that if we "proceed along our present
course for about 150 years . . . the atmosphere would begin to
warm up appreciably—let us say about three degrees. At this
point, however, the enormous multiplicative effects of further
exponential growth would suddenly descend upon us. For beyond that threshold, extinction beckons if exponential growth
continues for another generation or two." [3]

He is quite sure, moreover, that this industrial heat would
cause serious climatic changes long before the danger threshold is reached. But he cautions against any "prediction of
imminent disaster," for he believes an answer lies at our
fingertips in the form of solar energy which adds no heat to
the atmosphere which would not already be there.

"Thus imminent disaster is not the problem here," he concludes. "It is the inescapable need to limit industrial growth
that emerges as the central challenge . . . . The problem of
global thermal pollution, for all its awesome finality, therefore
stands as a warning rather than as an immediate challenge." [4]

The confirmed cooling trend seems to discredit Heilbroner's
hypothesis, but until a lot more evidence is in on either side I
am not willing to throw it out altogether. There are too few
"givens" and too many unknowables.

The scanty evidence presently available allows for several
theories. Some climatologists hold to the comic-sounding but
seriously held "wobble" theory. They believe a tiny bit of un-
steadiness in the earth's rotation alters the amount of sunlight
which strikes the surface, and this accounts for the temperature
variables.

Others think the same thing happens as a result of slight
changes in the earth's orbit around the sun, increasing or decreasing the planet's distance from the source of its energy.

Some scientists—notably astrophysicist Walter Orr Roberts
—think there is a connection between the eleven-year sunspot
cycle and earth's weather patterns, although none of them
attempt to theorize about just how the connection works. The
solar storms do disturb the earth's magnetic field and wreak

havoc with communications, but there is no confirmed link with weather. Roberts suspects, however, there is a relationship between the periodic lull in sunspot activity and recurring drought on the east side of the Rocky Mountains.

Another climatologist who rejects Bryson's pessimism is J. Murray Mitchell, Jr., of the National Oceanic and Atmospheric Administration. He accepts the cooling trends as real, but is unconvinced about the reason and the long-range projection. He thinks Mother Nature is just a capricious soul who will reverse the cooling trend all by herself—assisted, perhaps, by the greenhouse effect—in due time.

Meanwhile, far from Africa's Sahel, in the small village of Singhali in India's Gujarat state, a Moslem landowner watches a slight breeze whip up dust devils in his parched field. He had hoped the field would produce enough rice to feed his family until the next harvest, but the yield this year was less than 5 percent of normal.

He wonders if the monsoons will fail again next year. But more immediately he wonders how his family will eat for the next ten months. There will be no second crop this year because there is no water for irrigation. Life must somehow be sustained until the next monsoon—if it comes. Every family has long ago emptied the huge earthen jars used to store grain, because every other year has been a drought year for the past decade.

The people of Singhali never live far from the razor edge of disaster, but the village of two hundred families has not known famine like this since 1900—before the time of this present generation.

About a third of the villagers are landowners. The largest plot is one hundred acres. Most own from three to five acres, because the land has been divided to the sons generation after generation. The only way some of these have lived in times of scarcity is by mortgaging their land to the moneylender. At 20 percent interest, they will either be in debt for a long time or else will lose their land.

The rest of the people in Singhali are day laborers. Normally they work on the surrounding farms, but this year they are not needed. The only work available is on a temporary government-sponsored project to deepen the nearly dry water reservoir.

The digging is all done by hand and the dirt is removed in baskets carried on the villagers' heads. When a worker completes an area five feet deep by ten feet square he is given eight kilos of food grain. At the end of each day he also gets the equivalent of ten cents in cash, about enough for tea. It is hard work for healthy people, but it is sometimes killing for those whose bodies are already weakened by malnourishment.

When I ask what they will do when that project is finished, they merely echo my question, "Yes, what will we do?" No one knows.

It is a very bad year for Singhali, and the prospects for many families range from bleak to hopeless. I talked to one family for which hope has almost run out. The father's name is Gokal Whalji Christie. (The "Christie" part, I am told, was added to indicate their new faith when the family became Christian believers.) He is forty. His wife's name is Daruben. She is thirty. Both ages are approximate; they don't really know. There are four children; the oldest son is twelve and has been dumb since birth.

Gokal is a laborer, but he has had no work for more than six months. In normal times his family would have two meals a day. Now they are thankful when they have one.

Meal? Well, hardly. In the morning it's a cup of plain tea, no milk or sugar. In the afternoon—if there is an afternoon meal —it's a small millet cake (*bajari*) with tea and maybe a raw onion or other vegetable. This is not enough calories—less than a hundred—for bare survival, much less for work.

"How does this affect you physically?" I inquire through the interpreter.

As with all the answers to my questions, this one is a matter-of-fact understatement: "We don't have enough strength because we don't have enough food. To work in the fields would not be possible even if there were jobs. I can barely work around the house. We are not in good health and our children also have the same difficulty. They don't grow healthy because they don't get enough food."

Stark. Honest. Devastating. I am deeply moved even though I have heard it, oh, so many times.

How does hunger affect their sleep?

"The children sleep whether they are hungry or not. But we hold such feelings for them and we worry so for them, that we do not get enough sleep."

Do the children cry from hunger?

Tears fill the eyes of the mother as she says: "The children cry much of the time because they are hungry. It is hard for us not to weep with them."

It is another quiet, deep moment, like that I had experienced with the Tuareg chief. The mother continues: "For the next crop we will have to wait one more year. If God keeps us alive, we will remain alive. Otherwise we will go back to God, and that is what I expect."

For the first time in my life I am face-to-face with a fellow Christian who fully expects to die—soon—from starvation. The effect on my life then and later is incalculable. Never have I seen such serene faith and utter trust.

"We don't envy any of the others who may have food. Whatever God wants us to have today he will give to us. We still depend upon him. There is no sharing of food in the village because everybody has the same difficulty. Some may have a little more than others, but that also is not enough."

Might life be better somewhere else? In one of the cities perhaps?

"Life is hard in the other villages as well. We would like to move to a city, but we are told there are no jobs there also. If we go to another place we will have no house for the children. No, we have decided to stay in the village. If death comes, it is better to die among friends."

I talk about the children again. What hopes and aspirations do the parents have for them?

"We depend upon God for the children's future. Right now it is hard to make plans beyond survival."

I wonder how the children feel. Because the oldest can't speak, I turn to Julius, age seven. He is a shy lad, but with some gentle coaxing he begins to open up. He is one of the two children who go to school. The other is Naomi, age six.

"What do you want to be, Julius, when you grow up?" (A more accurate phrasing would be "if you grow up," but honesty would be too brutal.)

"I would like to become a preacher like my uncle."

Now comes a tough question.

"Julius, if you could have anything in the world you wanted, what would you wish for?"

It's an attempt to get down inside the mind and heart of a seven-year-old. He doesn't answer right away. I don't know if he's thinking or reluctant to say, so I ask the question again.

When it comes, his answer devastates me: "For today, I would like a meal, and for the future, an education."

Spoken without emotion, straight, honest. No fantasizing. I decide that even at seven, when you have to live with "life vs. death" as the daily issue, there is no time for childhood dreams. Happily for me, what Julius asks for is something I can give him because those are the exact needs World Vision meets.

While I am talking to the Christie family, a handsome, bearded Moslem steps out of the crowd and says something to the village chief. I am told he is the owner of one of the few wells still producing in Singhali, but it is nearly dry and must be deepened. One of the Christians tells me this man, facing disaster himself, has continued to share the water in his well with Moslem and Christian alike.

When I tell him that his well will be one of the first projects in the village with which we will help, his flow of speech stops in midsentence. He just stands with his mouth open. No words came, but his soul spoke richly through the pools which formed in his eyes. With no attempt to wipe them dry, he just stood there and sobbed. He clutched my hand and would not let go. In his eyes I saw the response to love—and his response was love also.

It was a good feeling.

But the overriding question still remains: Will the monsoons return next year? Some will not live until the end of June to find out. But Singhali waits—and hopes.

What do these villagers know about changes in the circumpolar vortex which caused those precious rains to be dropped into the oceans or in a place that already has too much rainfall? They only know that any year the monsoons fail, people like themselves who always live marginally are pushed over the brink.

In normal years—or, weatherwise, has their entire lifetime

been abnormal?—the monsoon unrolls from the south like a great cloudy carpet. It is both an awesome and beautiful thing to see. The June-to-October rains bring a moratorium on marriages and religious festivals in northern India because, as the Hindu legend goes, "the gods are sleeping."

But far more important is the monsoon's effect on the economy. India's rivers and irrigation systems together can water only about 23 percent of the productive land. Thus, the monsoon rains—with all their vagaries—play a larger part in the economics and politics of India than any other single factor. That is why the progress of those dense nimbus clouds from the southwest is watched by the six hundred million people on the subcontinent with such profound concern.

"The monsoon is the most memorable experience of our lives," wrote Kushwant Singh, one of the country's sages. "For others to know India and her people, they have to know the monsoon."

But does anybody really know the monsoon? Dr. Pancheti Koteswaram, director-general of the Indian Meteorological Service and the country's number one weatherman, says, "The monsoon is one of the world's unsolved mysteries."

Conventional wisdom says it occurs when the moist sea breezes which work their way up from below the equator hit the hotter Asian land mass. But that is a simplification of a very complex and interlocked weather system. According to the late celebrated mathematician John von Neumann, who pioneered the idea of computers for analyzing weather:

"The hydrodynamics of meteorology presents without doubt the most complicated series of interrelated problems not only that we know of but that we can imagine."

The process starts—if interrelated weather patterns can be said to start anywhere—as the air in the tropics, heated by that great atomic-powered furnace the sun, rises in kingsize updrafts, sucking up incredible quantities of water from the sea every day. On the uptake, this heavy air loses much of its moisture in the equatorial zone creating what is called "rain belts." Thus lightened, it acts like the air over your living room radiator when it reaches the ceiling and moves toward the cooler walls. In the earth's case, these "walls" are the North and South Poles.

The air descends after traveling about a third of the way to the poles, creating the high pressure belts at a point where most of the world's deserts are found. Some of it turns back toward the equator. The rest resumes its far-from-leisurely journey toward the poles, having been speeded up by the east-to-west spin of the earth. Whipped along by the earth's rotation—1,100 miles per hour at the equator—the air begins to blow more and more from the west as it moves toward the poles. The most commonly observed results of this are the prevailing westerlies at lower altitudes and the jet streams in the higher reaches.

None of this is irrelevant to the arrival or nonappearance of the monsoon in India, for ultimately the poleward-bound air bumps into the cold air extending out from the poles. This mixture is called the "circumpolar vortex" and it is this collision of air masses which produces most of the weather in the temperate zones.

To understand the influence of the circumpolar vortex in the northern hemisphere, try to imagine the full skirt of a Spanish dancer draped over the North Pole extending downward into our temperate zone. The bottom of the skirt is as full of waves and bounce as if the dancer were still wearing it, because the air movements are modified by every mountain range, every plateau, every body of water, every lowland.

The difference in polar and equatorial temperatures determines how far down the skirt extends. Because of the global cooling trend, the lower edge of the circumpolar vortex has not retreated in recent years as far toward the pole as in previous summers, thus blocking the monsoons out of the regions where they are vital to the survival of hundreds of millions of people.

In spite of the fact that Dr. Koteswaram noted in 1974 that the Indian monsoon had stalled on a line extending south of Bombay and into Uttar Pradesh and extreme eastern India, he does not believe it is permanently retreating.

"I personally have examined time series of rainfall in eighteen states of India going back to the mid-19th century," he said, adding: "I could confirm no trend of diminishing rainfall in areas of North India, as would have to occur if the monsoon were in fact receding.

"The only trend I could detect was that there has been a marked increase in rainfall in this century along the west coast from Bombay south and this seems to be related to sunspot activity." His conclusion puts him squarely with Walter O. Roberts and against Bryson.[5] So you can choose either theory and be sure of support.

I would merely point out that if the good doctor is wrong in his interpretation of the data, it will not be the first time a human mind has found it impossible to accept the unthinkable. And a long-range failure of the Indian monsoon, with its resultant staggering human disaster, is the most unthinkable of thoughts.

But whoever is right, the people of Singhali know the 1974 monsoon never did arrive. They don't debate the relative merits of the two theories because they never heard of them. They just wonder where they will get grain for tomorrow's *chapattis* and how long it takes to starve to death.

What good is it to explain to them—or to the Bengalis on the other side of the Hindustan Peninsula—that a capricious swirl on the hem of the circumpolar vortex pushed North India's seasonal monsoon nearly a thousand miles to the east and dumped the water on Bangladesh, creating disastrous floods?

Jobeda, who sits in a refugee camp in Dacca waiting for death to take the sixth of her seven children, knows only that this time the waters washed away the last thread of her hope. It had been holding tenuously ever since the cyclone of 1970 in which between a quarter and a half million people perished.

While none of Jobeda's family died then, that time marked the beginning of her sorrow. Marooned for days, she and her husband returned to a site from which their village had completely disappeared. All that remained were the children and the clothes on their backs. For this family and countless others, life became a process of deterioration and death. They couldn't even get a toehold for the climb back. The clothes grew threadbare; malnutrition and starvation took the children one by one.

Held together by the fatalism of her Islamic faith and the strength infused into the Bengali bloodline through centuries of struggling to survive, Jobeda managed to cling to life and sanity for four years. Then came the flood of 1974. It inundated two-thirds of the country and destroyed virtually all the season's rice crop. What would have been India's blessing was Bangladesh's curse.

Jobeda's husband was one of twenty-seven thousand deaths due to starvation reported as another result of the flood. It was too much for her. She pulled her few rags together, picked up a clay pot, gathered her remaining two children and went to Dacca in a last desperate effort to keep them alive. There she became a refugee statistic—one of twelve hundred in this camp —just as her husband and five of her children had become starvation statistics.

When we saw her sitting stoically in the corner of a makeshift hospital, she was emotionally wiped out. Jobeda had no tears left to cry. Lying at her feet, the two remaining children were too weak from malnutrition and sickness to do more than whimper.

In some ways, this family was Bangladesh in microcosm. Called the "basket case of the world," the country of eighty-three million people cannot rise to its feet before it is flattened again by either man or nature.

Mother Nature doesn't always seem to be mankind's friend. Her calamities and uncertainties add enormous, unpredictable problems to the already gigantic task of feeding a hungry world. Cyclones in Bangladesh and northern Australia are only one symptom of a freakish weather system which can be alternately kind and brutal. There are hurricanes in the Caribbean and southeastern United States. Drought in Africa, South Asia and Central America. Killer floods in the Philippines and Pakistan, as well as in Bangladesh. Eight inches of August snow on western Canada's wheat fields. Unusually bitter winters in America's northwest and Siberia, coupled with unprecedented winter warmth in the northeastern United States and European Russia.

At this point nobody can say for sure what it all means. It seems likely that the gigantic witches' brew being concocted in the twenty-mile-deep atmospheric blanket which holds our weather contains a lot more surprises. And any disruption of the norm is generally considered bad, since man and the environment will both have to make traumatic adjustments to accommodate the change.

Of all the ingredients in the agricultural mix, weather is the one about which the least can be done.

However, modern technology may make the future brighter than the past. We already possess abilities to make some modifications in weather's most radical and destructive deviations. Dams can be constructed to harness runaway floods. Although cloud seeding to produce rain is far from being an exact science, it is being done with some notable success. Tornadoes can be warned against. Hurricane watches now give us enough time to "batten down the hatches," and recent experiments give hope that we may be able to weaken the fury of the winds.

The calamitous tropical cyclone which started Jobeda's sorrow on November 12, 1970, had been spotted on satellite pictures. But it was easier to get the message from the satellite to the receiving station than to deliver it to the crowded populations of the coastal islands which lay in its path. As a consequence of this glaring communications gap, uncounted thousands of people were drowned by mammoth tidal surges in the greatest natural catastrophe of this century.

Maybe someday soon we will fashion a terrestrial communications system that will match in speed and efficiency our already incredible celestial transmissions.

Man's own inadvertent contributions to climate problems are also not without some solutions. Writing in the journal *Science*, Drs. S. I. Rasool and S. H. Schneider suggest that within fifty years we can reduce atmospheric pollution enough to reverse the cooling trend by changing over from polluting fossil fuels to clean nuclear power in energy production.

Some of nature's calamities which contribute to the problem of hunger already can be blunted by using existing technology. Modifications of hailstorms is one example. Total losses from hail in this country alone run as high as $300 million. Hailstones can strip a corn field to ribbons and level to the ground a field of wheat. Experiments in the Soviet Union with cloud seeding have proven remarkably effective. So much so, in fact, that antiaircraft batteries have been set up in the wheat fields of the Caucasus. When an embryonic hailstorm is detected by radar, the guns fire explosive charges filled with silver iodide into the clouds. The crystals turn the water vapor into relatively harmless sleet before it can form into deadly hailstones.

The Russians claim that use of this method has reduced hail damage by 85 percent in some areas.

There is considerable hope for improvement in long-range weather forecasting, which at present is a notoriously inaccurate science. Those who have had their picnics or parades rained on would argue that frequently the short-range predictions aren't much better. One irate housewife telephoned a Washington television weatherman on a wintry morning and acidly told him: "I wish you'd come out here and scoop this six inches of 'partly cloudy' off my driveway!"

But the truth is that today's scientific forecasting is light years ahead of the folklore of earlier times when we depended on rheumatic joints or the behavior of birds to give us our weather clues. Moreover, long-range prognostication is going to get a lot better.

New patterns are being discovered that can tip us off to future weather trends. For instance, there appears to be an unexplained relationship between ocean temperatures and weather. A meteorologist with California's Scripps Institution of Oceanography has found that the appearance of hot and cold patches in certain parts of the Pacific Ocean seem to be followed by colder-than-usual winters in the eastern United States and milder-than-usual winters in the west.

This and other studies which are going on may one day give the farmer enough advance notice so that he can select the right seed variety and time its planting to fit next year's growing season.

The Bible is not speaking metaphorically as it tells of a future time when "the desert shall rejoice, and blossom as a rose," when "the parched ground shall become a pool, and the thirsty land springs of water." [6]

We are told only the fact, not the time.

It could come, if God blesses man's efforts, on some early tomorrow. Thankfully, some technology to modify the weather and make it more beneficent is already here. New discoveries are on the way and some breakthroughs may be just around the next cyclone.

Or the next drought.

I hope my Tuareg friends and Jobeda and the people in Singhali can make it till then.

I told them a lot of people would be trying to help.

Chapter 4
Dispossession: The Hungry Travelers

THE MOVEMENTS OF THE HUMAN FAMILY across the earth have always had less to do with wanderlust than with its search for food.

Archaeologists and historians are revising old theories about the fall of ancient civilizations such as the Indus Valley, the Hittite, the Mycenaean, and the Mali empire of Africa. New evidence indicates the cause of their collapse may have been due more to the deteriorating climate-food situation than to barbarian invaders.

The entire history of the Jewish people has nearly as much to do with Jacob and his sons settling in Egypt to escape the famine in Canaan as it does with Abraham moving from Ur. The plot of that dramatic story of Jacob, Joseph and the brothers hinges on hunger—the years of famine which struck not only Egypt where Joseph ruled as prime minister, but all the surrounding lands as well.

In his novel, *The Grapes of Wrath,* John Steinbeck movingly chronicled the migration of the Joads and their Okie cousins from the midwestern dustbowl of the 1930s to the "promised land" of California's fertile San Joaquin valley.

It is hunger in today's Sahel that drives the nomad from his desert home in the hope that he will find greener grass on the other side of the sand dune.

Hunger is both a cause and consequence of dispossession. Some have become hungry wanderers because the land of their ancestors could no longer sustain them. Others are without food—or, at least, without enough food—not because the land won't produce, but because they have been driven from it by war, tribal conflicts or political dealings.

Consider the case of the Palestinians.

Victims both of war and international political decisions over which they had no control, these people have been without a homeland—and most of them without a home—since 1948 when the United Nations created the state of Israel and decreed the end of Palestine. I will not argue the rightness or wrongness of that decision, for political questions of that nature are beyond the scope of this book. However, there can be no questioning by even the most committed Zionist of the enormous human tragedy which resulted from it.

In 1974, twenty-six years later, the United States Committee on Refugees reported over two million Palestinians still displaced in the Middle East. Most of them are dispersed in Jordan, Lebanon, Syria and Israel (or the Gaza Strip and Jordan-West Bank for those who prefer not to recognize the territorial conquests of the Six-Day War).

Many, like the Abu Oweimer family, have been there from the beginning. For the Oweimers, dispossession is now a way of life. Three generations have made their home in Shelter 65, Block B, Maghazi camp in the Gaza Strip for nearly a quarter-century. It is barely distinguishable from the hundreds of others which house about 8,500 of their fellow countrymen. A rough door in the mud-brick wall, dignified with the Koranic inscription, "In the name of God the all-merciful and compassionate," opens off a narrow alley onto a sandy courtyard and two small rooms.

Nine people live here.

One of the rooms, its floor area not more than ten square yards, serves as kitchen, working and eating area and a place to sit when it is cold or wet outside. The other is the communal sleeping room, where mattresses are rolled up during the day to make extra space for sitting or study.

The hot, dry summers make outdoor living possible for five months of the year, but the heat is searing and there is little

shade. An outside tap brings water into the home—a luxury
not shared by all the residents—and a private latrine has been
installed. Kerosene oil provides fuel for the small stove which
serves for both cooking and heating, and the lamp gives a little
light in the dark evenings.

The Abu Oweimers were never a wealthy family. Of Bedouin
stock, they established themselves in Beersheba where citrus
fruits and vegetables grown on the plot of land around their
home provided a small income. But it was an independent
livelihood and a guarantee that the sons would be cared for in
the future in a modest way.

The events of 1948 shattered this way of life which had
seemed so solidly based. When their land was lost, the family
fled westward to the Gaza Strip, a sadly congested enclave
where today some four hundred thousand people, nearly three-
fourths of them Palestinian refugees, are crowded into less
than one hundred forty square miles.

Here for twenty-five years the Abu Oweimers have lived the
life of the dispossessed—a life made empty by grinding poverty, pervading hunger, soul-killing boredom and shameful
dependency.

From time to time they have been joined by others who
come in waves with each Arab-Israeli conflict. Tens of thousands have been born in the camps. Pawns in a political
struggle to which they see no end, not a few have turned to
spectacular violence in an effort to force the world to take
some notice of the futility of their lives.

Plane hijackings, embassy shootings, the massacres at Lod
airport in Tel Aviv and the 1972 Olympic Games in Munich—
these and more were spawned in the camps of a dispossessed
people who have no home and no hope.

As rash, repugnant, inexcusable and tragic as these acts
are, they are not senseless. Not to a trapped people who feel
they have nothing left to lose. And they are not likely to stop,
given the desperate state of mind of these guerrillas, until
world opinion has forced governments to look beyond the
symptomatic fever of violence to the disease of their displacement.

Listen to a refugee college teacher:

"I think any American would die for his country when the

time comes. And I feel that we have such a worthy cause that it is very hard for a Palestinian not to be doubly committed because of the injustice . . . I am talking from my heart really. Sometimes when I eat, I think 'here I am eating' and there are so many people thrown out on the desert. Houses are demolished and they don't have any place to go. So we suffer very deeply." [1]

A businessman describes the emotional trauma of being dispossessed:

"We had to leave that part of the world just overnight and leave everything, our property, our business, our belongings, even our sentimental belongings. Sometimes I miss that little tree behind the house or that tomb of my father, my mother, or grandfather. These things are not of any material value, but they are of tremendous sentimental traditional value to me as a Palestinian. That is why we will not forget that part of the world and we will work very hard . . . " [2]

The suffering is physical as well as emotional. The camps can provide only the minimum needed for survival—minimum space, minimum shelter, minimum food. Many families still have to depend on some international relief agency for their next meal. The largest of these agencies is UNRWA (United Nations Relief and Works Agency), but it is able to spend only thirteen cents a day per person to provide housing, food, medical care and education.

Many refugees are still in tents with only one thickness of canvas to keep out the brutal summer sun and the harsh desert winter. Others have graduated to simple concrete block shelters, but life is only a bit less grim than in the tent cities. Everywhere there is scant water supply and inadequate sanitary facilities. Hunger, while not acute for most, is as constant as the blowing sand.

It is a life they share with more than fourteen million other displaced persons in the world, down from a high of over eighteen million in 1970. About 60 percent of them are found in Asia, with the war in South Vietnam and Cambodia accounting for some seven million. There are still about sixty-four thousand Tibetan refugees, mostly in India, who fled the 1951 Chinese occupation of their country.

Africa accounts for just over a million of the total, with the victims of the Sahel drought being the latest additions. The Western Hemisphere has almost one and a half million refugees, including three hundred twenty-six thousand Cubans in the United States and a reported three hundred thousand Haitians in the Dominican Republic.

If all these refugees were brought together into one nation, it would have a population larger than most of the countries of Europe or Latin America. To get an idea of the magnitude of this festering social and economic problem, try to imagine the total populations of Illinois and Wisconsin being uprooted and sent scrambling over the state lines with nothing but the clothes on their backs and—maybe—a cooking pot.

In addition to the staggering personal costs, think about what that would mean to the adjoining states of Minnesota, Nebraska, Iowa and Indiana. Refugees from the earlier collapsing civilizations were often able to migrate to sparsely inhabited areas and start all over again. Today's crowded world offers no such prospect, and even if it did, the reality of political divisions and national boundaries would make mass migrations impossible except in the most primitive areas.

The presence of ten million unwanted and burdensome Bengali refugees on her territory was one of the reasons for India's entry into the war for independence in Bangladesh. Suddenly, in almost one wave, India received into her already crowded eastern states of West Bengal, Bihar and Meghalaya the equivalent of two-thirds of an entire year's new population growth. Faced with chronic food shortages of her own, how could Mother India provide for these uninvited waifs of a civil war?

For many months she tried to, at a cost to her own marginal economy of $3 million a day, but that didn't meet even the basic needs of the rising flood of humanity. So India attacked the Pakistani army in Bangladesh, not primarily because of the antipathy between the two countries, but to open up the territory and reverse the tide of refugees. In today's shoulder-to-shoulder world, dispossession for any reason has serious political consequences.

But always the most terrible price is the human one. Hunger, disease and suffering inevitably follow in the wake

of such migrations. *Time* magazine (August 2, 1971) describes the agony of the displaced Bengalis:

> Over the rivers and down the highways and along countless jungle paths, the population of East Pakistan continues to hemorrhage into India: an endless unorganized flow of refugees with a few tin kettles, cardboard boxes and ragged clothes piled on their heads, carrying their sick children and their old.
>
> . . . Many are sick and covered with sores. Others have cholera, and when they die by the roadside there is no one to bury them. The Hindus, when they can, put a hot coal in the mouths of their dead or singe the body in lieu of cremation. The dogs, the vultures and the crows do the rest.
>
> . . . The column pushing into India never ends, day or night. . . . Hundreds of thousands of these are still wandering about the countryside without food and shelter. Near the border, some have taken over schools to sleep in; others stay with villagers or sleep out in the fields and under the trees.
>
> . . . Says one doctor: "The people are not even crying any more." Perhaps because what they flee from is even worse.

A farmer named Simari Bjundan was one of nearly fifty thousand who crossed the border on a day when I was there with a load of baby food. His family was more fortunate than most I saw. Most carried nothing, while he pushed a handcart on which were piled a few of their belongings—some pots, two blankets, a chicken, a shovel, a plow and a sack of rice. By leaving ahead of the advancing Pakistani army they had time to gather a few possessions.

The chicken was stolen in a few days, the rice was gone in a month, but his exile was to last a year.

So Simari, his wife and their four children joined the army of hungry travelers. But they were drafted; it wasn't a voluntary enlistment.

In fact, no one chooses to be a refugee. By definition, a refugee is a displaced person who is the victim of social unrest, intolerance, natural disasters, or war. In its 1972 report, the U.S. Committee for Refugees said:

"[The refugee's] decision to leave his home and seek asylum, with all the pain and courage which that involves for himself

and his family—his decision was his response to something
that happened, something that was decided outside himself
which frightened or repelled him irrevocably. He may be in
flight from a fire bombing of his village in Vietnam or Cambodia or Laos, and is running in mortal fear of his very life.
His decision may be more measured because of a prolonged
harassment of his spirit, as in Eastern Europe or China or
Haiti. In either case, he has been violated as a person and
has the right to asylum and to any help he can get.

" . . . beneath the statistics and arguments about cause and
effect there are people—children and men and women who eat
and breathe and pray and hope like us, and their right to our
help in their circumstances can only be denied if we deny the
God who gave us life and embrothered them to us."

Those who have been victimized by war, social unrest or
political decisions have voted with the only ballot frequently
left to them—their feet. This vote for life or breatheable air
may take the refugee halfway around the world. Or it may take
him no further than over a barbed wire fence or just across
a river. Nearly half the population of Cambodia (Khmer Republic) are refugees in their own country. An estimated three
million people have been uprooted in four years of fighting,
and upwards of a million have descended on the capital city
of Phnom Penh, more than doubling its peacetime population.

Horrendous nutritional problems have resulted. A people
who were self-sufficient in food now depend on rice—when
they have it—shipped from the fields of Arkansas and Texas.
(Ironically, the polished American rice, stripped of Vitamin
B, is causing an increasing incidence of beriberi among the
refugees!) Reasonably well-nourished when there were fish
for the catching, vegetables for the growing, and chickens for
the raising—that is, when the people were on the land—their
state of health and nutrition daily deteriorates in the refugee
camps.

The children are especially vulnerable. Many fathers are
dead. Others have been kidnapped and forced into servitude
by the Khmer Rouge (Cambodian Communist insurgents) and
North Vietnamese. Most of the rest are with the government
forces. Mothers try to eke out the family livelihood in a multi-

tude of ways, all of which usually mean her absence from dawn to dusk. The youngest children are looked after by the older ones.

Food is scarce; money scarcer.

Result: childhood nutritional disaster.

Two case histories from the World Vision nutrition center in the Tuol Kauk area of the city are typical. The center has room for about seventy-five children and it is always full. These are the worst cases, brought from camps all around the city. Thousands of others are given special feeding in the camps.

The nutrition center was a natural and necessary outgrowth of World Vision's medical program among refugees. Many children are so far gone by the time a doctor sees them, they cannot make it without special care.

At the center, Dr. Penelope Key, a British doctor who heads a team of sixty-eight Khmer nationals and expatriates, points out to me a desperately ill child. Kim Hong is twelve to eighteen months old. Nobody knows for sure. He was found in a camp being "cared for" by his ten-year-old sister. The grandmother was the only adult sharing the hovel, but every day she must go out to work. The only way to find such cases is to search them out, for how would a ten-year-old know to bring him to the clinic? Kim Hong has marasmus (an extreme form of malnutrition), pneumonia and severe diarrhea. During the month he has been at the center, the child has nearly died several times. Until three days ago he was on intravenous feeding. Now he must be fed every two hours, right through the night. Normally that is the responsibility of a family member who stays with each nonorphaned child, but the overworked nurses just don't have the heart to wake the older sister, so they do her job during the night hours.

While we stand there, the tiny-girl-trying-to-be-grownup is spooning milk into the mouth of her very sick baby brother. I ask about her family. She says her father was taken by the VC (meaning Vietcong, a term applied to the enemy, even though most of the fighting is done by Khmers, not Vietnamese). Mother? Disappeared, doesn't know if she is alive or not. There were nine children, she tells us, and she presumes the rest are "with the VC."

She is sad about it, but she obviously takes pride in her role as surrogate mother.

Dr. Key points to another child. Yam Bunthoeun is six years old, one of four children. His father died in a rocket attack three years ago. When the boy was brought to the center six weeks before, he weighed less than thirty pounds and was too weak to walk. His arms measured only four inches in circumference. Now he has gained five pounds and the doctor is confident he will make it.

Not all do make it. The mortality rate at the center is 15 percent, not bad considering the marginal state of most of those brought in. But the nurses are appalled by it. I have seen them cry when they arrive for duty and are told which ones didn't make it through the night.

With only slight variations, the stories from Tuol Kauk nutrition center could be repeated thousands of times. They comprise one of the least-talked-about of war's many tragedies. Malnutrition induced by war's displacement may not be as spectacular as an exploding rocket, but it can be just as deadly.

The cities of Africa's Sahel are also overflowing with refugees, not running from a war but fleeing before the black horse of famine and his rider. Nouakchott, the sand-swept capital of Mauritania, has an estimated 120,000 people living there, three times its usual population. Mopti, a city in Mali with a normal population of about 55,000 now has about 110,000 people living in and around it. Fabled Timbuktu has also doubled in population—from 12,000 to 24,000.

In India the situation doesn't seem to be as bad, but there are reports of migration from dry countryside areas to the cities, perhaps involving hundreds of thousands of people.

In the countries of the Sahel, however, an estimated four to five million people were put on the move by drought. Hundreds of villages were abandoned for a less satisfying but more assured life in the camps.

Into one of the nomad camps that ring the city of Nouakchott, Ehel Idi has brought his family of six. Life is sustained by the distribution of American-provided sorghum grain and occasionally some powdered milk. But Mr. Idi and millions more can no longer be productive and have become a drain on the world's economy. He had never met city people before, for his world was the edge of the desert. His life was herding cattle and until a few years ago he owned three hundred head. Now he's down to ten sheep and an emaciated goat. He longs to go back to the life he knows.

"But I am forced to stay here," Mr. Idi told an AID worker. "I tried to survive. We had finally thirty-five cattle left. I cut down trees for them to eat the leaves and keep them alive. But it was no use. They all died and this is what I have left. I didn't want to come to the city even then, but others told me I must live. I could stay alive and find food for the family if we came here."

He would like to work, but is handicapped by having only one leg. He cut off the other leg himself when it was broken from a fall down a well.

"I want no pity. I want to live away from here and herd cattle. Maybe when the rains come . . . "

His words trail off, but they are picked up and echoed by Ehel Lemeounek, a camel herder and head of a family of fifteen. Once he owned two hundred camels. Now he has none.

"My whole life is herding camels," he says. "I know no other life. I want to go back to camel herding. I would work as a guard if I could get a job, but I would rather take care of five camels than anything else in the world."

Most of the hot windy days he spends under his sheepskin tent with his family. What do they do? He shrugs his shoulders and says:

"We meditate."

Neither of these men fit the image which many of us in the West have of such people. Too often we think of them as lazy, incompetent, worthless beggars who would like to remain on the international dole forever. If that caricature fits any of them, it is certainly no higher percentage of the total than would be found in any other country, including the United States. For the majority, it is grossly inaccurate and cruelly unfair.

Remember, except for those who have fled their homeland over matters of conscience, no one chooses to be a refugee.

There are groups, however, which do not fit the standard definition of refugees yet must be mentioned in this chapter because they are displaced and they are living marginally, albeit more or less voluntarily. They are not as much dispossessed as transplanted. These are the tens of thousands involved in national programs of resettlement designed to relieve population overcrowding.

These transmigrants do not cross national boundaries and in most instances they are offered some financial inducement by their governments, either in cash or land grants. In addition to distributing the population of a country more evenly, these movements also have secondary benefits for governments in that they open up virgin territory for future expansion and development.

The concept certainly has validity, and in most cases the programs have a long-range salutary effect on some of the pressing national problems. However, it must be honestly recognized that the early years are hard and bitter indeed for most transmigrants. For that reason they must be counted among the planet's hungry travelers.

In Brazil the resettlement program is taking place under the government's policy of "national integration," which includes the colonization of Amazonia. This vast jungle region covers 42 percent of Brazil's land mass, but has only 4 percent of the population. This has prompted the government to begin a campaign to recruit new citizens for the Amazon basin.

Officially, the government says the plan is meant "to open up a horizon for the population surpluses of the Brazilian Northeast, for descendants of Europeans who are now experiencing the distresses of Southern *minifundios,* or for Northeastern migrants who are increasing the dramatic situation of the large Southern megalopolis by lacking qualification for confronting the competition of the urban labor market."

I'll translate: the settling of Amazonia is basically for three purposes—to relieve population and economic pressures in the arid Northeast, to thin out the marginal farmers in the South, and to keep the unskilled peasants in the Northeast from migrating South into a surfeited labor market.

The only thing debatable is the part about relieving population pressures. That is yet to be proven.

To make life in the primitive region more liveable, the

Trans-Amazon Highway is under construction from the coast into the interior. Cities are being built at intervals to serve the more basic settlement units which contain fifty to sixty families. The government says it will provide basic facilities and services.

Over half the colonists thus far have come from Northeast Brazil, recruited by announcements on radio and television and through posters. The government provides either air or bus transportation. It is an attractive offer for many illiterate or semiliterate peasants who have never been above the subsistence level and most of the time below it.

But the Garden of Eden it isn't, as they soon find out. In fact, many have died who arrived already weak and sick from years of malnourishment. There is a high incidence of malaria, and clearing the jungle can break even a healthy man.

Disappointingly, both to settlers and scientists who had hoped Amazonia might help feed the world, the land is not nearly as fertile and productive as was originally thought. When the protective growth is cleared away and the land is laid bare to the elements, the colonists find the soil becomes badly leached from the frequent rains.

Whatever are the long-range benefits to a nation from transmigration, they are achieved at the price of privation, hardship and hunger paid by the migrants.

For some the price is too high and they bail out of the project. There are no figures on the desertion rate among transmigrants in Indonesia, but it undoubtedly would be much higher if the way back home were across land instead of water. The Indonesian experiment was begun by the Dutch government in 1902 in an effort to relieve the pressure of an overcrowded Java. It is still going on under the national government for exactly the same reason.

With eighty million people, the island of Java, which is roughly the size of the state of New York, is the most densely populated area of its size in the world. The average density is over seven hundred per square mile, while in some areas like Central Java it is more than three thousand per square mile. If the United States had that density, our population would exceed that of the world! Being rich in islands—including Borneo, the third largest in the world—and with some of them relatively uninhabited compared to Java (Borneo, for example, has a density of only 6.7 per square mile), the government has continued what seems to be the logical process of transmigration.

Some 148 projects have been established in 17 of the country's 26 provinces, according to government figures. Each migrant gets four things:

1. Transport for his family from their home to their island destination.

2. A very simple house, valued at around $25.00.

3. Two hectares (five acres) of land on which to build the house and grow crops, as well as tools, seeds and fertilizer for one crop.

4. Food supply for up to a year in the event of crop failure, which is more the rule than the exception during the first year.

Since most of the projects are located in very poor, marginal type land districts, failures are common. In South Kalimantan, for instance, tidal action in the low-lying land assigned to transmigrants makes the land salty and marshy, guaranteeing scant harvests or crop failure. The people must work long, hard hours for minimal returns. For this reason the projects are generally unpopular and not a few abandon them, preferring at least the poverty of familiar surroundings.

The Surip family decided to stay. It wasn't too hard a decision to make, because here at least Mr. Surip had hope. His life in central Java was a dead-end street. Central Kalimantan offered hard work, but promise. When he first saw the land though, his heart sank. It was still half-jungle. The large trees had been felled, but their stumps were still in the ground. He would have to clear the land himself. He hadn't known that.

His first priority was a vegetable garden. Then he must clear enough land for rice. It is the hardest work he has ever done and there are times when he wonders if it will ever be finished.

With the family's efforts totally concentrated on producing enough food to stay alive, there is little if any time for improving the quality of life. Children are rarely in school, not only because teachers don't want to leave Java for the frontier, but also because the children are needed to help in the fields.

Normally it takes five years to get the first food crop from virgin land, and up to twenty years for the project to be fully self-supporting. To suffer so much and wait so long, a migrant must be possessed with an inexhaustible supply of hope.

Amazingly, that seems to be the quality which stretches the furthest among all the dispossessed. I can confirm Pope's observation, "Hope springs eternal in the human breast." Over and over again I have seen hope vigorous and unshaken in spite of circumstances which should break a man.

Beside a lonely road in the Sahel on a blistering day, several young men appeared to be plowing a dry, powdery field with scrawny cattle stumbling in the dust.

What could they be doing? Planting? There was no moisture in the soil. The seeds would certainly blow away. The farmer, whose sons were driving the cattle, smiled when asked what was going on.

"No," he said, "We are not plowing yet. We have not had rain for a whole year." He looked up at the cloudless sky, then down at the sizzling ground.

"We have survived," he said. "And we still have these cattle. We have the American sorghum and one way or another we will continue to live."

He smiled again, and nodded toward his sons driving the cattle around the dusty field in the broiling sun.

"No, we are not plowing now. But these animals have not had a harness on for a year now. We are getting them ready. We are practicing.

"When the rains come," he said, "we will be ready."

As long as the indomitable human spirit refuses to be crushed, there is hope for a hungry world.

Chapter 5
Urbanization: The Fatal Lure of the City

Prostitutes in Carapebuce are no more rare than fish in a lake. It exists for them. Located about ten miles outside the center of Vitória, capital of the state of Espírito Santo in Brazil, it was founded a few years ago to get vice out of the heart of the city.

Although not officially approved, it is officially ignored. The economy of Carapebuce is based on the "oldest profession," which is practiced openly. In an area covering several blocks, there are more than one hundred buildings classified as hotels, bars and nightclubs.

The town is right out of the old West. Rows of one-story adobe buildings line the unpaved streets. Girls slouch in the open doorways and sit in the windows. Even though the nights are chilly, the dress is minimum and the exposure maximum.

A group of girls crouch around a fire in the road. Among them is Ana. She was born a few miles away in São Torquato, the toughest district in Vitória. She is the oldest of nine children. Her father disappeared when the youngest, now ten months old, was born. Because she was always hungry and her mother had more mouths than she could possibly feed, Ana left soon after her father disappeared.

Inevitably she wound up at Carapebuce and joined an estimated two thousand of her sisters in the trade in this one district alone.

That might not seem so strange, except that Ana is just twelve years old. As one of thousands of child prostitutes in the teeming cities of Brazil, Ana is part of one of the country's gravest social problems.

It is particularly acute where poverty is the harshest. That would include most of the urban areas of the Northeast, especially Recife, Fortaleza and Belém, as well as Manaus which is a thousand miles into the Amazon forest.

Most people do not see the child prostitutes. Afraid of a run-in with police or being picked up by child welfare officers, they keep to the shadows, tense and nervous as fawns. But they are there. In a series of raids over a two-month period in 1974, more than twelve hundred girls from eleven to seventeen were found working as prostitutes in Carapebuce alone.

Where else in the world could a twelve-year-old earn 4,000 cruzeiros (about $600) a month, which is ten times what an adult man would get for working all day in a factory? Some families live on these earnings entirely. Sometimes a girl might support two families by hiring a youngster from another family to take care of her children.

"Once a girl of twelve or thirteen has earned that kind of money, you haven't much hope of getting her out of prostitution," says Luis Geraldo Calmon Ferreira da Silva, a young lawyer of the Espírito Santo Foundation for the Well Being of Minors. "Usually she has no education, no training. There is nothing you can offer her that will pay her anything like the same money."

He says they are lucky if they can rehabilitate 15 percent of the child prostitutes.

Foundation president Luiz Fernando Garcia Marques says the problem springs from the massive move to the cities from the land in the past three decades.

"In 1940, 65 percent of Brazil's population was rural and 35 percent urban," he explains, "now it's exactly the reverse. Most of those people who have moved into the cities have little education and no preparation for city life. Some are absorbed by industry, but the number of persons on the margin is growing rapidly."

In those words, Marques had described a worldwide phenomenon which is making a catastrophic contribution to world hunger.

The question asked in a World War I vintage song, "How'ya gonna keep 'em down on the farm?" is now a universal dilemma. The trend to urbanization is as old as the tower of Babel, but with the growth in world population this related problem has reached unprecedented proportions. So much so, in fact, that estimates indicate all of the net increase over the past fifteen years has gone into the cities.

In 1850, according to Alvin Toffler, only 4 cities on the face of the earth had a population of one million or more. By 1900 the number had increased to 19, and by 1960 there were 141.[1] Today he says, somewhat more than 25 percent of the earth's population can be found in the industrialized cities.[2]

For those of us in the industrialized West, this trend to urbanization may not seem to be a problem. Our nation, which a century ago was about 25 percent urban is today about 25 percent rural, and this fantastic shift has occurred without any major economic or social upheaval. But it must be pointed out that in the developed world, as industrialization replaces agriculture and as agriculture becomes more mechanized, this is a normal trend.

In the Third and Fourth Worlds, however, it creates chaotic conditions because (1) it reduces the number of people involved in food production without a comparable rise in mechanization and (2) there are not enough jobs in the cities for the masses that arrive daily. The results are totally predictable: unemployment, followed by poverty, followed by hunger, followed by malnourishment. Following inevitably then, are slums, crime and political unrest.

If the cities have always been pools of unemployment, in the developing countries today the pools have become an ocean. Although there are no accurate figures available to compare rural and urban unemployment in the LDCs, the International Labor Organization (ILO) in Geneva has compiled an index that gives some idea of the situation.

Since it is impossible to get reliable data from many developing countries, the figures given below are valuable only as a basis for comparison. However, the ratios shown in this unemployment index do reflect the magnitude of the problem. The unemployed figure under "Rural" is the index base; the figure under "Urban" indicates the differential ratio:

UNEMPLOYMENT INDEX

	Rural	*Urban*	
Indonesia	100	250	
Iran	100	200	
Korea	100	450	
Philippines	100	200	
Thailand	100	1600	(*this figure is for Bangkok and Thonburi; for other cities it is 800*)

If this trend continues, the ILO says, in twenty years there will be more unemployed people in cities than employed!

Socioeconomist Robert Heilbroner makes the same point and mentions the frightening implications:

"Rapidly increasing populations in the rural areas of technologically static societies create unemployable surpluses of manpower that stream into cities in search of work. . . . In many such cities unemployment has already reached levels of 25 percent, and it will inevitably rise as the city populace swells. The cesspool of Calcutta thus becomes more and more the image of urban degradation toward which the dynamics of population growth are pushing the poorest lands." [3]

To see what this means in human terms you only have to go to Calcutta's Sealdah railway station. Here live some of the most wretched of Calcutta's homeless hordes. Even though there is food in the countryside, they have left because they could not afford to buy it. The city offers more places to beg and scavenge. Not far from the station there is a market where cabbage leaves and cauliflower stems are left in the street when the vendors close their stalls. There are also garbage dumps where they can fight with the crows for rotting scraps of food.

Thousands of people pass through Sealdah station daily, but no one has ever taken a census of its permanent residents. Why should anyone bother with a few hundred un-

fortunates, when in the city there are more than two hundred thousand people living and sleeping on the streets who are no better off—or only slightly so—than their brothers-in-poverty at the railway station?

To go from Sealdah station to the streets is only to pass from one degree of total despair to another.

Babu Lal has never lived anywhere but in the streets. He has been a pavement-dweller since he was born over fifty years ago to a mother who was a sweeper and a father who did odd jobs. Like so many others, he scratches a living of sorts from the garbage heaps of the city.

His day begins about dawn when the street starts to come alive and the traffic begins to move. The thin cotton *dhoti* which has covered him during the night is readjusted around his body to become his only garment. He sifts through the trash piles until around eleven o'clock, pouching his finds—rags, papers, broken glass—in a bag slung over his shoulder.

As noon approaches, Babu Lal heads for the scrap merchants to sell his morning's collection. It nets him about twelve cents, enough for a meager lunch. Then it is back to the streets again where he hopes to find enough junk to pay for dinner. And so goes the day—every day.

No one knows how many of the ragpickers there are competing for Calcutta's leftovers, but Babu Lal says the city's seven and a half million inhabitants produce enough garbage to go around and make it possible for the scavengers to stay alive. Unofficial estimates place the total at over twenty thousand pounds a day. But in the economic order of the developing countries, one man's junk is another man's livelihood.

A nation's refuse heaps are an accurate, if mute, witness to its relative wealth. In the United States we must dispose of a hundred fifty million tons of trash and garbage annually. In packaging materials alone, that includes fifty-five billion cans, twenty-six billion bottles and jars, sixty-five billion metal and plastic bottle caps as well as more than half a billion dollars worth of other materials used in packaging consumer products.

We junk seven million automobiles every year. Paul Ehrlich says if current trends continue, sometime in the next decade every man, woman and child in the United States will, on the average, be producing a ton of refuse annually.[4]

Calcutta's ragpickers could make a comfortable living recycling what the average American city throws away.

In another of his books, Ehrlich shows how the United States in trying to help India, unwittingly contributed to its urbanization problems. He says that in 1966 the United States shipped one-quarter of its wheat crop—nine billion tons—to India. Thousands migrated to port cities in order to be close to the centers of grain distribution—and never went back home.[5] As a result, the distribution of India's population was permanently altered. At the turn of the century about 11 percent of India's population was urban. Today more than 20 percent of India's people live in cities. That is roughly one hundred twenty million people. Jobless and hungry, they are some of the prime contributors to India's political ferment.

Calcutta is a hotbed of ultraradical Marxist activity. It is the center of the Naxalite movement, a violent and anarchist group of young leftists. The hungry street-dwellers and tens of thousands of others are ripe for their propaganda. Some time ago I landed in Calcutta and was met by an Indian friend. Because of a strike and a "squat-in" on the streets by the workers, it took us nearly two hours to get from the airport to my hotel. As we crept along, my friend gave me a lesson in Indian economics, sociology and politics.

"When the average coolie can work, which may be as much as half the time," my friend told me, "he earns the equivalent of about thirty cents a day. That is not enough to buy rice for his family. He leaves his home every morning with the cries of his hungry children echoing in his ears. It shouldn't be surprising that when the Communist organizer comes along and says, 'Workers, arise, all you have to lose is your chains!' he finds it a believable promise. He is sure nothing could be worse than the status quo.

"So he becomes a Communist," my friend said, "not because he believes the ideology, but because he wants to feed his family."

It is interesting, I think, that at least in parts of Latin America I found exactly the opposite. In the barrios around

Bogotá, the Communists find few recruits. I had thought it would be otherwise. I think I had gotten this impression from reading statements by Latin governments who seem to always blame disturbances by the poor on "Communist agitators." Like many other North Americans, this fitted my preconceptions. Consequently, I didn't question it until I visited the barrio of Altamira.

Altamira is a part of Bogotá's "misery belt," a ring of slums perched on the sides of the mountains which surround the city. The mayor says they make up about 40 percent of Bogotá's population of three million.

It took us about half an hour to make the climb to Altamira where Padre Miguel Mosset was waiting for us. We were near nine thousand feet and a sharp, cold wind was blowing, but this Spanish priest warmed us with cups of black Colombian coffee and his own gentle spirit. No black suit and clerical collar for this priest of the people. A worn green sweater covered a nondescript shirt and topped a pair of rumpled trousers.

Somehow he didn't come across as being the radical the Catholic church makes him out to be or the troublemaker the government says he is. I asked him about it.

A sigh precedes his answer, as if he has heard it, oh, so many times. Then softly: "No, I am not a radical. I am only for the people. Nor are the people of Altamira radical. They are disillusioned and resentful, but only because of so many unfulfilled promises."

"Does this disillusionment make them susceptible to Communist propaganda?" I inquire.

Father Miguel just shakes his head. "They don't even listen," he says, "They tell the Communists, oh, you're just gringos, too."

Father Miguel knows the attitudes of his people. He came to Altamira ten years ago over the protest of his superiors who didn't want a church in that slum. He has received not one peso from the church, either for his salary or the simple building he has erected as a place of worship. To them he is a "bad" priest because he has helped motivate the barrio to form an organization and press the government to provide community services. In Colombia, where 5 percent of the people control the country's politics and economics, it is "bad" to challenge the establishment and the status quo.

From that elevated position at the top of the economic pecking order, it is easy for the rich to look at the people of Altamira and the other twenty-one barrios around Bogotá and blame their poverty on laziness, lack of initiative, climatic conditioning or inherited class weakness. When Father Miguel talks about this, it is the only time in more than three hours of conversation that he raises his voice. Now it has a sarcastic edge:

"To say that people don't progress because of hunger is a subversive statement to most people. They will say that cannot be the reason—that you have lost your faith in God. Let them come and see. The lethargy in Altamira is the result of diet, not culture.

"Mostly the people eat rice and potatoes. Meat even once a week is a luxury. A school boy starts the day with only a cup of black coffee and maybe a thin potato soup. By ten o'clock hunger is gnawing at his stomach and in his mind. it affects his total life—his mental response, his sex drive, his ability to concentrate."

Across the road live Raphael Bello, his wife and five children who confirm Father Miguel's statement. Mr. Bello is a truck driver and member of the small evangelical church in the barrio.

The diet for the Bello family is maize, bread, potatoes and rice. All starch and carbohydrates. They try to have meat twice a month.

"The Catholics and evangelicals here are united," Mr. Bello tells me, "and Padre Miguel is our friend."

Our friend. Perhaps that is what the disfranchised in urban slums need most. Someone to help them speak up—to touch the sources of power. Yet because they have been exploited and disappointed so many times, it is not easy to be their friend. Suspicious of all outsiders, their trust and confidence must be earned.

In Bombay, on the other side of the world, a young Indian is just beginning to gain the trust of the 120 families who live in Jaffer Baba Colony, one of the city's 525 slum areas. (The Bombay city government prefers to call its slums "hutment colonies," an inoffensive euphemism that covers 1.5 million people.)

Rajam Singh—twenty-seven years old, bearded and strikingly handsome—had been working in this particular slum for eight months when I met him. In order to more fully identify with the needs of the people, he moved into a hutment among them two and a half months before. On the day that I walked through Jaffer Baba Colony with him, an almost carnival atmosphere prevailed among its thousand inhabitants. The next day was going to bring a happy break in a life of hardship. The colony was getting water! There would be no more need to carry cans up and down the steep hill. Water would flow through a pipe right to the slum. The people had collected enough among themselves to build the brick-and-cement platform where the water would flow.

But more importantly, by helping them make their petition to the city for the water line, Raj Singh had shown them what joint community action could achieve. He was as proud of them as they were of him.

Like Padre Miguel, Raj is soft-spoken and self-effacing. Also like the Latin priest, he rejects the word "radical" when applied to himself. A former medical worker and seminary dropout, Raj told me, "I simply can't afford to live in a luxurious flat with air conditioning when so many in this one city live in these abject poverty conditions, but each person has to set his priorities. Once I told a group of parents, 'Whom do you call a blessed son? One who educates himself, does well in life and looks after his parents in their old age. What about the young man who left home at thirty, roamed around, associated with social outcasts, got into the bad graces of the religious leaders and was executed? What about him? He was God's own Son, you know.'"

As a worker for the Bombay Urban Industrial League for Development (BUILD), an organization of the local churches, Raj dreams of changing the whole structure of the slums by helping people organize themselves around improvement goals.

One of those goals in Bombay and every other crowded

city has to be housing. Whether you call these slums *hutment colonies, favelas* (Brazil), *barriados* (Peru), *townships* (South Africa) or *urban blight* (U.S.A.), there is a monotonous sameness about their poverty. Very rarely is there a qualitative change in slum life. Sometimes the people will try to cosmetize their life style to make it appear more middle class than it is —remember the television antenna which seems so incongruous sticking out of the roof of a jerrybuilt slum shack?—but down inside nothing really changes.

Everything still marks it as a slum: narrow streets, inadequate housing, little or no services, poor sanitation, incredible congestion.

Most urban slum dwellers are squatters. They settle on government land, unused speculator land, and undesirable land —swamps and lowlands in Bangkok, flood areas in Baghdad, steep hillsides in Rio de Janeiro giving them the most beautiful views in the city if they look over the *favela* itself.

Dwellings vary from straw and mud hovels, to bamboo and scrap lumber huts, to tin and cardboard shacks. In Latin America they tend toward the latter, using packing cases or odd scraps of lumber for walls; zinc sheeting, canvas, or flattened oil cans for roofs; and bare earth for floors. The floor space is aproximately eight by fourteen feet, sometimes divided into two rooms to house from five to ten people. There is no electricity or water.

In 1969, Paul Ehrlich estimated that if ten thousand houses were built each day for the next ten years in Latin America, at the end of that time some hundred million of our southern neighbors (more than one-fifth of the expected population) would still be inadequately housed.[6] Six years later there is no need to revise that estimate.

Indonesia is trying to do something about its capital city, Jakarta, literally legislating to "keep them down on the farm." The chairman of the National Board of Family Planning has said that from 1977, Jakarta will be a "closed" city. That is, nobody from other parts of the country may move to the capital, and the birth rate must equal the death rate. It is estimated that by 1977 the population of Jakarta will be six million, representing a density of ten thousand per square kilometer.

Theoretically, each couple will be restricted to two children and the government hopes to achieve this by educating the present school children on the value of small families.

One can only wish them more success than they have had with the transmigration program.

In an address to the U.N. Economic and Social Council in 1969, Robert S. McNamara, president of the World Bank, said:

"The cities of the developing countries are the centers which ought to serve as the basis of both industrial growth and social change. Instead, with a growing proportion of their inhabitants living at the margin of existence, and the quality of life deteriorating for all, the cities are spawning a culture of poverty that threatens the economic health of entire nations." [7]

Nowhere is that gloomy prophecy being fulfilled more surely than in Africa. Although it remains the least urbanized of all the continents, the rate of increase of urban growth in Africa is two to three times that of most other areas of the world. According to the United Nations, about 25 percent of the world's population are city-dwellers. In North America the figure is 42 percent; in Latin America it is 32 percent, and in Africa it is only about 14 percent. But the growth rate of the sixty cities in tropical Africa that have more than a hundred thousand residents is 9 percent a year, three times the world average.

Overall population growth on the continent is between 2 percent and 3 percent a year, but its urban growth rate is double that, about 5.5 percent. Since 1960, Africa has experienced what may be the greatest short-term migration in its history. From Addis Ababa to Abidjan, the cities of Africa are being inundated by a rising tide of people leaving the villages for what is supposed to be the better life.

Interestingly, in virtually every country the growth is concentrated and sometimes confined to one city—almost always the political capital.

Kinshasa, capital of the Zaire Republic (formerly the Congo), has a population of over one and a half million and is growing at the astounding rate of 14 percent a year. The Nigerian city of Lagos, the other tropical African city with a population of over one million, is exploding at a similar rate.

The Ivory Coast capital of Abidjan now has about seven hundred fifty thousand residents, a tenfold increase in the past twenty years.

Another striking pattern of the growth of Africa's cities is that the coming of independence to many countries has coincided with the continent's period of greatest urban expansion. It seems likely the two things have a direct relationship.

"A lot of people thought that independence meant they would get free homes, free medicine, free cars. They started to come to the capital to see what this independence was about," an Ivory Coast official is quoted in *The Washington Post* (November 28, 1971).

"Instead they found a lot of guys sitting in air-conditioned offices and looking like they were doing no work. So they said, 'Why should we go back to the village when these people are enjoying themselves in the cities? We want to enjoy ourselves, too.' Are we who are already here to tell them to go back?"

So in Dakar, Accra and Nairobi hordes of young men from the countryside walk the streets of burgeoning business districts looking in vain for work. There are almost no jobs available for the estimated five million untrained villagers pouring into the cities annually. It is only a little better for those who have received some education. In fact, some who left the villages to go to secondary school are worse off than before. A group of tribal elders in southwestern Ethiopia sadly told me that most of their young people who had gone to Addis Ababa for a high school education cannot find employment in the city after graduation, but are too spoiled by their diploma and exposure to city life to return to tribal living.

As a result, both the cities and the villages suffer. The countryside loses its manpower in agricultural production and the cities must somehow try to provide minimal social services to these armies of unemployed which encircle them in the shantytowns. Of course, not all of this population shift is the result of the economic pull of the cities. Many of the new urban dwellers are pushed from an undeveloped rural economy which has lagged behind even the slow development of the urban areas.

There are other reasons for the flow toward the cities, too. We have already seen that drought is a big factor. Tribal tensions and warfare sometimes send whole villages into the cities for security. There are many individual reasons, but they are all like tributaries which feed a swollen stream of humanity being dumped into a stormy urban sea of social and economic problems. Abidjan has close to 50 percent of the registered unemployed in the Ivory Coast. In Lagos, 30 percent of the work force is estimated to be without jobs. At least 10 percent of Kinshasa's population has no visible means of support.

Overcrowding of the shantytowns has become a major problem because little new low-income housing has been built in the past decade. Newcomers crowd in with already crowded relatives or friends. In Accra the average house has four rooms and the average number of persons living in each house has risen from 14.2 to 21.6. In many other cities the majority of families live in one room.

The resulting human misery—of which hunger is only one cruel facet—is predictable and alarming. The brutalizing effect on the human spirit, especially of the children, can only mean a compounding of our urban woes in the years ahead.

The high incidence of child prostitution has already been mentioned. Streetboys are another phenomenon spawned out of these urban hells. Deprived of love and a meaningful home, boys by the thousands—some as young as seven and eight years old—take to the streets and to crime. It is the story of Fagan and his gang all over again. I have seen them in Addis Ababa where a friend of mine, Jack Smith, operates Hope for Boys where he tries to rehabilitate many of them. In Saigon, where streetboys are known as *bui doi*—nobodies—World Vision is helping hundreds to become somebodies. On a lesser scale we are doing the same in Bogotá with a project called Future Youth.

Recently while talking with a Colombian social welfare official, he took me to the window of his fifth-floor office in downtown Bogotá and pointed to an abandoned excavated construction site across the street. It was dotted with several shacks made from scrap materials and tarpaper. These, he told me, represented the center for one of the many streetboy subcultures in the city.

That very day the newspaper, *el tiempo*, had carried an in-

terview with a former streetboy. It revealed the loss of inno-
cence and subsequent terrifying life of a boy who took to the
streets at the age of seven and described it as living "at the edge
of hell."

Called "Frijolito" (little bean) because of his size, he never
slept in a bed for two years. His bed was under the fountains
of Bolivar Square or among the columns of the capitol building.

"The homosexuals offered us silver," the former streetboy
said, "and if we didn't agree they would take us by force. The
prostitutes took many boys to watch them in their sexual acts
with degenerates.

"I passed uncountable nights awake suffering from cold and
hunger. When you're hungry, cold hits harder. I waited for
dawn and attacked the leftovers on the tables of the night
watchmen. . . . One day I cried bitterly. In front of me a woman
served warm milk to her dog. She covered him with a special
wool coat. Later she served him a biscuit and bread and covered
him with scented powder. He had an identification tag around
his neck and a pendant and the woman took him to her chauf-
feur-driven car.

"I was hungry, and it was obvious. I smelled bad and didn't
have warm milk or a wool shirt. I discovered that my life meant
less than that of a dog."

That discovery by little Frijolito is still being made by increasing numbers who have lost their identity with the rural
past and cannot establish another in an unfamiliar urbanized
setting. They are the flotsam and jetsam on a very troubled
sea.

What are the answers? At the moment there are no sure
ones—only guesses. Speaking of Africa, a university professor
in Nairobi who deals with urban affairs, said: "Many of the
problems probably defy solutions, given our current economic
resources and the fragmented approach of Africa to the problems."

In some cases, a complete social restructuring will be needed
in the villages to stop the drift of young people to the urban
areas. Large numbers of these young people say one reason
they leave the villages is to escape the autocratic methods of
traditional rulers and the privileges awarded to older people in

most tribal societies. But nobody expects these customs of the centuries to pass overnight.

At the other end of the urbanizing stream, greater industrialization does not seem to be the answer. This would require capital, a trained labor force, and overseas markets—none of which are available in the quantity needed. And even if they were, some economists and government leaders are skeptical that the creation of more jobs in the cities would create an even greater influx of job-seekers, in an unending cycle.

Nor is decentralization a realistic approach at this moment. In most developing countries there is little infrastructure in the interior. Roads, electricity and methods of communications needed for factories are scarce outside the major cities.

Rural development seems to hold out the greatest promise, but this, too, has its problems. Some efforts to develop the countryside seem to have turned out quite differently than planned. When roads were paved into Liberia's remote regions, the people fled instead of staying to rejoice. They were afraid it would be easier for tax collectors and government labor recruiters to get to them.

One answer which I believe holds promise and which ought to be seriously tried is the integration of the agricultural and industrial sectors within geographical regions so that each supports and contributes to the other. It is fatal not to recognize that most of the world is still rural and agricultural. Facilities for processing agricultural products and factories for producing simple agricultural implements and tools should be located close enough to the farming areas to make the creation of transportation and communication infrastructures possible. In this way the two sectors of the economy—agricultural and industrial—draw from and feed each other. Surplus processed foods and other products could then be sent to major distribution points for export or redistribution throughout the country.

The manufacture of luxury items for export to the affluent nations, even though they may mean prestige and profit for a few, must take a lower priority to the production, processing and distribution of food.

Every such scheme should concentrate on labor-intensive projects which utilize the flooded labor market rather than capital-intensive programs which employ technology instead of people. This description of the integration of the two sectors is a simplified one, of course, but it seems obvious that given the realities which exist today a large part of the answer lies in some kind of intersectoral relationship.

This concept will be discussed in more detail in the chapter on development, but one cannot avoid here the conclusion that no matter how much money a development program may generate, it cannot be said to be a success until and unless it contributes in a positive way to the reduction of hunger and malnutrition in the land.

Chapter 6
"The System": Creating Hunger Amidst Plenty

I T IS DIFFICULT, IF NOT IMPOSSIBLE, for the average middle class American to disbelieve that every person in the world could make it like he did if only that person would (a) apply himself, (b) work hard, (c) grab the opportunities, and (d) save his money.

After all, every schoolboy knows it is the application of those virtues that made America wealthy and great. If they work here, they'll work anywhere.

And we really believe that.

It is hard for us to believe that the differences between the U.S.A. and the rest of the world are qualitative and real, not merely quantitative and cosmetic.

We think everybody is playing the survival game in the same league. It just isn't so—you've got the major league teams and the sandlot teams. And most of us in the majors don't even know what the sandlots look like where the other teams play, much less how the players live.

But if we are serious about becoming agents of change, we must know empathetically the life styles of those who play in the Third World sandlots. If we would understand the root causes of poverty and hunger in the world, we must see how the rules of the games are stacked against the weaker teams.

But let me caution you that the facts are likely to challenge
and contradict many of our sentimentally held notions.

At the heart of the problems of poverty and hunger, injustice
and inequity, are human systems which ignore, mistreat and
exploit man made in the image of God. If humanity is to be
served, if the hungry are to be fed, if the poor are to share in
God's bestowed abundance, some of the systems will require
drastic adjustments while others will have to be scrapped altogether.

Let it be said in our behalf that most of us probably never
stopped to think that the arrangements of world trade and commerce, which are so profitable and convenient for us, may be
unfair and oppressive for those on the other end. So let us now
consider that possibility.

Tomorrow morning while you are enjoying your second
cup of coffee might be a good time to contemplate the case of
Juan Díaz, a coffee worker in the Central American Republic
of El Salvador. We could choose a worker in the production of
any other primary commodity—sugar, tea or cocoa—but coffee
is a universal pleasure shared by rich and poor alike, and it
provides a useful example of how the patterns of world trade
bind the peoples of all nations together.

Juan's daily struggle for mere survival is hardly the TV
commercial image of life on the hacienda. He and three of his
five daughters spend long, hard days in the coffee fields of
Montenango. On a good day, Juan picks enough coffee to earn
$1.44; his daughters make a total of $3.35. With $1.24 of
these wages, Juan and his wife, Paula, are able to feed their
family for one day. In bad times, Juan and his daughters make
as little as $.56 a day—less than half the money they need
just to eat.

At the end of the six-week coffee season, Juan does odd jobs
around the hacienda—provided there is work to be done. He
can earn about $.90 there for an eight-hour day. Paula de Díaz
supplements her husband's earnings by working in the market. When people have enough money to purchase the toma-
toes, cabbages and other home-grown vegetables she sells,
Paula can make about $.40 a day.

The hacienda provides a simple dwelling for the Díaz family,

but no modern facilities. Candles are used for light, water has
to be hauled from a well and furnishings consist of little more
than a table and some chairs. Aside from a dress and shoes for
each of the girls during the coffee season, the family has not
been able to buy much else in the last five years. Whatever
money doesn't go for food is spent for visits to the health
clinic ($.40 each time), the high interest on bills at the com-
pany store, expenses for the children in school, and for the
burial of Juan's father, who died last year.

"You know, I look forward to a better life for my children,"
Juan says, "I dream that if it is possible—if I can possibly afford it—my children will not follow in my footsteps, that they
will break out of this terrible way of life. But the money problems we face every day blot out those dreams. I feel bad,
nervous, I don't sleep nights worrying about how I'll get something for them to eat. I think and think but don't find any
answers. I work hard; my wife and daughters do, too. We all
do. But still we suffer. Why?" [1]

What would you say to Juan? Probably he would get a variety of answers—you aren't industrious enough; you are lazy,
uneducated; you are inferior by nature; there aren't enough
resources to go around, or that is just your fate.

But he wouldn't likely hear anyone blame "the system," and
if he did, he would have to ask them what they meant. He
doesn't have time to be preoccupied with the national and international systems—economic, political, societal, military—
which govern his life and the development of his country. But
suppose he did and suppose he could understand them. Here is
what Juan would see.

When he looks at Hacienda Santa Barbara, the plantation
where he works, he sees no chains which bind him to it, but
he knows he is not free to exercise any significant control over
most things that affect his life. Juan owns almost nothing; he
has no savings; he has bills at the company store; and he has
a family to feed, clothe and educate.

Forming a union to press for higher wages and increased
benefits is not a practical option, for he fears such agitation
would result in his being fired and replaced by one of his many
fellow countrymen who are literally begging for jobs.

If Juan could get out of debt to the company store and save a little money, he might leave the plantation and try to find work elsewhere. But this is also impractical for he never has had a chance to get an education or develop other skills. Besides, he would soon find that life in the city is no better than at the hacienda. As a result, he is held by chains as binding as any forged from steel.

When Juan looks at his country, he sees here, too, that the system is stacked against him. Virtually all the wealth and income, land and industry, political and military power rest in the hands of a small ruling minority. One-third of El Salvador's wealth is controlled by 5 percent of the people. The annual income of a person in this privileged class is twelve times that of the poorer two-thirds. The disparity is even greater—thirty to one—for the poorest 10 percent.

This imbalance in the distribution of wealth and income carries over into the consumption of goods and services. Those who are better off consume disproportionately more—up to thirteen times as much.

The distribution of farmland in El Salvador is weighted in the same way. More than 40 percent of the arable land is controlled by an elite 1 percent of the people, while 78 percent of the poorer agricultural population share only 11 percent of the land. The very poor must either work on the lands of the rich or scratch out a bare living on small, unproductive plots of ground.

Juan Díaz can't even begin to understand the system which keeps him poor and hungry, much less know how to try to change it. One day if he and all the other Juans over the world strike out in blind rage at the system and those who perpetuate it, don't be too surprised. You could hardly expect from them a sophisticated and reasoned response.

Although Juan knows nothing about the international forces which affect him so deeply, they are very real and they serve to support the internal situation in which he finds himself. These powers extract from his country and the rest of the developing world their wealth and natural resources—a part of the system which has been going on for centuries and which made it possible for the Western nations to accelerate their industrialization.

It was the plunder mentality of such civilized countries as

Spain, Portugal, England, France and Holland in the sixteenth and seventeenth centuries that started the rich and naturally endowed lands of Latin America down the road to present-day underdevelopment. Gold, silver and other precious resources were removed from these colonies and used to enrich the mother countries.

Even after independence in the nineteenth century, the more industrially advanced countries wielded enormous power over the newly independent Latin American nations because (1) they dominated the international systems of trade; (2) they controlled the international monetary system; (3) they supplied most of the new investment capital, and (4) they used their political and military power to preserve the status quo.

Thus the flow of resources out of Latin America continued. The patterns set hundreds of years ago are not terribly different today. Plundering, although more sophisticated, is no less rapacious. But now other countries of Western Europe, as well as the Communist countries, Japan and the United States have come into the picture. By means of trade, financial investments and economic assistance, these nations pursue their own ends —with some unfortunate consequences for Latin America and its people.

It is small comfort—and no excuse—that the systems were not intentionally designed to handicap the poor. It changes nothing to say they were not put together with malice. However they developed, it is time to take a more objective and compassionate look at the global systems—to examine who bears the costs as well as who reaps the benefits.

And what does all this have to do with your morning cup of coffee?

Well, El Salvador and twelve other Latin American countries emerged from their colonial past with one-crop economies. They depend on the sale of a single commodity for over 40 percent of their export earnings. Five of these countries, including El Salvador, depend on the sale of coffee alone for a substantial portion of these earnings. Coffee, however, makes up only 1 percent of the volume of world trade; and, to make matters worse, it is not an item of absolute importance to an industrialized economy.

But for Juan Díaz and the 350,000 other coffee workers in El Salvador, the price of coffee on the world market can literally mean the difference between life and death. It has been estimated that a decline of even one cent per pound in the price of "green coffee" means an annual loss of about $65 million for the coffee-producing countries.

While the developing nations like El Salvador have little besides primary products to sell, 79 percent of what they purchase abroad consists of manufactured goods. The steadily increasing prices of these goods from industrialized nations are due partly to inflation and partly to increased wages resulting from successful efforts by unionized labor in industrialized countries. (You couldn't have known that your last raise negotiated by the union hit Juan Díaz right in his already flat billfold, but that's how closely linked are the world trade systems.)

As you brew your morning cup of coffee, ships set sail, goods are being exported and imported, capital is being invested, and Juan and his daughters begin another grueling day in the coffee fields. Broadside denunciations of the system in which Juan is trapped will not lighten his burden; far less will denials of the root causes of his plight.[2]

What is needed is conscious effort, based on truth and compassion, to make fundamental changes in the system. And no beginning is too small. Youth delegates to the Second World Food Congress sponsored by the U.N. Food and Agricultural Organization said: "It is not enough to free man from the hunger imposed on him by an insufficiency of food. Man must be freed of all the forces that oppress him, of the natural, economic and political order." [3]

We must be open to rethink words and concepts which heretofore may have seemed threatening to us, and not simply salivate like Pavlov's dogs because of prior semantic conditioning.

Take the word *radical*, for instance.

To be radical simply means to get at the root of things. That is what we mean by radical surgery—it doesn't stop at dealing with symptoms. The trouble with many of the so-called radical causes is they are not radical enough. Violence is not radical; it is reactionary. Only forgiving and serving love is radical. Communism as an answer for the world's economic ills is not

radical at all—it deals only with superficialities and never touches the deep roots of alienation and selfishness. Neither does capitalism, for that matter. Nor socialism. No system that ignores the sin problem in man and society and that values machines and production quotas over human beings can pass the test as an adequate answer.

For that reason I believe the people of God have a radical and unique contribution to make toward the restructuring of the old systems and the creation of new ones. In fact, so absolutely essential to an accurate understanding of both the problems and solutions is the Judaeo-Christian concept of man as a creation of God, I am appalled that it is so often ignored.

The fault, I am convinced, lies largely with those who hold this view. When we should be the vanguard of change, why are we more often the rearguard preservers of the status quo? It seems that we deliberately misunderstand Jesus' words, "You always have the poor with you," as confirming poverty and discrimination as a perpetual God-arranged state for some. Jesus' words, however, are no invitation to resignation and inactivity, for he continues, ". . . and whenever you will, you can do good to them." [4]

Should not doing good include working for systemic change as well as delivering a Christmas basket, making a contribution on Worldwide Communion Sunday, or writing a check to the United Way?

Speaking to this issue some time ago, three hundred Roman Catholic priests in Brazil issued a statement that stabs deeply into the Christian conscience. It said in part:

It is in the framework of paternalism that many people, including church authorities, approach present-day realities and social problems. They attempt to solve them by appealing to the duty of paternal charity. They establish countless charitable organizations, social programs and money campaigns. They unwisely launch philanthropic initiatives that are dear to the middle class, because the latter can thereby work off their feeling of guilt and the responsibility they bear for the gap which separates their standard of living from that of the impoverished people around them. People try to alleviate the effects produced without tackling the causes behind them. In practice, the Church's life of action makes her an accomplice in the brutal exploitation of the people and in the misguided effort to solve poverty and illness on an individual basis.[5]

Edgar Snow said it in fewer words: "I want nothing to do with any religion concerned with keeping the masses satisfied to live in hunger, filth, and ignorance." [6]

Granted that Snow was no defender of piety, he apparently did see a yawning credibility gap which still has not been closed. I will not defend the church's failures. It would only widen the credibility gap.

Where the church has failed, let it repent and do the works demanded by a just and righteous God: " . . . seek judgment, relieve the oppressed; judge the fatherless, plead for the widow." The God of morality and right insists that aesthetic worship is no substitute for moral honesty: "Bring no more vain oblations; incense is an abomination unto me; . . . Your new moons and your appointed feasts my soul hateth: they are a trouble unto me; I am weary to bear them. . . . your hands are full of blood." [7]

God loathes a church that revels in an impractical and unapplied piety.

I believe the church's prescribed activities can be grouped into three areas: Worship and Teaching, Evangelism and Mission, Service and Social Action. I prefer these to the usual dual breakdown of Faith and Order—Life and Work, for I think that kind of simple division leads both to misunderstanding and mispractice.

It is not that the three are self-contained and unrelated. They are more like the three legs of a stool. Two out of three are not enough. Most often, however, evangelicals have grabbed the first and second while liberals have grabbed the first and third. Tragically, both have gone charging away with wobbly stools. Little wonder the record of success has been spotty and discouraging. How could it have been otherwise with so shaky a foundation?

The time is ripe for the church to rediscover its total mandate. Since it is not my purpose in this book to argue the case of evangelism and mission, I leave that for another time and place. Here I am dealing with the sins within systems which produce hunger, economic discrimination, human exploitation and the abuse of resources and which the church condones or ignores simply because—as we say—this is the "isness" of things.

In this case, "isness" is the name of the dragon that must be slain because it holds captive the fair maidens of liberation, justice and dignity. Isn't it sad to see a mighty church standing before the dragon, intimidated by all the fire and smoke? But isn't it sadder still to see that church turn from the battle and occupy itself by jousting with windmills while the dragon continues to devastate the planet?

And the church must do something more than tell government and business what their responsibilities are. True, the church must apply the standard of judgment to secular institutions, but I think most of them are sick of pious frauds passing resolutions for them in ecclesiastical assemblies while completely ignoring their own inconsistent practices.

I think God may be sick of it, too.

I know I am.

The church has had so little influence in political and economic matters recently that I still see the story of Wilberforce's efforts to free the slaves in England one hundred fifty years ago used as the most contemporary illustration of its involvement.

If God is on the side of the poor and oppressed, where is the church? Maybe we need to rewrite Mother Goose:

Rise up, O Church, and blow your prophet's horn,
Speculators are driving up the price of wheat
    and corn!
Where is the Church that looks after God's sheep?
Under the haystack fast asleep.

That's where it seemed to be in Ethiopia while over the centuries an aristocracy built and perpetuated a feudal system to which the recent famine in the country can be heavily traced. Or maybe it was only pretending to be asleep, because actually the Ethiopian Orthodox Church—by owning 30 percent of the land in the country—was an active participant in the heartless system.

Consider this: Although over 90 percent of the population of Ethiopia must earn their living from the land, these peasants share ownership of only about 10 percent of the land. Apart from what the church holds, the aristocracy owns the remaining 60 percent. The system requires share tenancy, with the peasant paying his rent in money, produce or crops.

But here is the crusher. The law of the land (1960 Civil Code of Ethiopia, Article 2988) states that rent is presumed to be 50 percent of the produce of the rented land. And that isn't all—the peasant must pay tenancy fees, a tithe, and a land tax which is a fee for the right to rent! Together these can eat up 90 percent of what the poor farmer earns.

How can he possibly afford fertilizer or irrigation? He can barely live. Many didn't during the famine. An estimated hundred thousand died.

A lot of people blamed the weather, but a young Canadian nurse named Betty Friesen gave me the wisest and most insightful analysis I have heard. In response to my question about what caused the famine, she replied: "Years and years and years of doing things wrong."

Funny, I didn't hear anyone else blame the system. The drought was most frequently cited as the culprit, but it was only the straw that broke the already burdened backs of the peasants.

Ethiopia is not an isolated example of a discriminatory system of land distribution. Latin America provides many more. In Chile, 1 percent of the plantation owners have 43 percent of the land. Guatemala, where 0.2 percent of the landholders have 40.8 percent of all property, is even worse. In Bolivia, before the last reform, 6.3 percent of the population owned 91.9 percent of all the land.[8]

In the same book from which those figures are taken, Father Rosier says he doesn't believe the answer necessarily is to be found in parceling out the land in small chunks—the uneconomical *minifundios* of southern Brazil and the inadequate 1.7 acre plots in Bangladesh tend to support this view—but he does think that exploiting the land and underpaying the workers should be made a punishable social crime.

Father Rosier may well be right, and I would suggest there are some other crimes—those committed by governments against their people—that ought to be punished somehow this side of Judgment Day. Crimes like preserving the national image over the lives of starving people. Emperor Haile Selassie of Ethiopia got his comeuppance, at least in part, for just such a reason. His establishment ignored the famine rather than let the world know what was happening.

The Far Eastern Economic Review (Nov. 15, 1974) reported that "India is trying its utmost to soft-pedal reports of famine in some parts of the country. New Delhi has sent strict instructions to its diplomatic missions abroad that they should blandly deny stories in the international press saying that the problem is reaching serious proportions. The envoys are required to tell foreign officials that the situation has been exaggerated in the media. . . . The Indian government, obviously worried about its sagging image overseas, has even asked charity organizations, such as Oxfam, not to dramatise the hunger problem . . . they have been advised to collect money discreetly."

The magazine must have been right because two weeks later the Minister of State for Agriculture and Irrigation, A. P. Shinde, accused the foreign press of "exaggerating" famine conditions and trying to defame India.

That attitude of governments, I insist, ought to be a punishable crime.

But even if judgment comes to the top, as it did to Haile Selassie in the form of a coup which toppled him, things rarely change at the bottom. That seems to be in the nature of systems. Ethiopia took heart when the new Provisional Military Administrative Council promised democratic reforms. Only God and the peasants knew how badly they were needed. With an average annual income of $80 and a 3 percent literacy rate, it is one of the poorest and least literate nations on earth.

The peasants were overjoyed at the promise of land reform. They waited hopefully. When it was finally announced eleven months later, the reform consisted of a decree imposing state control over virtually all the land in Ethiopia! Only the landlord had changed. Now the rent goes to the state instead of the despised aristocracy.

I know what Father Rosier meant when he told me that rainy night in his apartment in Bogotá, "The poor no longer believe in promises." I asked him what they did believe in.

His answer: "God—and the lottery."

The lottery because it offers the illusion of immediate relief and God because he is their only hope of ultimate justice.

But some injustices cannot wait until the final reckoning. Prime Minister Pierre Trudeau of Canada has written: "Never before in history has the disparity between the rich and the poor, the comfortable and the starving, been so extreme; never before have mass communications so vividly informed the sufferers of the extent of their misery, never before have the privileged societies possessed weapons so powerful that their employment in the defense of privilege would destroy the haves and the have-nots indiscriminately. We are faced with an overwhelming challenge." [9]

The challenge is to change the system fundamentally. There is no single human task facing mankind today which has a higher priority. Let us be done with tinkering. Within nations, agrarian reforms must be tackled resolutely. Sensibly, but resolutely. The poor must be franchised into the economy. Between nations, trade policies must be adopted which benefit all, not just the self-chosen few. It is obvious that the present patterns, rigged so favorably in the interest of the developed minority, cannot continue.

Cartels are already being formed by Third World suppliers of raw materials to confront industrialized nations. OPEC (Organization of Petroleum Exporting Countries) is only the first, and what it has done to the price of oil will be duplicated with other primary products as the cartels become effective.

As suicidal as these trends may be, they are an understandable retaliation for the stranglehold which the developed West has kept on the economic throats of the Third World. But the present course is both disruptive and dangerous. As Prime Minister Trudeau pointed out, weapons used to protect privilege kill indiscriminately. Even our so-called "smart" bombs can't tell the rich from the poor. Yet our government has left the door open for military action if the Middle East oilfields are shut down or an embargo on oil shipments threatens to strangle the American economy.

I simply plead in the name of God let us exhaust all the positive measures first. It is a good time to remember some words of Pope Paul VI: "If you want peace, work for justice."

And justice is what the Third World feels it has been denied. No more eloquent and knowledgeable spokesman for that point of view has emerged than Mubashir Hasan, Pakistan's minister of finance, planning and development. In a 1974 speech to the United Nations he called on the industrialized nations "to make suitable adjustments in the economic order that has brought them the highest standards of affluence ever attained by man in the history of civilization."

Contrasting that with the nonindustrialized world, he says: "Out of every three children born in the developing countries, one succumbs before the age of five. For those who survive it is a life of deprivation, desperation and degradation. Theirs is a subhuman existence. It is an intense, but, mercifully, short struggle, as their life expectancy is no more than 30 years."

How did this disparity happen? By "an unceasing transfer of resources . . . from the poor to the rich nations." And by exploitation of cheap labor which takes literally billions of dollars out of the pockets of "nearly two-thirds of mankind, who toil from dawn to dusk, from childhood to old age."

Mr. Hasan lists five principal elements in what he calls the "inequitable transfer of resources":

—Unfair tariffs imposed by developed countries, which become more unfavorable to the developing countries as the degree of processing increases.
—Exorbitant interest on capital and excessive profits on investments in the developed countries.
—Prices of raw materials from the developing countries depressed through monopolies, cartels and unfair trade practices.
—A virtual monopoly exercised by developed countries on ocean and air transport.
—International financial processes that work in favor of developed countries—clearance of money transactions, insurance and coinsurance schemes and fixing of freight rates.[10]

If you have any doubts about Mr. Hasan as an objective source, let me cite some facts quoted by Senator Mark Hatfield which absolutely support the gentleman from Pakistan. The senator says that from 1959 to 1969, the United States invested $16.23 billion in Europe and $10.9 billion in Canada. During that ten-year period we repatriated profits from those

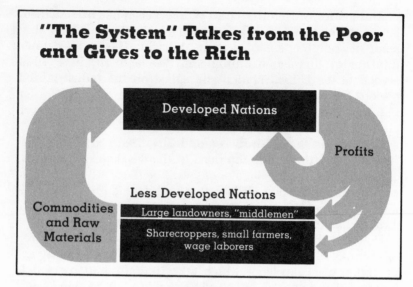

Figure 1

investments of $7.3 billion and $4.7 billion, respectively. Large, but not exorbitant.

During the same ten-year span, we invested $5.8 billion in the Third World countries of Latin America, Africa and the Middle East. Our repatriated profits from those investments were $15.1 billion—a whopping 250 percent return!

It is with enormous justification, then, that Mr. Hasan concludes: "The antagonism between the rich and poor is natural. You have to be poor to realize it. The poor are increasingly beginning to believe that the rich have not become rich by divine desire but by expropriating the fruits of their labor; that some nations are affluent and others are impoverished as a result of the cumulative effect of the years of imperialism, colonialism and neo-colonialism, and not because of any inherent defect in themselves."

His point being: the only way we can live together peacefully on the same planet is for you to stop exploiting us and to help us catch up by making basic reforms in the system which put us where we are.

A modest enough request, it seems to me.

In a speech of his own given at the James H. Oliphant Forum in New York near the end of 1974, Senator Hatfield offered a concise and practical analysis of the action required.

He said: "If we share the goal of eliminating hunger in the world . . . then we would be wise to begin the transfer [of resources] now, before we regard them as exclusively 'ours' and the transfer becomes 'expropriation.'

"What will be required is what has always been most difficult to accomplish without violence: A redistribution of power, and the wealth that brings power; an end to pre-emption of resources by the rich; and a replacement for the kind of economics which divides the world into potential consumers and expendable workers for the sake of acquiring more money. Developing that sort of political economic meaning will be a tremendous task, for it requires grasping a new reality through experience, understanding, and no small amount of sacrifice. It will take, as Claude Levi-Strauss has said, 'a spiritual revolution as great as that which led to the advent of Christianity.' "

Senator Hatfield is talking about a journey of a thousand miles, but as the Chinese proverb says, even such a journey begins with one step.

Perhaps the first step is a sober reevaluation of our personal life styles, to be followed ultimately by a renunciation of our unrestrained pursuit of superaffluence.

The place to start is here.

The time to start is now.

The person to do it?

Me.

PART TWO

PERSPECTIVES ON HUNGER

Chapter 7
Population: Is the Stork Outrunning the Plow?

I T WAS AN ANGRY LETTER.

The lady admitted it was.

She had taken one look at a recent issue of our *World Vision* magazine and had thrown it in the trash can. Her comment to me, essentially, was: "I'm fed up with seeing appeals to feed starving people and I won't give any more money to help them until a birth control pill is given out with each gift of food."

I understand her frustration. The growing world population and its consequences concern me, too. A lot of people are feeling it, if I can judge by the mail I receive. One letter had a carefully worked out mathematical equation and graph to demonstrate the futility of humanitarian food relief. What these letter writers are saying is that we should not feed hungry people in poorer nations because they are reproducing themselves too rapidly and the world's resources cannot stand the strain of their fecundity.

Are they right? Is there really a population-resource problem? Is the stork outrunning the plow?

Consider three statements made in Bucharest in 1974 at the first world population conference ever convened:

"If population continues at the present rate, we will destroy the species," U.S. Secretary of Health, Education and Welfare

Caspar Weinberger quoted Nobel laureate and father of the Green Revolution, Dr. Norman Borlaug.

Snorted Nigeria's Dr. Dora Obe Chizea: "You cannot scare us by saying that we will die of hunger, because we die of hunger every day."

Opined China's Hsu Shou-yen blithely: "Pessimistic views are groundless. The future of mankind is infinitely bright."

Who is right? How can you know for sure?

Let's state three obvious things. First, we live on a finite and nonexpandable planet. What you see is all there is. Second, many of earth's resources are nonrenewable and they are being exhausted at an alarming rate. Third, given the truth of those two statements, some limit on population is inevitable and essential.

With those statements most of the world powers would agree. Go beyond those elemental facts, however, and you get sharp division. There are even serious differences on the implication of the basic facts themselves. Generally, the divisions occur somewhat along these lines:

(1) The developed West stoutly insists that among social programs, population control must have the highest priority.

(2) More than a few nations in both the Third and Fourth Worlds—Rumania, Brazil and Argentina among them—feel they are underpopulated and want to stimulate births rather than curtail them.

(3) The others, including India with the second largest population, are willing to put some stress on family planning only if it is tied to a radical redistribution of wealth between rich and poor nations.

Virtually everybody wishes the answer could be as easy as that suggested by my irate letter-writer. Unfortunately, not even the problem can be stated that simply.

If my experiences in the developing nations have taught me anything, it is that the problem isn't as simple as "overpopulation" nor is the answer as easy as "birth control."

How Much Is Too Many?

"Too many people" is a dangerous generalization that doesn't really describe anything. "Too many" must refer to something.

In this case, it means the relationship between people and the availability of food or the ability to produce it. But not all developing countries are overpopulated in relation to their resources. Take the case of Cambodia. If it were not for the war, Cambodia would be a rice-exporting nation and its almost eight million people would have adequate room in which to distribute themselves and make a living.

Some very crowded developing countries have still managed to reduce their population growth and also feed their people. Taiwan, with fifteen million people, has a per acre output of basic foods of over thirty-three hundred pounds, actually slightly higher than output in the United States. Sudan and Nigeria have great potential for feeding their own people and for exporting food. And the list doesn't stop there.

When I recently visited the West African country of Niger, a government official told me the only population problem in his country was keeping alive those who were starving.

"There is something about the developing countries which really bothers us," he told me candidly. "Whenever anything is in vogue in the West, you want to impose it on us. Right now population control and zero growth are big on your agenda, but we get tired of having others tell us what our problems are and what our interests should be.

"Unfortunately, the drought in the Sahel and the lack of medical facilities in the country are controlling our population more than we desire. Our interest is to feed the people we have," he said.

This same official agreed, however, that the level of interest in population control would and should be much higher in other Third World countries such as poor India and crowded Bangladesh. His plea simply was not to assign the same level of priorities to every nation.

In Niger, he said, food production, not population control, heads the list of priorities.

My own involvement in the country has convinced me that with assistance, Niger has the potential to feed itself. Even along the rich banks of the Niger River there are tens of thousands of acres of good land which could be made arable at a minimum of expense. World Vision is jointly engaged with Lilly Endowment in a land utilization-irrigation project in that area which, within five years, holds the promise of providing a large proportion of the food the country needs.

The term *overpopulation* then, really does not describe the true situation everywhere throughout the developing world.

One has to ask, "How many is too many?"

The Coming Four Billion

None of this is to be construed as an invitation to sanguinity. The world is certainly not out of trouble. Babies are weighing in on this fragile planet at the astonishing rate of three hundred fifty thousand every day. That's a new Tulsa, Oklahoma, or Calgary, Alberta, every twenty-four hours. Any second now, one of these hungry newcomers could turn up the world's people-counter to a massive four billion.

From the original two we've come a long way. *The Population Bulletin* (April 1971) reports that "from the 'time of Adam and Eve' until now, man's population has doubled 31 times." In early 1975, population growth was occurring at the rate of 2.1 percent a year, according to a U.N. report. That sounds very innocuous and nonthreatening. However, at that rate we add another million people to the total in less than five days, a billion people in no more than a dozen years, and will double the population by the year 2007.

U.N. Secretary General Kurt Waldheim told the Bucharest conference, "The next 30 to 35 years may well be the most challenging in the history of mankind . . . for it is virtually certain that the world's population will double [to eight billion]."

Look where we've come from. It took from the beginning of man until 1830 for one billion people to inhabit the earth. It took only one century to double that to two billion, and only thirty years to climb to three billion. The next leap to five billion will take place in only a twenty-four-year time span. That is what the Club of Rome report, *Limits to Growth,* calls "super-exponential" growth. It means that not only are we increasing, says the Club, a group of noted scientists, but the rate of increase is also increasing.

Think about it this way. Most of us usually conceive of growth as being *linear,* such as when a child becomes an inch taller each year. Population growth, however, is *exponential* because it maintains a constant percentage of the whole in a constant time period. An illustration of that is the growth in a colony of yeast cells as each cell divides into two cells every ten minutes.[1] We know what this does to bread dough.

Now if you add to that concept the fact that the rate of growth has also been growing, says the Club of Rome, you have "super-exponential" growth, a new hazard to the health and happiness of the world.

If the world's population were to double another sixteen times—remember it has already happened thirty-one times—there would be only one square yard for every man, woman and child on earth.[2]

So you see, there are limits to exponential growth. Only the most insanely optimistic could deny this. Most demographers and socioeconomists project a population-resource doomsday. The dates vary, but only slightly. An M.I.T. study cited in *Limits to Growth* projects that it will happen "sometime within the next hundred years."[3]

Remember, though, that is only a guess and there are lots of other guessers.

The Guessing Game

Nobody thought much about doomsday or resource depletion until nearly eighteen centuries after Christ. During the 1,650 years from the time of Christ to the times of Cromwell and Bunyan, the world population grew quietly and unnoticed from three hundred fifty million to five hundred million. By that time, however, it was calling attention to itself with a quickening pace that produced a doubling to one billion by 1850.

During that time, a British clergyman and economist, Thomas Malthus, took notice of it. Maybe others did, too, but in 1798 Malthus wrote his observations in a book, *Essay on the Principle of Population*. It is one of the most important books ever written on the subject, and has had such a pervasive influence on modern demographers that they classify themselves as Malthusians, anti-Malthusians, or neo-Malthusians. As his

theories are refined in the light of contemporary situations, the last category is increasing.

And what did Malthus say that was so important? He said that population unchecked increases in a geometrical ratio— 2, 4, 8, 16, 32, 64, 128 and so on—while sustenance increases in an arithmetical ratio—1, 2, 3, 4, 5, 6 and so on.

That is what started the guessing game about doomsday. Malthus assumed that: (1) food is necessary to man's existence; (2) passions between the sexes will never change; (3) the rate of population increase is greater than the power in the earth to produce sustenance.

But the respected prelate made two serious mistakes. He didn't anticipate the widespread use of contraceptives and he failed to see the greatly increasing productivity of the land. But those who would dismiss him entirely because he was wrong in these particulars have not been able to demonstrate his error in principle.

If, in fact, Malthus was right in principle, then our increasing population and diminishing resources are on a collision course somewhere out there, and that is what the highly pessimistic Club of Rome's report is all about.

When?

So the guessing game goes on, with neo-Malthusians making midcourse corrections in their calculations as new facts and evidence emerge. Some say the two lines on the chart could meet as early as 2025. Others think they may be kept apart indefinitely if we combine population control with increased food production.

Professor Philip Hauser, editor of *The Population Dilemma,* who has presided over some of the most prestigious population and census bureaus in the United States, claims that a 2 percent annual growth will produce "a population whose weight would match that of the earth in about 15½ centuries." [4]

Speaking of the world population, economic and political outlook to the end of this century, he says:

"Given the present outlook, only the faithful who believe in miracles from heaven, the optimistic who anticipate superwonders from science, the parochials who expect they can continue to exist in islands of affluence in a sea of world poverty, and the naïve who can anticipate nothing can look to the end of this century with equanimity." [5]

Is There Any Good News?

In the short term, Professor Hauser may well be right. Even if we started doing all the right things tomorrow, it will take time to decelerate the momentum of rapid population growth. It is like a fast-moving car that continues its motion long after the brakes are applied.

A fast-growing population is not subject to short-term manipulation. There are two basic reasons. One is that you can't eliminate social and economic forces which for millennia have encouraged high fertility. The other is that rapidly growing populations have a majority of young people who are yet to achieve parenthood. [6]

Paul Ehrlich, in *The Population Bomb*, says: "These youngsters are . . . the gunpowder for the population explosion." He cites the fact that 40 percent of the population in the developing countries are under fifteen years of age, and concludes: "As that mass of young people moves into its reproductive years during the next decade, we're going to see the greatest baby boom of all time. [They] are the reason for all the ominous predictions for the year 2000." [7]

But if the foreground of the picture seems flawed, things look better out in the distance. Although we are a long way from the desired—at least by some—zero growth, birth rates are declining in some developing countries. Paradoxically, one of the reasons for the detectable decline is also one of the reasons for the present population problem—improved health care with the resultant falling death rate.

That is ironic because it doesn't fit our simplistic interpretation of things. Helping people live longer should increase population growth, not reduce it. Try dropping this statement into a conversation sometime: "Did you know that better health care in the poor countries actually contributes to a reduced population growth?" Chances are you will either be pronounced crazy or offered fantastic odds to prove the statement.

You can.

"At least a dozen developing countries of small to moderate size can unambiguously document a substantial decline in birthrates only a few decades after the onset of substantial declines in mortality," according to a respected demographer and author, Dr. Michael S. Teitelbaum.

He lists among them Singapore, South Korea, Sri Lanka, West Malaysia, Chile, Costa Rica, Puerto Rico, Egypt, and Tunisia. Another nine have shown a possible decline, and Dr. Teitelbaum has the statistics to back up his argument.[8]

The evidence is strong that there is some causal relationship between improved health services and fertility decline. While the current evidence from developing countries is modest enough, any change in the trend is encouraging and welcome.

A second factor which offers heartening news is the demonstrated relationship between overall development and birthrate decline.

Dr. Teitelbaum says, "The present world distribution of birthrates is so closely related to development status that the birthrate itself can be used as an efficient way of distinguishing developing from developed countries. There are few exceptions to the rule of thumb that developing countries have birthrates above 30 per thousand while developed countries have birthrates well below 30 per thousand."[9]

Even the few exceptions to that rule are instructive as supporting examples of the rule itself, for they are developing countries, such as Taiwan and South Korea, which have made marked progress toward both development and population control.

This is what the Third World was trying to say at the Bucharest conference, but which most of the West couldn't hear because of their hang-ups with birth control methods and family planning. They were saying, "Help us achieve development and you will have helped us control our populations."

History supports them, for the record shows that even where family planning services are available, human fertility does not begin to show a decline until certain basic social needs have been met.

"Birth rates do not normally drop voluntarily in the absence of an assured food supply, reduced infant mortality rates,

literacy, and at least rudimentary health services," says Lester
R. Brown, a former senior fellow at the Overseas Development
Council in Washington. "Thus despite their critical importance,
family planning services alone, even if made universally available, will not be enough. Far more attention must also be given
to designing economic and social policies that spread these fundamental improvements in well-being more equitably within
national populations, even in nations where per capita income
is still meager." [10]

Or, as the Latins say, "The table of the poor is meager, but
fertile is the bed of misery."

In his classic work of a lifetime, *The Geography of Hunger*,
written more than twenty years ago, Dr. Josué de Castro makes
the point that "hunger, far from leading to *de*population, tends
to bring about *over*population."

Noting the historical fact that "following periods of calamity, famine and pestilence, populations always increase their
rate of growth," the respected Brazilian scholar recalls that
"the ancient Romans had a word for those who, on a starvation
diet, had many offspring, or *proles*—'proletarians.' "

Dr. de Castro asserts—and supports with historical and
medical data—that "the hunger for proteins can cause a high
fertility index in both man and animal, and that liberal doses
of protein rapidly bring that index down." [11]

It all seems to say that the preaching of birth control and
family planning should be accompanied by the practice of
feeding the hungry and alleviating the human misery which
makes a bed fertile.

A Word about a Lifeboat

I know that some would insist we don't have that kind of
responsibility. I call it the "taking-care-of-old-Number-One"
syndrome.

It was never expressed more crassly than in an opinion
piece in *Newsweek* (December 23, 1974) by a California
lawyer. The writer, Johnson Montgomery, takes a very simplistic, elitist view of himself, his family and the world.

His thesis is, "The United States should remain an island
of plenty in a sea of hunger."

He wrote that he and his wife had made a conscious—and, by implication, intelligent—decision to restrict their family to the perfect number of two children so they would be able to give them more, and he'd be damned if he'd deprive his children for any ignorant so-and-sos who didn't have enough sense or desire to limit their progeny.

They could just make it the best way they could.

Sink or swim.

Exclamation point.

He makes a plausible case, if you happen to believe in the "lifeboat" theory—which I don't. I find it a grotesque and misleading analogy which caters to callous irresponsibility. But it does come in a neat, concise little package which allows for no intruding complexities, so it seems tailor-made for a lot of shallow American minds.

As I mentioned earlier it goes something like this. Each rich country is a lifeboat full of comparatively rich people. In the ocean outside each lifeboat swim the poor of the world, who would like to get in. When a boat is full, the fortunate ones on board are faced with the onerous—but understandably necessary—task of pushing away the others who are doomed to drown.

The theory has only one flaw, but it is a fatal one.

No country is a lifeboat.

If Mr. Montgomery really thinks we are, he should start living without things made from Chilean copper, Indonesian lumber, Malaysian rubber, Japanese synthetics and cheap Hong Kong labor. He should also quit drinking Costa Rican coffee, Ceylonese tea and Dominican cocoa.

Oh, yes, and stop using Arab oil.

That would change his life style!

It might even deprive his children.

But Mr. Montgomery doesn't have to do that because he is not in a lifeboat. With all the rest of us, he is on a ship which has a leak and is slowly sinking. What absolute idiocy for him or any of us to pretend that what is happening to the ship isn't happening to us.

I see two choices.

We can continue to sit in the first-class section and make our daisy chains, ignoring what is happening down in steerage.

Or we can get busy and help man the pumps. Even though we do owe something to those down in steerage who have helped make it possible for us to enjoy the comforts of first class, it isn't just a matter of saving their part of the ship. Global cooperation in this task is also a matter of enlightened self-interest.

I believe we have the capacity to bail out the vessel and the resources to repair the leak.

Personally, I prefer that to going down with the ship.

Of Whom Are There Too Many?

In talking about first class and steerage—us and them—there is always the tendency to think about the respective numbers.

Of "us" in the United States there are about two hundred ten million. In the whole developed world there are just over a billion people. The unclassified, misty world of communism numbers just over a billion. Of "them"—all the developing peoples—there are a few less than two billion.

Obviously, there are too many of them.

Or are there? To whom is it obvious?

Might it be possible there are too many of us?

That's worth thinking about.

Population researcher Pierre Pradervand asks: "If we claim that there are too many people on the earth, then why are we so sure that we are not the excess ones? We Westerners who individually consume and pollute as much as 50 or more African or Indian peasants? . . . I have never once heard a member of the population establishment say that there were too many upper-middle class, white, Anglo-Saxon Protestants in the world." [12]

When the rest of the world looks at our national life style and then hears our demands for universal birth control, they are inclined to suspect our motives. In an article in *Ceres,* a publication of the U.N. Food and Agriculture Organization (November-December 1973), French agronomist René Dumont points out: "The United States utilizes one-third of the energy consumed in the world, and utilizes from 14 to 40 percent of its production of materials, yet it counts less than

six percent of the global population. Blessed with land as vast
as it is rich, . . . the Americans still are the most massive importers of other people's riches. . . .

"An Indian," Dumont goes on, "utilizes roughly one-twenty-
fifth as much energy and scarce materials as a North American
does. Five hundred and seventy million Indians waste and
pollute one-eleventh as much as America's 210 million citizens."

In fact, even the poorest Americans will outconsume much
of the rest of the world. Professor Harold Shane of Indiana
University has said: "Even now the purchasing power of
Americans at the U.S. *poverty* level is above the consumption
level of the top 25 percent of whole populations in the so-
called underdeveloped countries." [13]

The next time you look at a baby, think about this: "Each
American baby will consume in a 70-year life span, directly
or indirectly: 26 million gallons of water, 21,000 gallons of
gasoline, 10,000 pounds of meat, 28,000 pounds of milk and
cream, $5,000 to $8,000 in school building materials, $6,300
worth of clothing and $7,000 worth of furniture! It's not a
baby, it's a Superconsumer!" [14]

There are no comparable figures for the rest of the world,
but you can be sure they would represent only a fraction of
that. Just consider that American necessity, the automobile.
It is estimated that from twenty to fifty cars pass through the
hands of an average American male in a lifetime.

In *The 99th Hour,* former U.S. Senator Stewart Udall tells
what one automobile means in terms of resources used: "An
average automobile represents a raw materials investment in
metals alone of the following irreplaceable resources: two
pounds of magnesium, 23 pounds of zinc, 32 pounds of lead,
36 pounds of copper and copper alloys, 76 pounds of alumi-
num and over 2,600 pounds of iron and steel." [15]

In terms of food, the average annual grain consumption of
an American is 1,850 pounds compared with 380 pounds for
an African or South Asian.

And on and on.

But the point is made.

As René Dumont says, America, with some 6 percent of the
world's population, consumes roughly one-third of the world's

resources. This means that with the resources available, only 18 percent of the world would be able to enjoy our living standard.

So perhaps the key question is not "How many are too many?" but "How much is too much?"

Why People Have Children

But that still doesn't satisfy our need to understand why it *seems*, at least, that the developing peoples have too many children. After all, their families are on the whole much larger than ours and there must be some reason in addition to the obvious biological one.

Why do *we* have children? Family name continuity, family business continuance, religious reasons, one child will be spoiled, trying for a boy or girl. These are just a few, but these and most of the others you would name are highly personal reasons.

An erudite, affluent woman in the United States has a baby for almost exclusively personal reasons—to materialize a deep love, to find fulfillment as a woman. For an increasing number of so-called "liberated" women, it is not even necessary to have the baby in the context of a marriage.

In the Third World there is a different set of reasons. For old-age security, international political prestige, to populate unsettled land, to create a cheap labor pool, to provide military strength, to build stronger families. The reasons grow more out of national or tribal concerns than purely personal ones. I am not arguing the validity of any or all of these reasons, but simply setting them forth. In his book, *One Hundred Countries, Two Billion People,* World Bank President Robert McNamara tries to shoot these down, but in my estimation most of his shots are wide of their mark. Logically and technically he may hit the target, but culturally he misses it because, to the people themselves in their situations, the reasons made good sense. You can't invalidate the reason unless you deal with the culture behind it.

In India, a woman may have personal reasons for wanting a child, but there are social, economic and religious reasons which completely overshadow them. She has a baby because there must be a son alive at the time of his father's death, and it is still necessary to have six children in order to be relatively certain that one male will survive. For generations without number, children have been a form of social security in countries which have no pensions or retirement programs.

Thus a baby is an economic bonus.

Then, too, a baby is potential labor. Being largely rural and without mechanical traction, most Third World families need children to provide labor on the farms. The land is not only the source of family survival; it is also a legacy from past generations. It must be preserved and made to produce.

This requires hands and the cheapest place to find those is in the mother's uterus. I can't forget a story told me by Dr. Ben R. Bringas in the Philippines. A father of eight brought in one of his children who was quite ill. The doctor prescribed, for a starter, ten injections of vitamin B-12 and the father asked how much it would cost.

When Dr. Bringas told him twenty-eight pesos (about four dollars), the father said, "I can't afford it. It is cheaper to have another baby."

We are horrified at that attitude, but I can assure you it makes sense to that father who has no possible way of putting his hands on twenty-eight pesos. That is why to export birth control methods without tackling some of the underlying social causes is an exercise in futility.

At one time it was thought that wholesale distribution of the simple and cheap intrauterine devices was a quick answer to population control. The problems developed in the fitting and retention of the coils, and with no professional help nearby, the discontinuance rates were high. Another factor contributing to decline in use is that women suffering from malnourishment have an increased tendency to bleed after IUD insertion.

You see, poverty has many by-products.

So do ignorance and illiteracy. No one knows how many hundreds of thousands of unwanted children are born simply because the parents didn't know how not to have them, apart from sexual abstinence which is hardly an option.

Most of the mothers in poor nations have only the most elementary understanding of human biology. When a peasant

woman in Haiti doesn't know that putting dust on the umbilical cord of her baby is likely to produce tetanus, how can we
expect her to know many of the sophisticated techniques to
prevent conception?

I was told in Brazil of a mother who visited a birth control
clinic to be fitted with a diaphragm. The nurse explained carefully how to use the contraceptive. Did the mother understand? Yes, she did. In at night, out in the morning to wash
it, in at night, out in the morning, etc.

Good. Very good.

Four months later the woman returned, obviously pregnant.

Nurse: "But I told you . . ."

Woman: "I know, and I did it just like you said. Every day.
In at night, out every morning to wash it."

Nurse: "I just don't understand!"

Woman: "Could the fact that my husband works nights and
is home days have anything to do with it?"

So the reasons why people have babies are different.

But the population clock isn't able to distinguish between
the wanted and unwanted. It just ticks madly away, trying
to keep up.

Time to Act

Having talked about some of the complexities surrounding
the issue, I come back to the basic premise on which there
is general agreement. The clock must be slowed. No longer
can every family on earth take as a personal mandate God's
words to the first family: "Be fruitful, and multiply."

Now God must be saying, "Be sensible, and plan."

A delegate from Bangladesh told the World Population
Conference in desperation: "Our part of the world is sinking
under the weight of population. Our growth rate is three percent. We are short of food, short of educational facilities, short
of everything. Every flood sinks us." [16]

Something must be done. Not for Bangladesh only, but for
the world.

But what?

Internationally, we need to attack on a broad front. It is
clearly in the interest of all to make an effort to satisfy basic

social needs everywhere. The resources are available in the world to launch programs aimed at increasing food production, providing health care and promoting literacy. Even a modest effort would help. The threshold at which the birthrate began dropping in Taiwan and Korea was reached at income levels under $200 per capita.

If the West demonstrated its willingness to make large amounts of money available for development projects when they were tied to family planning programs, I believe the developing countries would be ready to sit down and talk seriously. I do not view the Bucharest conference as a serious attempt at dialogue—countries were more interested in political posturing.

Robert McNamara was right when he said: "The almost universal fact is that parents want [family planning assistance] . . . often far more than their own political leaders comprehend." [17]

To those who see overpopulation as a child whose bones are malformed, whose mind is caged in a primitive world, whose teeth decay, whose eyesight is impaired, whose education is sporadic or nonexistent, it doesn't take too much of a selling job to put across family planning. Where it is coupled with improvement in the social context, population control planning can even overcome deep-seated religious prejudice.

Some governments are considering legislation restricting the size of families, with a negative income penalty or tax on all children over the official limit. If that sounds like an invasion of personal liberties, don't forget that most governments have already made bigamy illegal.

One member of a discussion group made this comment: "Maybe if you told people that the only way they will be living in the United States thirty years from now is to have the government controlling the number of children you can have and which days you can go to the grocery store and what type of food you can buy—maybe this would scare people into controlling population." [18]

Lester Brown has proposed a program which would stabilize the world population at just below six billion by the year 2015. He writes: "Some knowledgeable observers may well declare the target proposed for the less developed nations to be 'unattainable.' However, consideration of the population size with which many nations will be burdened *even if they meet these stringent goals* makes the prospect of not meeting them equally impossible to imagine." [19]

He bases his proposal on the fact that nearly a score of developed countries already are below replacement-level fertility. With only a bit more effort they can achieve zero growth. Brown thinks this could happen by 1985, and that by the same target date the developing countries should be able to reduce birthrates to twenty-five per thousand. He admits that will be tough, but insists it is possible.

The result of this latter step means that a smaller number of young people will reach their reproductive peak between 2005 and 2015. That is the time, Brown says, when the developing countries should lunge for the desired goal—bringing birth and death rates into balance.

It just might work.

Certainly we need to be trying something while we wait for the final resolution of the population problem in heaven. As I understand it, there we'll have ultimate population control. Sexual affinities maybe, but no breeding. It is a closed system —by reservation only—and it would have to be.

Otherwise, where would the Creator get enough planets for the overflow?

Don't Forget Those Already Here

And meanwhile, back on the only planet we have now, hungry people are already born. The birth control pill won't solve the problems of today's starving and malnourished. It won't give them buying power, or education, or health. It won't remove discrimination and unfair practices by landowners or oppressive governments.

The pill will have little or no short-term effect on world food consumption or resource depletion.

So what shall we do about the now?

Senator Hatfield has a suggestion. The "pie," he says, must be shared more equitably.

"The world produces enough food to feed all its inhabitants," the senator said in an address to a church group. "But when one-third of the world's population—all those who are comparatively the 'rich'—consume two-thirds of the world's protein resources, then millions of the other two-thirds of the world suffer, starve and die."

Quoting Gandhi, Senator Hatfield said: "The earth provides enough for every man's need, but not for every man's greed."

He goes on: "The world will be fed only by the sharing of resources which the rich of the world have assumed to be their unquestioned possession, and through the changing of values and patterns of life which the affluent have barely even questioned." [20]

What the senator is saying, in a sense, is that Jonathan Swift's eighteenth-century "modest proposal" is actually happening.

Did you hear about it?

When the plight of the poor in Ireland became intolerable to eighteenth-century England, Swift published *A Modest Proposal* in which he suggested that if the rich would fatten and eat the children of the poor, both food and population problems would be solved!

Now I must ask myself if my affluent life style is quite literally "eating" the children of the poor. I may be supporting churches, charities and humanitarian projects, but am I also supporting a famine by the way I live?

Paul Ehrlich says that "few Americans could sit in the same room with a child and watch it starve to death." [21]

Please try this exercise. Visualize just one of the ten thousand people who will die today as a result of starvation or diseases related to malnutrition. Make it a child.

Carry her in your arms and place her on your living room couch. It's too late for food. Too late for her to play with the Barbie doll someone has handed her.

Think of it, there are more than thirteen million Barbie dolls in the world with thirteen million wardrobes of beautiful clothes, and this child has never owned a new dress.

You try to interest her in the family pet, but . . .

. . . you realize this child would not be dying in front of your eyes if she could have had the cat's daily diet of protein.

You know it's just an exercise, but a troubling one because it represents so much reality.

Some social consciences are awakened gradually. Some with a single event. Either way, the awakening marks a time when action must replace academic exercises.

Because of individual and collective action there are encouraging, modest signs that we may be slowing down the stork.

Now if we can just speed up the plow.

Chapter 8

Food Production: And Who Shall Feed This World?

SAWAHREJO IS THE THIRD WORLD IN MICROCOSM.

In this hamlet in central Java, the gap between the plow and the stork is painfully evident.

The families here number 420—about two thousand people—and they live on 673 acres, a little more than a square mile. Of the households, 78 own no land and 284 farm less than half an acre.

Sawahrejo means "lush rice fields," and the name is immediately enhanced by one look at the green, irrigated paddies and the abundant and exotic fruit trees. But both the name and the scenery belie the reality.

The truth is, most of the village lives on the edge of hunger.

Take the case of Kayin—like most Indonesians, he has only one name—who, along with 184 of his fellow villagers, owns a mere fifth of an acre. It is more a garden than a farm, but in a good season Mr. Kayin can harvest about five hundred pounds of rice from it. That is barely enough to sustain himself, his wife and their two surviving children. (Three other children died; in Java, one-fourth of all deaths are children less than a year old.)

His problems are shared by virtually every small farmer in every developing country.

He doesn't ever expect to be able to penetrate the cash

155

economy because he can sell only enough rice to buy seed for the next season and small amounts of fertilizer. All he could afford this year was nine pounds of fertilizer, bought on the black market for less than one dollar.

He has given up all hope of being able to buy high-yield seeds, insecticide, and fertilizer in sufficient quantity to dramatically increase his output.

One problem was solved for him this year when repairs were made to an irrigation canal that flows near his field. Built during the days of Dutch rule, it had silted up and fallen into disuse, leaving plots like his subject to the vagaries of weather. At least, now he has a permanent supply of water.

He wishes he had permanent work, for that is his only opportunity for a cash income. The going rate for a day laborer —and Mr. Kayin has never been able to find work for more than 120 days a year—is about twelve cents a day, plus meals. Nearly all of this goes for cassava, the starchy root eaten by most Javanese to supplement their rice diet, since most of the fruit is sold. Cassava has little nutrition, but its bulk does help stave off hunger.

Mr. Kayin and the other smallest landholders own only 5 percent of the land. More than half is owned by a few relatively prosperous farmers who can afford the new seeds and techniques that have raised their yields by as much as 50 percent.

One of those is Supadi, a retired police officer, who has five irrigated acres and five and a half for which he must depend upon rain. He is one of the three biggest landowners in the hamlet.

His money has gone into the hamlet's nicest house. It is a comfortable whitewashed structure with a bricked-in terrace where he has planted an orange tree. But Mr. Supadi is a bit nervous about it all, for he senses that his prosperity is threatened by the deteriorating village economy.

"In the coming twenty years," he says, "the situation will get worse and worse. If the landless and poor have nothing to eat, they will become robbers, they will become hoodlums."

Although rice production on Java as a whole is expanding faster than population, and even with record harvests in the country in 1973, self-sufficiency is still an elusive goal. That same year Indonesia had to import 1.6 million tons of rice, more than any other country in the region.

For the very poor in Sawahrejo, it is obvious that statistics about increased production and consumption are meaningless. If you cannot afford the minimum, what difference does it make to know that others are producing and eating more?

Birth control pills and the intrauterine device, the loop, were introduced in the village in 1972. The record shows that fifty-two women accepted the loop and forty-five women started on the pill. The pill-takers gave up within a few months, however, complaining of headaches, and no loops were accepted after the first year.

It isn't so much resistance to the idea of birth control as it is skepticism of the methods and a certain religious fatalism about the results. With the high density of population, it is not hard for the people to see the advantages of small families. But by Asian standards the rate of population increase in central Java—1.7 percent a year—is relatively low.

High infant mortality is one of the reasons for that modest percentage and it also undercuts the very notion of family planning.

If the lifeboat metaphor mentioned earlier has an application anywhere in the world, it might best fit in the hamlet of Sawahrejo. In the final analysis, each of these small holdings is an overcrowded lifeboat—self-sufficient simply because there is no means to be anything else.

One young farmer was asked how many people had to be sustained on the slightly more than an acre and a half that his father had farmed.

He recited twenty-two names.[1]

Who shall feed the lifeboats in Sawahrejo?

And who shall feed this world?

Where Did All the Surplus Go?

It was only a few years ago that the United States was awash in food surpluses. With not enough storage facilities, the streets of some wheat-growing Kansas towns were piled high with the golden grain.

America's cornucopia was full and running over. Boosted

by genetic seed improvements and the wholesale use of fertilizer and pesticides, our own unheralded "green revolution" was inundating us with its overflow.

The question then was, "Who shall consume all this food?"

It was both good news and bad news. The good news was that yields per acre were soaring; corn production trebled. The bad news was that it couldn't be sold on the world market profitably because most countries didn't have hard currency with which to buy.

In order to end the staggering storage costs, we did three things: (1) Passed in 1954 a law with a "Food for Peace" provision which allowed us to give surplus food—nearly $25 billion worth—away as foreign aid, (2) paid farmers to hold land out of production—$3.6 billion in 1972 alone, almost three times the amount of our present food-aid program—and, (3) went on a waste binge as a society, from which the hangover is likely to last a long time.

Oh, yes, and we relaxed.

Unbelievably, we were still relaxing in 1972. Now we wonder how we could have missed the rather clear warning signals. Lester Brown, a senior fellow of the Overseas Development Council, says, "In 1970, not one of the 100 economists anticipated that by 1974 the U.S. would plant all its farmlands and having done so, we'd still be hanging on by our fingernails." [2]

But here we are, wondering what happened.

What happened was a small change in production and a big change in demand which triggered off the potentially catastrophic events of 1974 and brought the world to the brink of famine.

In 1972, for the first time in twenty years, the output of cereals—wheat, coarse grains and rice—declined throughout the world. The effect of this decline was exacerbated by the inexorably growing population, wars and natural disasters. Cambodia became an importer of rice instead of an exporter. India used up some of her normal nine million tons of grain reserve to help feed the twelve million refugees from Bangladesh which crossed her borders and as food aid to the new nation. The Sahel went on starvation rations.

The Russians got into the picture, too. Instead of tightening their collective belts to get them through a lean year, the usual policy, they joined the other affluent nations as grain importers. According to the *National Observer* (March 30, 1974), "The Soviets imported more food in 1973 than any other country ever has in history."

But something else even more incredible happened. For the first time, the producing Americans began to compete with foreigners for scarce food.

When the dust settled, the American surplus was gone and wheat prices had tripled to more than five dollars a bushel. As a result, India and many other poor countries were virtually driven out of the market.

Famine!

How many died? For India, there are no figures. The government doesn't even want to talk about it. Mrs. Gandhi is quoted as saying, "Whenever anyone dies in India, whether it is from

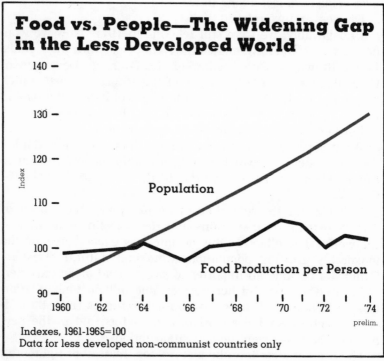

Figure 2

TB or whatever, the foreign press says they starved to death." The respected prime minister notwithstanding, it cannot be responsibly disputed that upwards of hundreds of thousands of Indians died from the food shortage in 1973–74.

Bangladesh has a similar internal political problem, so famine deaths are always minimized. However, foreign newspapers in Dacca reported that more than one hundred thousand Bengalis starved to death in a two-week period at the end of October 1974, and they were estimating deaths before the next rice harvest at possibly one million.

In Africa's famine regions, accurate figures are impossible to come by, but responsible estimates put the death figure at two hundred thousand—half of them in Ethiopia alone.

Famine! And even the 1973 bumper crops and 1974's barely adequate yields did not dent the problem because growing populations and a growing taste for meat consumed the entire harvests.

In 1961, the world stockpile of grain amounted to a ninety-five-day supply. In 1970, it was down to sixty-nine days. At the end of 1974, it stood at an alarming twenty-six days.

And that is the sad story of the shrinking surplus.

The Growing Capacity to Grow

With surpluses virtually gone, the hope for each year ahead lies in the ground. But it is a precarious and scary way for millions to live. The slightest disruption in any of a series of factors could send millions tumbling over the brink.

There are essentially two ways to expand the world food supply. One is to increase the land under cultivation and the other is to improve the present yield of cultivated land.

Both are possibilities.

Both have problems.

But first a look back before looking ahead.

From the time agriculture began about ten thousand years ago, Mother Earth has yielded up more and more of her good things to man's technological advances, as God surely intended. It is generally conceded there were six major technological breakthroughs which have accounted for the several hundredfold increase in the earth's food-producing capacity.

Chronologically, these were the use of irrigation, the discovery of animal traction, the cross-planting of crops between the Old World and the New, introduction of fertilizers and pesticides, breakthroughs in genetics, and the invention of the gasoline engine.

Each of these brought about quantum growth at the time of its introduction. Despite these advances, however, hunger remains the daily lot of much of mankind, for expansion of the food supply has permitted population to increase and the growing population absorbs—at least in the poor countries—all the increases in food production, leaving little food for improving diets.

Faced with something of an agricultural-population stalemate, is it possible that we can find or make more arable land somewhere on this planet?

The answer is a qualified yes. Comments Lester Brown: "If you are willing to pay the price, you can farm the slope of Mt. Everest." But even Brown admits that much unused land could be made productive at much less cost than his overdrawn example. Presently, about half of the potentially arable land— 3.5 billion acres—is under cultivation. That represents about 11 percent of the world's total land surface, but it includes practically all the best farmland.

Other lands which are being looked at are marginal. The most promising among them are:

1. The Amazon River basin in Northeast Brazil.

2. A band of about 1.7 billion acres across Central Africa.

3. Potential grazing lands in Colombia, Venezuela, Ecuador and Brazil.

4. Jungle areas in Indonesia, Thailand, Malaysia and Burma.

5. The Mekong River basin in Southeast Asia.

None of them are without problems. The Mekong runs through a politically unstable area, Central Africa is infested with the tsetse fly, special grasses would need to be developed for the high-acid soil of the Latin American savannahs, and land in the tropics deteriorates rapidly when the protective jungle cover is removed.

To make this land productive would require enormous capital investments on the order of $200 to $400 per acre. It has been estimated that the cost of putting all potentially arable land outside the humid tropics into cultivation would be between $500 billion and $1,000 billion. The top figure is about equal to the annual gross national product of the U.S., and twice that of all the developing countries combined.[3]

Cultural problems would also undoubtedly arise, reminiscent of the cattleman-farmer conflicts of America's West. Nomads would not take kindly to the idea of their traditional grazing land being turned into high-intensity agricultural production.

The idea of making large sections of unused land arable is not an impossible dream, but it does have nightmarish difficulties connected with it.

However, technological advances to increase the yield of present farmlands have certainly not run their course.

D. Gale Johnson, agriculture economist at the University of Chicago is optimistic. "I am confident," he says, "that the world has the capacity to increase food production more rapidly than the growth of population, as it has for the past two decades."

It was during that time the "green revolution" occurred.

The development of the high-yielding dwarf wheats in Mexico and a similar rice strain in the Philippines may not have been a quantum breakthrough, but it was a giant step forward. The research teams who worked on these projects said they were never intended as a final solution to the food problem. One team member explained: "It was a means of buying time, perhaps an additional fifteen or twenty years during which the brakes could be applied to population growth. The green revolution can be properly assessed only when we ask what things would have been like in its absence."

And while these high-yield varieties of grain have spread their benefits across the world, research has continued on other new plants. Scientists at the International Corn and Wheat Improvement Center in Mexico are working on a hypothetical hybrid that would combine the drought tolerance and disease resistance of barley, the self-fertilizing root system of the soybean and the high yield and food value of wheat.

A veritable Superplant!

The first hurdle, arising out of the fact that these are not closely related species, has already been leaped. The scientists have found that injections of the same drugs used to combat rejection of transplanted organs make it possible to overcome the biological barriers.

"It is futuristic," admits Dr. Armando Campos who is conducting the research. "If there's a payoff, it won't come for many years, but I know this—many, many years from now we are going to need to increase our food production still more. We must start now if we are going to be ready then."

Other scientists are talking about essentially redesigning plants to present more leaf area to the sun, as researchers already have by stimulating growth of a "flag leaf" on the top of rice plants.

Noting that increased carbon dioxide enhances plant growth dramatically in greenhouse settings, another group proposes that work be done to find ways of surrounding field crops with that gas, so basic to the process of photosynthesis.

A study released by the agriculture division of the National Academy of Sciences calls for expanded research aimed at replacing agricultural insecticides with insect hormones and pheromones—chemicals produced by the insect pests themselves.

The study also talks about using plain plastic tubing, perforated at strategic points and stretched out to irrigate a planted field only where water is needed—at the roots of the plants. The new method would use about one-twentieth of the water needed for conventional irrigation. Although the system is expensive, it waters only the crop, not the weeds.

For the future, Marion Clawson of the Washington think tank, Resources for the Future, Inc., advises, "There won't be any breakthroughs but a combination of things. . . . There are lots of possibilities for trouble, but lots of possibilities for solution."

One of the least costly ways of making the earth produce more is to increase the per acre yields in populous food-short countries. Rice yields per acre in India and Nigeria still are only one-third those of Japan; corn yields in Thailand and Brazil are less than one-third those of the United States.

If rice production in Bangladesh could be made to equal Japanese yields, it would jump fourfold from 10 million to 40 million metric tons. India now reaps approximately 100 million metric tons of cereal grains each year. If the yield levels equalled those of the United States, that figure would climb to 230 million tons. Simply by doubling its cultivated area without raising its current low yield levels, Brazil could produce an additional 22 million tons of grain.

The achievements and the dreams speak hopefully, and what they say is this:

The land's ability to produce and man's ingenuity for discovery and invention can be combined to give the earth a growing capacity to grow.

Water, Water Everywhere

Looking at the cornfield standing under three feet of water in our agricultural project on the banks of the Niger River, I had trouble remembering the terrible drought I had seen throughout the country six months earlier. As Oumarou Youssoufou and I looked at the swollen river, we both knew this did not mean the drought was broken in Niger. It only meant that another year's marginal rains were being drained into the sea.

Oumarou told me: "If we could conserve the rainfall we get instead of seeing it rush down to Nigeria and the Atlantic Ocean, we would have no water problems."

It was a refrain I heard everywhere around the hunger belt— from Ouagadougou in Upper Volta to Natal in Northeast Brazil. The Indian state of Gujarat had killing floods one year and deadly drought the next. Bangladesh could be described as just a spillway for the Ganges and Brahmaputra rivers.

It is the same, sad story in the Philippines—cyclical typhoon floods and drought, all in the same year.

As I flew across central India and drove over the Deccan Plateau, again the need was obvious. Watershed development. Catch basins. Dams. Wells. Everything, anything to preserve the precious monsoon rains and prevent their useless flow into the Indian Ocean.

Pure drinking water is a critical need. The *Times of India* has reported that nearly three hundred thousand villages with combined populations of over two hundred million people either have no source for drinking water or use sources declared unsafe.

The need is worldwide. The "World Environment Newsletter" department of *Saturday Review/World* estimates that five hundred million people suffer disabling diseases caused by unsafe water and that five million infants die each year from intestinal illnesses largely attributed to polluted water.[4]

The mayor of Tacloban City on the island of Leyte in the Philippines told me the greatest need in all the barrios of the East Visayas was pure drinking water. Mostly the people are drinking surface water, he said, leaving them with endemic debilitating diseases.

In the eighty national reports submitted to the United Nations Conference on the Human Environment, water was the major concern of the largest number of countries.

For drinking purposes, for flood control, for hydroelectric energy, for irrigation—for all these reasons and more, water conservation and control is an essential element in global development.

Most rivers flow to the sea almost unused by man, and more than half the water evaporating from the continents plays little part in human life. Irrigation takes only a fraction of the available supply. Less than 4 percent of the total river flow is used, in fact, and that irrigates only about 1 percent of the land area of the earth.

Interestingly, irrigation was the earliest agricultural innovation, being closely associated with the emergence of early civilizations in the Middle East. Since then, it has revolutionized agricultural production in many places. Today about one-seventh of all cultivated land is irrigated.

This interruption of the hydrological cycle has turned California's dry San Joaquin and Imperial valleys into some of the richest land in the world. There is evidence the same thing could happen in other parts of the world. H. D. Johns, an agricultural missionary with twenty-five years in India, told me if the water runoff from the Deccan Plateau in central India could be conserved for irrigation, much of the land could produce three crops a year.

Dams and irrigation projects would require no new technology, although in some areas they might create new problems. Disease is one of them. Schistosomiasis, commonly called "snail fever," is environmentally induced by conditions created by man. Caused by the larvae of a blood fluke that burrows into the flesh of those working in water-covered fields, its incidence has risen sharply as more land is irrigated. Affecting an estimated two hundred fifty million people, it now surpasses malaria as the world's most prevalent infectious disease.

Silting of lakes and irrigation canals is another problem, but this is no argument against doing them. It only underscores the necessity of maintaining a balance in the ecosystem around the projects.

The main limit now on the wider use of the miracle seeds of the "green revolution" is the availability of water. The U.N. Food and Agriculture Organization (FAO) estimates that demand for water will increase a whopping 240 percent in the next twenty-five years, yet the easiest big dam-and-irrigation projects are already completed.

Writing in *The Futurist,* Graham T. T. Molitor, an official of General Mills, says, "Water, not land, could become the principal restraint on the world's food production." [5]

Suggesting that available water be used more efficiently, *Time* (November 11, 1974) points out that wheat yields more calories than rice for the same input of water and that—in terms of water—one pound of beef is 2,500 times more expensive than one pound of bread!

That's something to remember about the use of water while we're waiting for the engineers to build all those dams.

Farming the Seas

While we are talking about water, let's look at that long-held dream of food experts—farming the seas. The best that can be said is that the dream is fading.

It was long thought the oceans were an almost limitless source of protein, either in the form of fish or algae. The world fish catch tripled to sixty-three million tons from 1950 to 1968, far exceeding the population growth rate. Then the catch declined in 1969 and has been as erratic as the stock market since then, with considerably more investment of time and money required each year to keep the production up.

Many marine biologists feel that the catches of table-grade fish have reached maximum sustainable levels, and indeed, that some of the thirty or so leading species may currently be overfished.

With the world clamoring for more protein, competition in world fishing beds has sharpened and clashes at sea and in world capitals have already occurred. Iceland wants the British to stay out of her traditional fishing waters, American fishermen complain about Soviet trawlers operating just beyond the twelve-mile offshore limits along the East Coast, and our own boats are in constant conflict with Ecuador and Peru.

The Japanese and Russian fishing fleets compete directly with each other in the North Pacific because in each of these countries, fish is an important source of protein. In fact, the "fish and rice" diet in Japan is the direct result of the country's efforts in the late nineteenth and twentieth centuries to feed a growing population with limited land resources. They turned to the sea for most of their animal protein so that today the average Japanese eats seventy pounds of fish per year, the highest of any major country.

Contrast that with our own per capita direct consumption of 14 pounds of fish per year. Then compare that with the amount of beef in our 1972 diet (109 pounds), pork (61 pounds), and poultry (50 pounds). Of course, we do account for more fish and consumption than that indirectly because we feed fish meal to our pigs and chickens.

It was once thought that plankton from the sea was our ultimate security against global famine. "Exploiting it, however, would require enormous efforts," according to the *Population Bulletin* (June 1970), "since a cubic meter of seawater contains a mere cubic centimeter of algal substance which in its raw form is unfit for human consumption."

Perhaps the color of the best crop to be obtained from the sea is not green, but black. When you consider the huge proven oil reserves which are under the ocean floor, the sea's greatest contribution to world food supplies may be through petroleum and its byproduct, fertilizer.

"Farming the sea" in this way may ultimately make it easier and more productive to farm the land.

Reforming the Farms

Land reform is one of the most promised and least achieved benefits of new governments in poor countries. Many have ridden to power on that promise alone, only to be subverted by the landed establishment once they arrived there, leaving the landless peasants still disfranchised. While not solely responsible for low agricultural production, the feudal system of landholder-sharecropper is undoubtedly a heavy contributing factor.

Says *Newsweek:* "After World War II, the U.S. occupation of Japan put an end to the ownership of farms by absentee landlords and placed land in the hands of the tillers. As a result, though Japanese farms are small (averaging one one-hundredth the size in the U.S.), the incentive derived from private ownership and a native industriousness have made Japanese farmers four times as productive as other Asians." [6]

Output also went up substantially when similar reform measures were taken in Taiwan, Egypt and Mexico.

In Latin America and Asia, however, huge areas of farmland are still owned by absentee landlords, and as long as the rent is paid they couldn't care less about productivity. Even if the sharecroppers had the incentive, they lack the means to increase the yield.

El Salvador illustrates the point. The country is mostly hills and mountains; its good farmland is limited to a coastal strip and scattered level spots in the interior. Owned by large commercial operators, this first-class land is devoted almost exclusively to plantation crops—cotton, sugar cane and coffee. These are all grown for commercial export. (Remember Juan Díaz in chapter six?)

That leaves only the barren hills to some three hundred fifty-two thousand *campesinos* for subsistence food growing. With their families, these peasants make up about two-thirds of the population of the country—about two million people.

Much of the land they cultivate is so steep that it has to be planted with a stick. It is impossible to plow with oxen, which most *campesinos* don't own anyway.

The rent is high—twenty to forty dollars for a plot less than two acres. Mostly the farmers grow maize on these hills, getting a yield of eleven to fourteen bushels per acre. Frequently the crop must be sold at sacrifice prices even before it is harvested. This grosses the family less than two hundred dollars, and out of that the landlord and moneylender must be paid.

They live on the rest, plus whatever they can earn picking coffee or working on one of the other commercial plantations.

Simply breaking up the plantations and distributing the land to the peasants may be too simplistic an answer. Father Gerard Rosier of Colombia's National University thinks so. He writes: "It is doubtful that a distribution and greater sub-division of the land would result in a more equitable distribution of well-being among the people."

He thinks "the wrong in Latin America isn't that land is in the hands of a few, but rather that these few misuse the land, plan production badly, don't use modern techniques, and pay their workers badly." [7]

A part of his thesis is debatable, however, when you consider that acquisition of land by large agri-businesses is the first step in a process in which the benefits are entirely on their side. Instead of producing food for consumption within the country, the land is turned to commercial cash crops, mostly for export.

When I was in Colombia, the sugar industry was busy buying small farms in order to plant more sugar cane and cash in on the escalating world market price. The little marginal farmers who were selling out would most certainly join the urban migrants, winding up in the jobless pools in Bogotá, Medellín or Barranquilla.

The changeover might contribute something to the nation's foreign exchange, but it will subtract a great deal more from the nutritional levels of its people.

However, land reform need not always be thought of in terms of redistribution. A "regrouping" strategy in the form of growing and marketing cooperatives can also be an effective method of reform. This makes it possible for farmers to take advantage of outside expertise, technology, business management and group borrowing power.

It has proven to be an effective answer for the *campesinos* of

El Salvador. Through cooperatives, many small farmers are producing seventy-five to eighty bushels of corn per acre—sometimes up to one hundred bushels—on their marginal land. It is a long leap from the eleven to fourteen bushels of a few years ago.

Tanzania has developed its own cooperative system as part of its national socialism. Called *ujamaa,* it can best be described as something between China's communes and Israel's *kibbutzim.* It has had mixed success, but by the end of 1972 there were about five thousand *ujamaa* villages with a population of over two million, representing about 14 percent of the nation's people.

The size of agricultural plots is not really the key in land reform. In many instances, small family farms may indeed be inadequate and inefficient. On the other hand, neither can bigness be equated with effectiveness.

The key ingredient in reform is incentive. The Soviets and Chinese have both learned the hard way that even the committed in the communes work better if a measure of incentive is added to the ideology. Says Demetrius Christodoulou, an FAO specialist in agricultural reform: "A man is just more likely to have the will to work his own land." [8]

Provided, of course, he has help with the know-how.

Whatever is the form of reform, both incentive and know-how will be needed in large doses if the plow is to stay up with the stork.

Food in the Bank

Having seen the world at the brink of famine and still standing only a few inches away, an increasing number of voices are joining in a call for a Joseph. It was this far-sighted prime minister of ancient Egypt who planned and administered the world's most famous food stockpile. Accumulating it during the seven years of plenty, he fed not only Egypt but neighboring countries as well during the seven years of want which followed.

About the only voices which haven't joined in the call for a food stockpiling system today are the commodity futures speculators and members of the Farm Bureau. The former make their money gambling on shortages, and the farmers remember too well the depressed prices when the silos and streets were full of surplus grain.

In those days, however, the United States was practically the only nation playing banker. Recent years have taught us a great deal, and one of the things is that no one nation can carry the burden of feeding the world. Says Lester Brown: "Just as the U.S. dollar can no longer serve as the foundation of an international monetary system, so U.S. agriculture may no longer have sufficient excess capacity to ensure reasonable stability in the world food economy." [9]

Thus the need today is for an international Joseph with an international plan.

At the Rome food conference in late 1974, the FAO proposed establishing a "system of world food security" which would guarantee "that minimum supplies are always available to those needing them on reasonable commercial terms or on grant terms." Although it leaves open many questions, it is a worthy idea which needs to be implemented. Dr. Addeke H. Boerma, director-general of the FAO, has put it well: "This situation of living from year to year, with many millions of people subject to the fickleness of the weather for their basic food supplies, is simply not good enough." [10]

Such a "food bank" would help smooth out troubling fluctuations in price and even more disastrous fluctuations in supply. Its existence would facilitate the meeting of emergencies. It would indirectly benefit every nation.

Probably the stockpiles would be held nationally, but be subject to international monitoring and allocation. The United States should rightly insist that (1) the bank be tapped only for emergencies, (2) all major producing countries participate in "capitalizing" the bank with sixty to seventy million tons of grain—enough to feed three hundred million people for a year, and (3) all nations, including the Soviet Union and China, share in the cost of maintaining the reserves.

Such a bank would not be the whole answer any more than any other single act is complete in itself.

The whole answer to the question, "And who shall feed this

world?" can only be the sum of all the partial answers given here. But there is yet an even more basic question about which something must be said.

Can This World Be Fed?

Everything I know and understand causes me to come down on the optimistic side of this question. It can be done.

Not easily.

Not inexpensively.

Certainly not without some changes.

But it can be done.

It is not the way that is lacking. It is the will. The more you understand about the basic causes of hunger in the world today, the more you cannot avoid the conclusion that God has given man and the earth the capacity to conquer and control it.

If we treated all humanity with the dignity and love they are due as the offspring of God, if we acted toward the environment as its caretakers and not its ravishers, if we viewed the mandate to "tend and dress" the earth as the Creator's orders to us, men could live together in peace and the earth would bring forth its abundance.

That was God's plan.

Anything short of that is the result of man's sin—his sin against God, against his fellow man, against his environment.

It is history.

And it is prophecy.

The black horse of famine which rides across the pages of Revelation is not said to be the judgment of God upon the earth. His ravages are the work of man upon himself. Having sown the wind, man reaps the whirlwind. It is one of God's laws, built into the very fabric of creation.

Because of that sin which brought separation from God to both man and his physical environment, the whole creation now groans in agony, awaiting its final redemption at the return of Jesus Christ.

But until that time, if we have the capacity to relieve suffering and save life—and we do—and refuse to do it, that will undoubtedly be a part of our judgment.

There is a remarkable passage in Charles Dickens' *A Christmas Carol* when the Ghost of Christmas Present takes the miser Scrooge to observe Christmas at the home of his underpaid clerk Bob Cratchit, who has a crippled little son. Scrooge, whose heart is already being touched, asks if Tiny Tim will live.

"If these shadows remain unaltered by the Future, none other of my race," returned the Ghost, "will find him here. What then? If he be like to die, he had better do it, and decrease the surplus population."

Scrooge hung his head to hear his own words quoted by the Spirit, and was overcome with penitence and grief.

"Man," said the Ghost, "if man you be in heart, not adamant, forbear that wicked cant until you have discovered What the surplus is, and Where it is. Will you decide what men shall live, what men shall die? It may be, that in the sight of Heaven, you are more worthless and less fit to live than millions like this poor man's child. Oh, God! To hear the Insect on the leaf pronouncing on the too much life among his hungry brothers in the dust!"

And how shall this world be fed?

In his poem, *The Vision of Sir Launfal,* James Russell Lowell gives a clue. For the perceptive, perhaps nothing more than a clue is needed:

> Not what we give, but what we share—
> For the gift without the giver is bare;
> Who gives himself with his alms feeds three—
> Himself, his hungering neighbor, and me.

Chapter 9
Food Consumption: Overweight and Underfed

$\mathbf{A}$T SIULI BARI VILLAGE, 170 miles northwest of Calcutta, Adary Mal hunched over the little pot where the family's one meal for the day was cooking.

Bubbling in the pot was a wad of weeds.

One of her six children squatted beside her, picking through a handful of snails gathered from the fields that day.

This would be the only protein they would have.

"I am eating these things every day," said Dukhu Mal, looking at his wife's weeds. "What else can I eat? I have no choice. Look at my skin. Look at my bones."

Hunger has overtaken this village of 150 families. The landless laborers now have nothing to do except pick the weeds in front of their mud-and-thatch hovels to fill the swollen bellies of their starving children.

Rice prices have doubled and the farmers have sold their stocks to the traders for cash. There is nothing left for the local hungry at prices which they can afford.

Not far away at Bankura town, Habu Baury picks up cow dung, pats it into little cakes and sells it for fuel.

"Some days it's sold and some days there's no buyer," he said. "The day there is no sale, we starve. When there is no food, the children cry. How can they live without food? That's why they cry."

Meanwhile, in Los Angeles, the manager of a restaurant chain told a reporter who inquired about food waste that many people can't finish the food they are served, but in spite of this the restaurant tries to maintain a "healthy looking plate."

Bernard Thol of Hale Restaurants talked of the waste syndrome which afflicts the American culture, and admitted that restaurants were "caught up into it. Will it antagonize the customer if you cut [portions] down? We have tried to maintain this by increasing the price instead of cutting down portions."

Lee Davis, head chef of Lawry's in the same city, agrees there is waste, especially in such things as bread and butter. But they have to be served, he says, because "if you don't give it to them they think we are going cheap. We would much rather raise prices than cut portions."

"I throw away every night whole pieces of bread, maybe ten or fifteen pounds of it," says George Spanos, owner of Bryon's Restaurant in Richmond, Virginia. "It's a shame!"

Morrison's Cafeteria at Frankfort, Kentucky, serves about four to five hundred people during an average lunch hour. According to the manager, Ted Lance, the wasted food fills up two thirty-gallon garbage containers.

It's a similar story at Les Champs Restaurant in New York. Mel Dansky says the eatery dumps at least ten pounds of butter and a hundred pounds of meat each week.[1]

That amounts to two and a half tons of meat and one-quarter of a ton of butter each year. Wasted. In one restaurant.

The disparity of food consumption around the world is unquestionably one of the major causes of hunger, and American eating habits are undoubtedly a heavy contributing factor to that inequity.

Which leads me to ask a question.

Is There a Food Ethic?

That our eating habits are luxurious and even wasteful few would dispute. However, "waste" is a relative term. We begin to see just how wasteful our affluent diets are only when we relate them to (1) the amount of food necessary to sustain good health and (2) the hunger diets of the rest of the world.

Only God knows the amount of surplus fat the American public carries around, but it has to run in the millions of tons. Add to that the other millions of tons which are lost through dieting annually and regained by backsliding, and the total is mind-blowing.

We are an overfed nation, not only quantitatively but also qualitatively. On the average we get three hundred calories more per day than we need and, according to *Consumer Reports,* "many Americans routinely take in three to four times more protein than their bodies need." [2] Not only more than we *need,* but other sources estimate we regularly get twice as much protein as our bodies can even use as protein.

Apart from the health factor which we'll talk about later, can food consumption be treated simply as a matter of supply and demand—along, of course, with the ability to pay?

In *Diet for a Small Planet,* Frances Lappé raises the issue: "When your mother told you to eat everything on your plate because people were starving in India, you thought it was pretty silly. You knew the family dog would be the only one affected by what you did or didn't do. Since then you've probably continued to think that making any sort of *ethical* issue of eating is absurd. You ate what your family always ate, altered only perhaps by proddings from the food industry." [3]

Is it absurd to think of eating as an ethical issue? Or, in a world of scarcity and starvation, are we forced to face the question of a food ethic?

Early in the writing of this book, I was having a chat with Russell Chandler, religion writer for the *Los Angeles Times,* on this very subject. We couldn't escape the conclusion that ethical considerations are primary in dealing with an element so essential to life as is food. U.N. Secretary General Kurt Waldheim has called it "the one essential and undebatable precondition of a life of dignity and decency."

If there is a work ethic, in which many Americans still believe, and a sex ethic, in which fewer people seem to believe, then there must be a food ethic, even though it may hardly be recognized by anyone at all.

I went to the Bible, the best book I know for ethical guid-

ance. It was easy to find the sex ethic spelled out. The work
ethic, though a bit less defined, was also there. But where was
the food ethic?

I found charity and mercy to be great themes in the Old
Testament. The Jews were forbidden to gather the leftovers of
the harvest from the fields, for these were to be for "the
stranger, for the fatherless, and for the widow." [4]

The rich fool and his full barns were there. That story said
something about the use of abundance. Another rich man and
a beggar named Lazarus were there. We are told the rich man
"feasted in great magnificence every day" while poor Lazarus
"would have been glad to satisfy his hunger with the scraps
from the rich man's table." [5] That seemed to say something
about self-indulgence.

There was a great deal about sharing. The Good Samaritan.
The teachings in the epistles. But there seemed to be no definitive word about a food ethic. Was this another example of the
Bible's concern with broad principles rather than detailed rules
of behavior?

I believe so.

It is there, but it is embodied in the comprehensiveness of
the Christian life. Vernard Eller makes an illustrative point in
his *The Simple Life*. After quoting the words of Jesus in
Matthew 6:33 (NEB)—"Set your mind on God's kingdom and
his justice before everything else, and all the rest will come to
you as well"—he adds:

"Here is the absolutely essential premise upon which
thought, faith, and practice must build if the result is to
qualify as the simple life in any *Christian* sense. There is a
'first,' and there is an 'all the rest.' " [6]

So the food ethic comes under "all the rest." It is in mercy,
in charity, in love, in compassion, in Christlikeness, and in
respect for the dignity and worth of man. Like the sacredness
of life, it is woven into the fabric of human relationships by
the Creator God. It is an inescapable part of being our brother's
keeper.

Try praying, "Give *me* this day *my* daily bread." See how
unsatisfyingly one-dimensional it sounds? Only as you put
bread-winning and bread-eating in the context of mutuality—
"Give *us* . . . *our* daily bread"—are they authenticated as holy

acts. In any other setting they are subject only to the jungle law of tooth and claw and survival of the fittest.

I remember something told me by a friend who went to Germany not many years after World War II. She was engaged in teaching children who had grown up during the very lean years of postwar recovery. In response to her question, "What is sin?" the children would inevitably answer, "Sin is wasting food."

Perhaps scarcity and suffering sharpen the social conscience.

Gluttony—our comforting euphemism is "overeating"—may be as numbing to the conscience as it is deadly to the body.

But gluttony is well-chronicled in the human record.

Spit-Roasted Songbirds

The rich man in Jesus' story who indulged in his food orgies was neither the first nor the last of his kind.

According to the archives, a churchman in 1570 offered the following menu to his guests. Don't bother reading the whole thing unless you happen to be captivated by it, but please scan it because I want to make a point.

First Course—Cold Delicacies from the Sideboard

Pieces of marzipan and marzipan balls
Neapolitan spice cakes
Malaga wine and Piscan biscuits
Plain pastries made with milk and eggs
Fresh grapes
Spanish olives
Prosciutto cooked in wine and served with capers, grape pulp
    and sugar
Salted pork tongues cooked in wine, sliced
Spit-roasted songbirds, cold, with their tongues sliced over them
Sweet mustard

Second Course—Hot Foods from the Kitchen: Roasts

Fried veal sweetbreads and liver with a sauce of eggplant, salt,
    sugar and pepper
Spit-roasted skylarks with lemon sauce
Spit-roasted quails with sliced aubergines

Stuffed spit-roasted pigeons with sugar and capers sprinkled
over them

Spit-roasted rabbits, with sauce and crushed pine nuts

Partridges, larded and spit-roasted, served with lemon slices

Pastries filled with minced veal sweetbreads and served with
slices of prosciutto

Strongly seasoned poultry with lemon slices and sugar

Slices of veal, spit-roasted, with a sauce made from the juices

Leg of goat, spit-roasted, with a sauce made from the pieces of
three pigeons for each two goats

Soup of almond cream

Squares of meat aspic

*Third Course—Hot Foods from the Kitchen: Boiled Meats and
Stews*

Stuffed fat geese, boiled Lombard style and covered with sliced
almonds, served with cheese, sugar and cinnamon

Stuffed breast of veal, boiled, garnished with flowers

Milk calf, boiled, garnished with parsley

Almonds in garlic sauce

Turkish-style rice with milk, sprinkled with sugar and cinnamon

Stewed pigeons with mortadella sausage and whole onions

Cabbage soup with sausages

Poultry pie, two chickens to each pie

Fricasseed breast of goat dressed with fried onions

Pies filled with custard cream

Boiled calves feet with cheese and egg

Fourth Course—Delicacies from the Sideboard

Quince pastries, one quince per pastry

Pear tarts, the pears wrapped in marzipan

Parmesan cheese and Riviera cheese

Fresh almonds and vine leaves

Chestnuts roasted over the coals and served with salt, sugar and
pepper

Milk curds with sugar sprinkled over ring-shaped cakes

Wafers [7]

Care to take a guess as to the identity of the genial host?

Pope Pius V.

Are you horrified at such sybaritic overkill in the papal
palace? Associated with religion?

No anguished cries from Protestants, please. The point I want to make is this: the colossal variety of succulent foods available to us day in and day out appear every bit as lavish in the eyes of the world's hungry as does the papal menu to us.

Especially to those three and a half million persons already in line for the death rattle of starvation whose laughing, loving, hoping and living will abruptly end this year.

You would like to protest that at least you don't eat song-birds? Never mind. Our polluted environment does it for you. Just call it the Ecology of Mindless Affluence.

Inefficient Protein Factories

Americans who say they are hungry enough to eat a horse, rarely do, but they do eat walking "protein factories" without giving it a second thought.

These protein factories are steers.

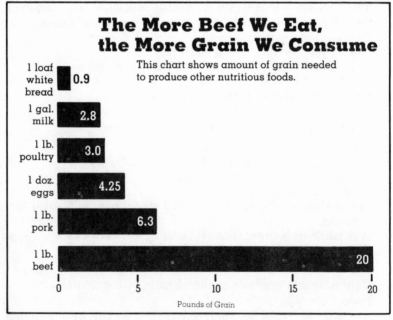

Figure 3

Actually, they are more like protein "reducers" than "factories" because, according to Frances Lappé, "the average steer is able to reduce 21 pounds of protein in feed to one pound of protein in the expensive steak or roast on our plate." [8] The other twenty pounds, she says, go into body energy, nonedible parts such as hair, and manure. In fact, the Department of Agriculture estimates that the manure from American livestock contains as much protein as our annual production of soybeans.

But animals are not the only protein wasters. So are humans. Especially American humans. As has already been noted, we now eat about twice the protein our bodies can use. It can't be stored, so the body exhausts it as energy or excretes it. So wasteful is our protein consumption that it has been estimated we could reduce our beef cattle by 25 percent and still feed every one of us half a pound of meat each day. That alone is enough to meet our total protein requirement, not to mention what we get from other food sources.

Maybe we need to get rid of some of our cows as badly as we think the Indians need to reduce their cattle population, especially since we now dispose of over half our farm produce by feeding it to our livestock. Not only feeding it, but force-feeding it. That's what they do in commercial feedlot operations where beef cattle are helped to gorge themselves by the use of hormones and antibiotics. And all this extra feed is not meant to add protein, but fat, so those well-marbled steaks and roasts can be graded "prime" and "choice."

Each steer puts away more than a ton of grain and several hundred pounds of high-protein feed made from milk products, fish meal and wheat germ.

And you probably will be surprised to learn that we don't produce all that cattle feed ourselves. Virtually all the fish meal comes from the Third World. Europe imports one-third of the African peanut crop to feed its livestock. In fact, Dr. Georg Borgstrom, in his latest book, *The Food and People Dilemma*,[9] concludes that the rich world is a net importer of protein from the poor world!

Can you believe our livestock consume as much grain in a year as do the entire populations of India and China? It's true.

And it's unnecessary. Cattle and pigs don't require valuable grain to make protein. They can produce meat and milk out of orange pulp and coffee grounds if a nitrogen source—such as urea—and a carbohydrate are added to convert cellulose to protein. Representative John Seiberling of Ohio is asking Congress to appropriate research funds to find ways to use some of society's waste as cattle feed. In addition to nonedible produce—corn stalks, vegetable tops, etc.—it has been proven that even treated cow manure and newspapers can be made appetizing to ruminants.

That would be the creative way to make our livestock truly protein factories instead of inefficient and wasteful protein reducers. It would also free up a lot of grain to feed the world's hungry.

And still you wouldn't have to give up all your steak.

Our Red-Meat Religion

Nutritionists and doctors, however, are sure we would all be healthier if we gave up some of the beef we eat.

"Meat consumption in this country is preposterously high, relative to need," according to Dr. D. Mark Hegsted of the Harvard School of Public Health, "and cannot be justified on a nutritional basis." [10]

That will shock a lot of Americans. Ever since the days of the cowboys and cattle drives we've thought the more beef you ate, the healthier you would be. The years of 1973 and 1974 were the first time in twenty years that beef consumption did not go up in this country. High prices and concern over saturated fat helped reduce it to 109 pounds per person, down from a peak of 116 pounds in 1972. That, however, was still an increase of 87 percent over the 62 pounds per capita consumption in 1952.[11]

The American Heart Association suggests that a three and a half ounce serving of beef is really adequate for most people, since it contains more than half the recommended daily allowance of protein. Then, too, the protein in other animal sources such as chicken, fish, cottage cheese and milk is every bit as useful to your body as the protein in red meats—with less grain required to produce it.

But over the years we've developed a kind of "red-meat"

religion in this country and it has helped turn America into the world's leading importer of beef! And all the time you thought your steak came from Texas.

Beef is certainly a tasty way to ingest protein—it is about 25 percent protein—but it is not necessarily the best source of the body-building substance. On a scale of 0 to 100, the FAO gives meat a protein quality of 67. True, that is higher than most plant proteins—except whole rice at 70—but it is below cheese (70), fish (80), milk (82), and eggs (95). In terms of land yield, the difference is even more pronounced. An acre of cereal grains can produce five times more protein than an acre devoted to meat production; legumes (peas, beans, lentils) can produce ten times more, and leafy vegetables fifteen times more.[12]

Beef has other disadvantages, too. Animal fats are highly suspect as a major contributor to heart disease, and beef—especially choice and prime grades—is heavily larded with saturated, cholesterol-producing fat. Studies are continuing on just how heart disease and cholesterol in the blood are related, but there is strong evidence they are closely linked.

Red meat can make you fat as well, since it is a major source of calories. An eight-ounce serving of round steak, for instance, contains 500 calories.

There are other less expensive, less fattening sources of high-quality protein. Nonfat dry milk is one. Soy protein is another. Cereal grains are the main source of protein for some 80 percent of the world's people.

We may be on the verge of discovering that all along our red-meat religion has been a false faith.

Middle America

I don't know how much relevance a statistic like this has but I think it's interesting.

The October 1974 issue of *Bits and Pieces*, a magazine devoted to miscellanea, reported: "The average American belt has expanded in the past 40 years from 31 inches to 34 inches, according to an industry survey."

Better nutrition?

Or overeating?

Counting Calories

Whichever it is, we are still engaging in one of our favorite American pastimes, counting calories. Even when we are doing it, however, we don't know too much about what it is we're counting.

"Calorie" is a term used to describe both a unit of energy and the quantity of food capable of producing such a unit of energy. But since it is only the measure of the fuel and energy value of food, it is not an adequate criterion by itself for judging the relative adequacy of a diet. Some deficiencies—especially a deficiency of protein—are not always obvious from caloric information alone.

The measurement is helpful, however, in looking at the relative nutritional state of the world if you remember it is only a part of the picture.

As a general rule, the human body needs 2,400 calories per day to maintain good health, although that figure can go up or down, depending on individual size, climate, energy exerted, etc. With as few as 1,500 calories, the body is in trouble. The trouble deepens as the figure gets lower, and generally the body will deteriorate and starve at any amount below 1,200 calories over a prolonged period.

That gives you some idea about the minimum and maximum requirements.

Guess where Americans fit on the scale. We don't. We're off the scale—at the top—3,300 calories per day.

"As a nation," says *The Futurist*, "we are on the brink of being overfed victims of abundance. . . . A daily intake of 3,000 calories is generally too much, with consistent consumption above that level causing obesity and contributing to various health-related problems."

Although our per capita consumption levels have declined somewhat in recent years, they have never gone below 3,000 calories per day. *The Futurist* says our food consumption is still geared to the needs of a bygone era:

"Less arduous and more sedentary work, shorter work weeks, longer vacations, earlier retirements, and the like all contribute to a lifestyle that requires less output of human energy. . . .

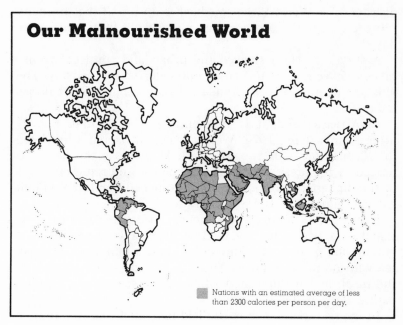

Our Malnourished World

Nations with an estimated average of less than 2300 calories per person per day.

Figure 4

Living in air conditioned homes, working in air conditioned offices, shopping in air conditioned malls, and enjoying controlled temperature climates during cooler months, Americans require fewer calories." [13]

With requirements lower and intake higher, we are literally eating ourselves sick.

While elsewhere in the world, people are literally starving themselves to death.

The *National Observer* (Sept. 21, 1974) reports: "If 2,400 calories are needed daily to maintain good health, then the average Indian is about 400 calories behind." However, in some places in the country and during certain seasons, the intake may be less than 800 calories for one or two months.

Ethiopia has a similar deficit. Indonesia is around 300 calories behind. So are the Philippines and Vietnam.

But don't forget these are averages. Millions are below the average.

The war in Cambodia has produced its own nutritional

disaster. The World Vision medical team found that in many refugee camps the average was more like 1,200 calories per day.

A survey in Haiti showed the urban and rural calorie intakes to have been 2,100 and 1,600 calories, respectively. The villagers of inland New Guinea get only about 1,500 calories a day.

In Africa's Sahel it is frequently less than that. Shortly after Thanksgiving 1974, World Vision sponsored a luncheon in Washington with Senator Mark Hatfield as the host. Attended by the press, members of Congress and representatives of the diplomatic corps, the event launched our FAST (Fight Against Starvation Today) program.

It was really more a nonluncheon because the meal consisted of a two-ounce fried millet cake, a very small boiled potato, one quarter of a raw onion, and a half glass of weak tea with no milk or sugar. There were sixty-seven calories in the meal, and it duplicated what I have seen many families eating across Asia and Africa.

In his remarks, Senator Hatfield indicated this was to be a symbolic meal so that we might more dramatically identify with hungry people around the world.

Asking to say a few words, the ambassador from Upper Volta movingly pointed out that for hundreds of thousands of people in the Sahel, this was not a symbolic meal.

"Except for the onion," he said, "this is the food which my people are forced to eat day after day. The onion is a luxury. Only a few would be able to afford it."

Across Africa and Asia, according to *Newsweek*, "nearly one-quarter of the 2.7 billion population (675 million) subsist on a diet far below the 1,000 calories a day that are needed for anything more energetic than just staying alive." [14]

But as we've seen, caloric intake alone cannot tell the full story. The key element in health and body-building is protein. Dr. Georg Borgstrom, member of the Department of Food Science and Human Nutrition at Michigan State University, believes that "the prime global deficiency is that of protein. . . . Indeed, 10 to 15 percent of the world is short of calories, or 'undernourished.' But vastly more people—perhaps 1.5 billion —suffer from the calamity of inadequate nutrients, or 'mal-

Malnutrition and Population

Estimated number of people with insufficient
protein-energy supply, 1970

Region	Population (millions)	Per Cent Fed Insufficiently
Developed Areas	1074	3%
Less Developed Areas (excluding Asian centrally planned economies)	1751	20%
Latin America	283	13%
Far East	1020	22%
Near East	171	20%
Africa	273	25%
WORLD (excluding Asian centrally planned economies)	2825	14%

Source: U.N. Economic and Social Council

Figure 5

nutrition.' A shortage of protein is the number one problem
everywhere in the hungry world." [15]

Here's what that means in human terms.

The Baricks of Calcutta

If you think you know something about stretching your food
dollar, you should meet the family of Gobar Dhan Barick.
You'll find their home down one of Calcutta's narrow lanes
that stink of urine and twist between mud walls.

Barick feeds a family of ten—counting his widowed sister
and her two children—on $9.50 a week. That averages out at
14¢ a day each.

Obviously, some things are missing from their diet. No
eggs—not at 50¢ a dozen. No flour. Grain is bought whole and
pounded. No milk; that can cost you 50¢ a quart if you insist

on having the buffalo milked at the door to make sure the milk isn't watered.

Here's how they do it:

Breakfast is a cup of tea and a rice biscuit the size and taste of an artificial dog bone. Sometimes only the children get the biscuits.

Immediately after breakfast as the sun is rising, Barick goes to the market with a small basket and returns with the day's vegetables. Mrs. Barick spends an hour and a half making an early lunch so her husband can eat before he goes to work at the print shop. She has no table in their one room, so she works on the cement floor, bringing her cooking pots out from under the bed.

Lunch is boiled rice; a vegetable fried lightly in mustard oil, or peanut oil if the former is not available; and soup called *dal,* made from the peas, beans, or lentils from which Indians get most of their protein.

Dinner preparation takes the same amount of time as lunch, and is prepared over a smoky pot of charcoal. The meal again is a fried vegetable and a heap of *chapatties,* made from whole wheat flour and water. Dessert, when they have it, is a lump of brown sugar.

They flavor their food with hot peppers and sometimes they have a salad of raw onions and tomato. On Sundays, Barick splurges on fish, buying ten or twelve ounces for about thirty cents. Occasionally, "if the pocket permits," Barick will get fruit on his way home from work. It is always locally grown bananas or mangoes.

The Baricks have peeled the dietary onion about as far as they can go. They get calories from grain, protein from *dal,* vitamins from fruits and vegetables, and fat from the oil their food is cooked in.[16]

Says a relief worker in Calcutta: "The marginal people spend 80 to 90 percent of their income on food, and they can only adjust to rising prices by buying less food. They always cut the most nutritious food first: meat goes out, milk goes out, vegetables go out, so they are left with only the staple, grain."

Malnutrition then becomes their constant companion. It's especially tough on the children. The tiny victims of maras-

mus—starvation—are common in the villages and slums.
They have sunken cheeks and loose skin wrinkled over matchstick limbs. For the most part, they are too lethargic and listless
to respond.

"He won't die, but he'll be stunted or retarded," says an
Indian doctor, examining one of the tiny victims. "In one
village around here, 3 percent of the kids go blind because of
lack of vitamin A."

Multiply that percentage around the world and the future is
not a happy prospect for millions of children.

The Saddest Brain Drain

Instead of counting sheep some night after overeating, try
counting children whose blindness is a direct result of never
having enough to eat. For a march past of Indian children
alone it would take almost eight hours at the rate of two
every second.

And blindness from xerophthalmia is only one tragedy.
There is beriberi. Scurvy. Rickets. And innumerable diseases
which attack weakened bodies.

A U.S. State Department official told a recent population
conference that "very conservative" predictions indicated some
six hundred fifty million children alone are already marked
for death or subhuman existence, and that close to *one billion*
are now living in the shadows of malnutrition and hunger.

I can still see the pert, smiling face of little six-year-old
Marli as she bounded around the playground of the Methodist
school and nutrition center in Rio de Janeiro.

Marli is just one of the billion, but I find it hard to visualize
a billion faces. I can relate to one.

Little Marli looked normal in every way. Healthy. Happy.
There was just one thing wrong with her, the director's wife
Anita Way told me. She couldn't learn. At first, the teachers
thought perhaps her difficulty was psychological, the result
of neglect in a family of eleven children. Her younger sister
had the same problem. But after careful observation and test-
ing, it was evident that Marli, a child of Brazil's poor and
wretched *favelas*, was unable to learn because as an infant her
malnourished body could not produce a healthy brain.

It was a sad diagnosis I heard repeated around the world. There are millions of children who because of chronic protein deficiency have suffered irreversible brain damage that consigns them forever to the cruel twilight world of mental cripples.

Children denied adequate protein in both the prenatal and early postnatal periods usually develop only half the number of brain cells as properly nourished children during the same period. *Time* magazine says, "At least 80 percent of all human brain growth occurs between conception and the age of two. This growth cannot take place in the fetus if the mother is malnourished, and it cannot be accomplished in the infant if he is starving." [17]

Doctors believe the lack of adequate protein during this period and even later prevents the full development of the myelin sheath which covers the nerve cells of the brain. They are confident this somehow relates to learning ability, although they do not yet understand the process.

For many of these children death would be a blessing, for they will never know a life. Not all the prayers of a thousand well-wishers, not all the money appropriated by Congress for food aid this year, not all the attention of the teachers in Latin America, not all the concern of all the mothers in the world can change Marli's sad and subnormal destiny.

Somebody sacrificed her God-given potential and subtracted all of life's meaning before she ever had a chance to say a word about it. Millions like her are locked into narrow cellblocks of mental retardation and the keys have been thrown away. For them, the doors will never open.

I believe their subhuman existence is the heaviest guilt which the affluent world must bear on its conscience.

I know I can't get Marli off mine.

Stages of Hunger

Mental damage can result long before there is any outward physical evidence of hunger. But ultimately the body also pays the price of this terrible tragedy.

There are pronounced and definable stages of physical deterioration between hunger and starvation. We need to understand something of the vocabulary of hunger.

The word *hunger* itself is the same as *undernutrition*. It has to do more with quantity than quality and refers primarily to a caloric insufficiency. It usually results in loss of weight, reduced activity and—in children—growth retardation.

Hunger in its qualitative form is called *malnutrition*, a state induced when the diet is lacking in some essential elements. It is most frequently the result of eating too much cereal grains and starchy foods, such as potatoes and cassava, and neglecting meat, milk, fruit and vegetables.

A severe protein-calorie deficiency is known as *marasmus*, and is more or less an advanced state of undernutrition, seen in a progressive wasting and emaciation of the body. It causes the bodies and faces of children to look incongruously old, since the flesh degenerates, causing the skin to wrinkle.

On the other hand, *kwashiorkor* is the result of severe protein deficiency; calories do not seem to be involved. Rather than producing emaciation, the body swells because the tissues are filled with fluid.

I remember such a boy in a refugee camp on the outskirts of Phnom Penh. He may have been twelve years old, but he looked more like six or eight. His face wasn't gaunt. It was full, almost cherubic. Dr. Penelope Key, head of World Vision's medical team, pointed out the swollen stomach, the puffy face, the scaly skin at ankles and wrists and explained these were the textbook symptoms of kwashiorkor.

I saw his struggled breathing. Each breath was a gigantic effort for him, not an automatic reflex, and it seemed that taking it required all the strength he had. This lad was so far gone that his body was feeding on the protein left in his blood. Without treatment, when this was exhausted he would die.

But the medical team was going to cheat death of this victim, for he had been found in time, and the vitamins and high protein powder which fortified his bowls of gruel served in the nutrition center would restore him completely.

In describing how hunger kills, *Time* reports: "The victim of starvation burns up his own body fats, muscles and tissues

for fuel. His body quite literally consumes itself and deteriorates rapidly. The kidneys, liver and endocrine system often
cease to function properly. A storage of carbohydrates, which
play a vital role in brain chemistry, affects the mind. Lassitude
and confusion set in, so that starvation victims often seem
unaware of their plight. The body's defenses drop; disease
kills most famine victims before they have time to starve to
death. An individual begins to starve when he has lost about
a third of his normal body weight. Once this loss exceeds 40
percent, death is almost inevitable." [18]

But for most, hunger doesn't kill.

It only makes life not worth living.

Food is a Celebration

One of the most graphic descriptions of the effects of hunger
occurs in the book, *Child of the Dark,* from which I have
quoted earlier. It is the diary of Carolina Maria de Jesus who,
like Marli, lived in one of Brazil's squalid *favelas.*

One of her daily battles with hunger she narrates this way:

"I didn't have any breakfast and walked around half dizzy.
The daze of hunger is worse than that of alcohol. The daze of
alcohol makes us sing, but the one of hunger makes us shake.
I know how horrible it is to only have air in the stomach.

"I began to have a bitter taste in my mouth. I thought: is
there no end to the bitterness of life? I think that when I was
born I was marked by fate to go hungry. I filled one sack of
paper. When I entered Paulo Guimarães Street, a woman
gave me some newspapers. They were clean and I went to the
junk yard picking up everything that I found. Steel, tin, coal,
everything serves the *favelado.* Leon weighed the paper and I
got six cruzeiros.

"I wanted to save the money to buy beans but I couldn't because my stomach was screaming and torturing me.

"I decided to do something about it and bought a bread
roll. What a surprising effect food has on our organisms. Before I ate, I saw the sky, the trees, and the birds all yellow,
but after I ate, everything was normal to my eyes.

"Food in the stomach is like fuel in machines. I was able to
work better. My body stopped weighing me down. I started to

walk faster. I had the feeling I was gliding in space. I started to smile as if I was witnessing a beautiful play. And will there ever be a drama more beautiful than that of eating? I felt that I was eating for the first time in my life." [19]

Carolina had discovered what someone else has said.

Food is a celebration.

I am just sad that so few have been invited to the party.

Chapter 10
Development: People-Building vs. Nation-Building

WHEN FARLIE WINSON came across the border in the north of Niger in 1973, he and his family were traveling on a forged passport. He was a man with a record on three continents and the West African country was just about the end of the line for Farlie, his wife Enid, and their three small children.

Today he is a citizen of the country, carries a real passport issued by the government of Niger, and is considered by leaders of that country as an ambassador-at-large.

What made the dramatic difference? Two things. First, out on the desert one night Winson had an encounter with Jesus Christ which radically changed his life. He became a new person. In the words of St. Paul, "Old things passed away; all things became new."

Second, his agricultural background helped him see food-producing possibilities in the famine-stricken country that could conceivably make it self-sufficient in food. For a country which is considered an international basket case by the United Nations, that would be some achievement!

It all started simply enough. Winson was introduced by World Vision staffer Bernard Barron to Oumarou Youssoufou, a young Nigerian leader and advisor to the president. Youssoufou, educated in a mission school, was a "brother." He helped the new believer find a job as supervisor of a peanut-seed producing program. A fertile valley near the Niger River had been chosen for the project, and European engineers had designed an irrigation plan to pump water over a range of hills to the location. It would be expensive, but worth it for the export potential of the peanuts.

Winson spent two weeks going over the area carefully on foot and by Land Rover. He discovered that the lay of the land along the river was such that, by digging a canal eighteen miles long, he could irrigate tens of thousands of acres by gravity flow—not only for peanut production, but also for precious grain of which the drought-prone country never had enough.

Niger embraces about 490,000 square miles of West African desert and scrub land. Two-thirds of the area is pure Sahara sand; the other third is largely Sahel. Just over four million people try to scratch out what even in the best of times could be called only a bare existence.

Rainfall in normal years will total from four to twenty inches. The summer heat goes to 120 degrees for months on end. It is ironic that one of the best rivers in Africa, the Niger, flows through the country for some 500 miles, yet is little used. After the rains come, the volume of the flowing Niger River can be compared to its sister, the Nile, but there is no way to conserve it as it rushes to the sea.

Winson's proposal to Youssoufou was delightfully simple. Why not use the abundant Niger River flatlands, enriched with centuries of alluvial soil, to grow food for the rest of the country? His survey had already proven the feasibility of inexpensive gravity-flow irrigation. Between Niamey, the capital, and Gaya, near the southern border, there are over sixty thousand acres of treeless land awaiting cultivation.

Providentially, in the country at that time was Charles Williams, vice president of Lilly Endowment, Inc., an Indianapolis-based philanthropy created and supported by the family which founded the pharmaceutical house of Eli Lilly and Company. The Lilly Endowment has given away millions of dollars to charitable and development programs in the U.S.A. and abroad.

Youssoufou took the idea to Williams who studied it and secured from the Endowment a grant of $250,000 to buy equipment and put the first 1,100 acres under cultivation. World Vision International was asked to manage the project.

The first crop of corn, which produced abundantly without fertilizer in the rich soil, was within days of harvesting when the river, fed by heavy rains at its headwaters in Mali, over-flowed for the first time in years. Although the fields were flooded, the crop was not lost because villagers, spurred by the memories of the recent hungry days, used canoes to harvest the fermenting corn.

But the floods were only a temporary setback. They could be controlled with simple dikes along the river. The important thing was that Winson's projections had been right. The land was rich. Water would make it produce. A year-round supply of the precious liquid was available in the river, and up-river canals could put it on the land without expensive pumping.

The project has exciting potential. At least two crops a year—conceivably three—can be grown on this fertile river lowland. The lands are remarkably flat and need no stump-removing or rock-clearing. If all the river lowlands within Niger were brought into production, it is estimated they would provide 50 percent of the grain requirements of the nation.

Williams is now looking for multinational partners to help fund stage two. The Niger government has given strong en-dorsement to the project. International funding bodies have expressed an interest in the cultivation of the entire lowland region when stage two—which is simply an expansion of the original 1,100 acres up to 12,000 acres—is completed.

Winson, who had no degrees but lots of practical savvy, is a hero in the country.

The project also has some important spin-offs. As the land is brought under cultivation, it will be turned over to the farmers in twelve-acre plots for continued agriculture produc-tion. New villages will have to be created in order to have enough people to work the land. Village resettlement, while respecting the rights of tribes who own land along the river, could bring better health, decrease infant mortality, improve the living standard, and bring an era of development to the lives of thousands of Niger's marginal rural families.

Health clinics and safe water supplies will be a priority in the settling of new villages. These can be done at a level which

does not destroy tribal customs and traditions, for no one wants to Westernize the concept.

New industries will be generated, but not on a Western scale. They would be simple industries like carpentry, brick-laying, and well-digging to meet local needs. New schools and other community services would be required.

To cultivate his land, each farmer would probably step up to animal traction—using animals to help him plow in place of the short-handled hoe he presently uses. This would generate more simple industries—blacksmithing, plowmaking, welding, leathercraft.

The artisans for all these basic trades will be trained at a vocational school on the site of the Tara Valley project. This, too, is a long-held dream of Youssoufou who saw a perfect opportunity to wed the two projects. What better place to train tradesmen than in the place where their newly learned skills could be utilized in building communities?

The final ingredient in this development mix is the formation of marketing cooperatives to help each farmer dispose of the surplus he produces on his plot. The plan is for the government of Niger to buy the grain from the cooperatives and to arrange for its distribution and sale in the nonproducing areas of the country.

One Step Beyond

The Tara Valley project is, from beginning to end, one of the most exciting examples of total development I have seen anywhere in the world. I begin this chapter with it because it demonstrates some points which need to be made about this little understood, but critically important, subject of development.

First, development is a necessary step beyond relief. Most relief programs begin with emergency needs. The emergencies may be created by natural or man-made causes, but relief is an after-the-fact response. For example, if a river overflows every year, it would be patently stupid to mount a relief campaign annually for the victims. It would be better for all concerned to use some of the relief money to dike the river in order to prevent the floods next year. That is development.

Relief in poor countries must inevitably lead to development, for causes must be dealt with while the symptoms are being treated.

Second, development must start with people where they are. Too frequently the process starts with where the developer— usually an expert from a Western nation—thinks the people ought to be. For instance, an outsider in Niger might first of all think about producing crops for export instead of helping plan for crops for local consumption.

Then, too, it is very hard for a Westerner who is accustomed to the finest in machinery and technology to bring himself down to the level of the short-handled hoe which must be developed into animal traction. This erroneous reading of where people actually are on the economic and social ladder may be the cause of failure for more development projects than any other single factor.

To succeed in building people, development programs must also recognize economic realities. Again, the Western expert usually has available to him huge sums—relatively speaking— for feasibility studies, pilot projects, etc. Before the project is even begun, it is already far beyond the local economic standards. This is not to say that money is not needed—and sometimes a lot of it—but a project is almost certainly doomed to failure when measured by its impact on people if money is substituted for local input and initiative.

Which brings me to the next thing about the Tara Valley project. The one thing Youssoufou has insisted on—rightly— is that his own country must be recognized as the controlling element in the project. Decisions are not the unilateral prerogative of any outsiders connected with the project—the decision-making process is a partnership with the Nigerian voices carrying at least as much weight as those of the expatriates.

There must be strong indigenous involvement if development is to be maximally effective. Youssoufou got slightly heated when he said to me, "Why should foreigners think they know more about our country than we do? Our people have lived here for centuries. Why should outsiders think they can ignore us when discussions are held regarding our future?"

Development must aim at meeting total human need. Development is not just one thing. It is a balanced combination of many elements. In Niger, it would not be enough simply to irrigate the land. Or provide vocational training. These are only part of a total development package that embraces education, medicine, agricultural methods, pure drinking water, land reform and vocational training.

The problems contributing to underdevelopment must be attacked on a broad front. The ultimate goal of development must be the enrichment of the total man—mentally, morally, economically, physically and spiritually.

In a word, its objective is to produce self-reliance. Tragically, the present world systems are not designed to meet that objective. The income gap is widening, and for hundreds of millions of people self-reliance is only an impossible dream. Yet we dare not settle for less. The international basket cases must be made to walk again. No one wants to carry them forever. To the countries themselves, international charity is degrading, demeaning, dehumanizing.

The only answer to putting them on their feet and making them self-reliant is the right kind of development. Because it is so essential to global wholeness, we can no longer leave development to the so-called experts. Development, like the correcting of so many other social ills, is everybody's business. That's why men like Farlie Winson, Oumarou Youssoufou and Charles Williams can dare to dream about making Niger self-sufficient in food. It is this kind of international teamwork—combining the financial resources of those who have, with the strong and committed indigenous leadership to be found in every country, and coupling this with the practical know-how of a man who knows land, farming, and Africa—that can be the genius behind successful development projects.

Development Is about People

A *New Yorker* magazine cartoon showed a native chieftain, dressed in a grass skirt, relaxing in the shade of a thatched hut. An American visitor nurses his drink across a plain wooden table. The chief says: "Actually, we don't think of our country as *under*-developed so much as we think of yours as *over*-developed."

That's worth thinking about.

But what is the median point which divides *over* from

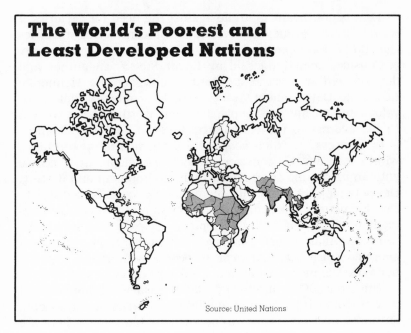

The World's Poorest and Least Developed Nations

Source: United Nations

Figure 6

under? Many Westerners equate development with industrialization. Certainly many people in the Third and Fourth Worlds
think of it in terms of the amount of consumer goods available.
Not a few vaguely think of development as the process by
which countries become as Westernized as possible. Perhaps
the reason is that *developed* and *underdeveloped* are terms used
almost synonymously with Western and non-Western nations.

Actually, development has nothing to do with industrializ-
ing or Westernizing. In fact, these things may impede true
development.

Development is about people, not things. I know that countries need cement plants, plastics factories and heavy industry.
But I also know that most often these high-investment ven-
tures meet few people needs. Smoke-belching factories cannot
be made the hallmark of successful development programs.
Most often they do more for their owners and for the nation's
GNP and its exports than they do for the masses of hungry
and disfranchised people.

That is not meant to argue against the need for factories. I would stoutly argue, however, against considering factories the end of developmental goals.

Consider something said by Edgar Stoesz, an author and development worker, at a recent meeting of the Mennonite Economic Development Association. He contends that if development "is not for people, it is not worthy of the name." In his address to the conference, Stoesz said: "Development is the process by which people are awakened to opportunities within their reach (conscientization). Development is people with an increasing control over their environment and destiny. Development is people with dignity and a sense of self-worth. Development is freedom and wholeness and justice. Development is quality of life. Development is people living in the full realization of their God-given potential. Development is a liberated spirit. Development is people with rising expectations. Development is the new word for peace."

This concept of developing people instead of nations will require some fundamental rethinking. Conventional wisdom on the subject has proven to be virtually bankrupt. There are no more experts. Some monuments to their memory in the form of disproven theories or abandoned projects still stand, but the breed is dead.

Don't cry.

Joe Kimmins of the American Freedom from Hunger Foundation asserts: "Development is too important a process to be left to 'development experts.' In their fascination with economic growth—their rhetoric of concern for the common man notwithstanding—and in their obeisance to a conventional wisdom derived from experience with highly productive, industrialized economies, their vision of the future has become far too narrow and too self-defeating to be allowed to dominate." [1]

It may be helpful to take a look at one of those monuments —a disproven theory which got racked up by reality.

The Leak in the Trickle

It had a captivating name—the "trickle-down" theory. It had

been around for a long time and seemed to have been proven beyond dispute in the Western societies. Although the name was new, the thesis was old, for Alexis de Tocqueville had made it the basis of his *Principle of Stratified Diffusion.*

"Trickle-down" was the way wealth had come to Europe and North America. This seemed to say that the most effective way of promoting everyone's development is to generate a nation's economic growth, and this is done by encouraging the best people—the educated, talented, dynamic elite—to make full use of their energies. As they led in economic development, the rest of society was supposed to benefit.

Almost all the experts held to this theory in the 1950s and 1960s. Aid programs were designed around this framework. Help the biggest and best and ultimately—somewhere at the end of the trickle—the least and poorest will get their share. So loans were made to start industries. Export businesses were especially favored because they contributed to the credit side of the national balance of payments.

The West thought it could have its cake and eat it, too. By financing industries and businesses which exploited the two things less developed countries had—raw materials and cheap labor—we thought we could maintain our life style and at the same time make it possible through trickle-down for the poor in these countries gradually to improve their living standard.

Guided by this kind of thinking, development projects were rarely aimed directly at the poor because the poor had less potential for growth. They remained objects of charity. They were outside the mainstream of development work. The stream would have to trickle to them through many economic and social strata.

The theory had only one flaw.

It didn't work.

There was a leak in the trickle. The educated, the landowners, the bureaucrats got richer while the poor became poorer. It was a paradox and unbelievable to the experts, but it happened just that way.

Referring to the poorest 40 percent in many developing countries, Robert S. McNamara, president of the World Bank, confirms that "development is simply not reaching them in any decisive degree. Their countries are growing in gross economic terms, but their individual lives are stagnating in human terms." [2]

Studies by the World Bank indicate that in ten countries with per capita incomes averaging $145, the poorest 40 percent of the people receive a per capita income of only $50 a year. In another ten countries with per capita incomes averaging $275, the poorest 40 percent receive only $80. In India, some two hundred million people subsist on incomes that average less than $40 a year.

Professor Tibor Mende, formerly a senior officer with the United Nations, points out that trickle-down did not work because the transmission belt from upper to lower classes was missing.

"The prosperity of the few," he said, "does not spread in concentric circles, as happened after the West's industrial revolution. The transmission belt is missing. This is largely so because, below a certain level, poverty cannot be attacked by indirect means." [3]

Growth, it is now seen, is not enough in itself. Economic indicators are not accurate measuring devices where the well-being of people is concerned. Because there are strong forces which work against the poorest in even the most fair-minded societies, a rising gross national product does not mean a more equitable distribution of wealth.

Under the trickle-down theory, it meant only a widening of the income gap, not a wider distribution of the economic resources.

Labor-Intensive vs. Capital-Intensive

Most contemporary development wisdom was born in the technological West, or has been largely influenced by it. I saw a perfect example of this on a small South Pacific island.

For years this tiny island with only a few hundred people had gotten by with a hand-operated telephone switchboard. It was totally adequate for the needs. And on an island where there aren't a lot of jobs, it provided employment for four operators. But some of the island fathers had been bitten by the technological bug from their exposure to the West and they wanted an automatic switchboard.

Application for a loan was made to the Asian Development Bank, a quasi-government agency. A costly study was made, the loan was approved, and the island telephone service was automated. Not necessarily improved; just automated. As a result, four people were unemployed and two of them had to leave the island in order to find work.

Yet this project was reported as a development "achievement." One cannot help but wonder what was really achieved when the project is measured against Mr. McNamara's words: "Development is about people. The only criterion for measuring its ultimate success or failure is what it does to enhance the lives of individual human beings." [4]

One of the reasons why the trickle-down theory didn't produce the desired results is that development funds were invested, for the most part, in capital-intensive programs—expensive projects designed to use modern technology and automation rather than people. In the developed West perhaps such a policy decision can be justified, but hardly in any over-populated and underemployed place in the rest of the world.

People not only need production; they need jobs. It was Mahatma Gandhi who said: "The poor of the world cannot be helped by mass production, only by production by the masses."

In 1974 World Vision entered into a well-digging and well-deepening program with the Andhra Christian Council in the Indian state of Andhra Pradesh. Rather than send in a well-drilling rig which could produce water on an assembly line basis, we urged our Indian counterparts to use as much local labor as possible to do the work.

It was slower. It was less efficient. But the projects employed thousands of people at the village level who had no work. The villages needed water, but the people also needed jobs.

During the height of the refugee problem in 1974 around Phnom Penh, Cambodia, a World Vision agriculturalist from New Zealand, Ben Webster, wanted to irrigate about two hundred acres for dry season rice farming. A canal several miles long was needed. Rather than do the job with a tractor,

Webster hired twelve hundred of the idle refugees to dig the canal.

Capital-intensive means of production may be the answer in an educated, mechanized and technological society, but not in countries where the unemployment rate is chronically at 25 percent or more. Streamlined and efficient production may have to be sacrificed for the higher goal of providing jobs and incomes for the unemployed masses in the less developed countries.

On the outskirts of Tanzania's capital city, Dar-es-Salaam, sits the country's largest factory. It is a textile mill which produces *khanga*, the wildly colorful sheets of cotton which the women wrap around themselves as a garment. Nearly a thousand looms are set up in a hall the size of two football fields. The factory employs 4,700 people. It could get by with half that number by using more modern machinery, but there has been a conscious decision not to do so. Labor is not as expensive as machinery. Besides that, people need jobs.

Wouldn't you guess it? The Chinese set it up.[5]

For nonprofit humanitarian agencies such as World Vision, we have one temporary answer in what we call "task relief" programs. Unemployed villagers are paid to work on projects which benefit the entire community. In addition to scores of wells in the Indian states of Andhra Pradesh and Gujarat, many miles of road have been built in Bangladesh through such programs. Labor-intensive programs have been used to construct dams and water reservoirs in India and West Africa.

Task relief beats putting families on the dole. It saves the dignity of able-bodied people. And it puts food on their tables.

In all my travels, I have never seen anyone perpetually hungry who had money with which to buy food.

The Role of Aid

There are two ways by which money flows from country to country. One is trade. The other is aid.

We have already seen that the trade system is stacked against the less developed countries. It is rigged in favor of the wealthy West.

But what about foreign aid? Surely that is all in favor of the recipient country?

Guess again. Aid, too, is pretty much rigged to favor the donor country. Consider these facts.

First, more than half the financial assistance given by the United States is in the form of loans which must be repaid with interest. It is still called "aid," but it is not a gift. Some of the money goes to the World Bank and other regional quasi-government banks.

Second, over half of our foreign aid appropriation is for what we call "security assistance"—military purposes. Some forty-two cents out of each aid dollar is marked for "development assistance" and another six cents is given for "welfare and emergency relief."

Third, as has already been pointed out, most of the aid money is spent more in the commercial interest of the donor country than it is to alter the social and economic picture in the recipient country. As late as 1965, the then president and chairman of the World Bank, Eugene Black, pointed out that "foreign aid" was enormously beneficial to the donor nations in at least three ways:

"1) Foreign aid provides a substantial and immediate market for U.S. goods and services.

"2) Foreign aid stimulates the development of new overseas markets for U.S. companies.

"3) Foreign aid orients national economies toward a free enterprise system in which the U.S. private firms can prosper." [6]

A relatively small percentage of aid ever really goes to improve the life of the common, hungry people abroad. Indeed, most of it is spent in the donor country to purchase war matériel and other goods, or to pay for expensive studies done by American think tanks or academicians which tell the Third and Fourth Worlds what their needs are.

When Galo Plaza was secretary general of the Organization of American States, he described U.S. aid to Latin America in these words: "Most U.S. aid under the Alliance for Progress is not a gift [but] is in the form of loans that are being repaid. . . . it is not at all unreasonable to turn the picture around, and think about the benefits accruing to the United States as a result of what we call aid. . . . Nearly all this [the loans] is being spent in the United States on United States goods." [7]

Loans are valuable for certain development projects, but we would have a lot more credibility if we would stop trying to kid ourselves and our friends into believing that this reflects our altruism.

As Michael Hudson says, "The net flow of foreign exchange over time is not from the United States to aid-borrowing countries, as implied in the modern connotation of the term 'aid,' but from the borrowers to the United States. . . . So-called foreign aid is, indeed, feudatory. Aid has imposed vassalage on developing countries . . ." [8]

Aid certainly has a crucial role to play in development, but it needs to be honestly labeled and creatively used. The facts indicate that neither is happening on a very impressive scale right now.

How Generous Are We?

No doubt many Americans are shocked at this revelation of truth regarding foreign aid. And disappointed. We have always been proud of our generosity. We remember how we fed our enemies after both World Wars. We know that millions of dollars are given annually to domestic charities and to private relief and development agencies.

In personal giving, Americans are still some of the most generous people on earth. In 1971, voluntary contributions from the American public amounted to almost $890 million, or two-thirds of the total international voluntary aid. U.S. voluntary contributions were second only to those of Sweden.

The recent revelations about world hunger have once again touched the sensitive nerve of compassion for millions and there has been a great outpouring of money to private organizations.

But if development is going to be done on the large scale necessary to change the face of the underdeveloped world, governments and corporations must also do their share. After the rebuilding of Europe at the end of World War II through the highly successful Marshall Plan, the concept of aid began to change. Now it is only a shadow of its original form, but the terms and labels are still the same. Maybe the truth in packaging law should apply to government programs as well as consumer products.

Proportionately, our government gives much less now for economic aid than at any time in the past 25 years. In 1949 we were giving 2.8 percent of our gross national product. In 1975 it is .25 percent of the GNP. This means for every $100 of total national output, our contribution to overseas economic aid is about 25 cents.

The Food for Peace program is being cut back as a result of higher agricultural prices, a decline in congressional appropriations, and an increase in domestic consumption. Food aid for 1974 was cut by one-third of the 1972 totals, and half of that reduced amount went to Indochina. At the same time the United States and Canada were benefiting by nearly $10 billion from higher priced food exports. So the oil companies weren't the only ones increasing profits in those days!

Those who feel the U.S. federal government is subtracting from domestic programs to provide foreign aid should consider that in the 1975 federal budget, 49 percent is devoted to what is called "human resources" (including health, education and welfare), slightly over 29 percent for "national defense," almost 9 percent for "physical resources" and *1.38 percent for all development assistance programs overseas.*

Development assistance from all sixteen nations who are members of the Development Assistance Committee (DAC) averages only about .36 percent of their combined gross national products, according to Robert McNamara. This compares with a U.N. target of .7 percent. To reach this goal, the developed nations need commit only about 1.5 percent of the amount by which they will grow richer during this decade. This leaves them 98.5 percent of their increased wealth to use for themselves. The small amount asked for would hardly bankrupt a rich nation, but it could make a remarkable improvement in the development of the poorer countries.[9]

The U.S. Chamber of Commerce reports that in 1972 Americans spent approximately $11 billion on their personal care (including barber and beauty shops), over $8 billion to buy

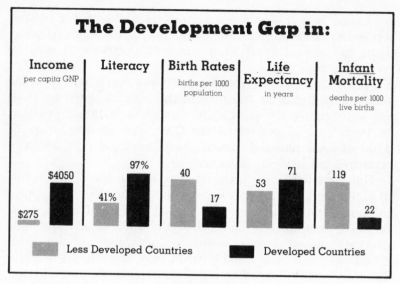

Figure 7

their shoes and keep them repaired, almost $48 billion on all forms of recreation, over $80 billion for new and used automobiles, and less than $3 billion for all forms of foreign assistance, much of which was military aid.

As generous as we may think we are, both personally and as a nation, the cold facts show that we still have a long way to go.

"No Choice but to Turn Inward"

When comparing income and life styles, people in the poorer nations may even feel they have the right to question our claim to generosity. With all our private and public aid, the income gap widens.

Development isn't keeping pace.

"The chase of Western living standards was illusory at best," says a senior economic advisor at the World Bank, Mahbub ul Haq. He says the average per capita income in the developed world now stands at $2,400, while in the developing countries it is $180. The gap, which is now $2,220, will widen by another $1,100 by 1980.

Short of a major transfer of resources—about which he is pessimistic—Haq says the developing countries don't have a breath of a chance of catching up.

His answer? "The developing countries have no choice but to turn inwards, much the same as Communist China . . . and to adopt a different style of life, seeking a consumption pattern more consistent with their own poverty—pots and pans and bicycles and simple consumption habits—without being seduced by the life styles of the rich.

"This requires a redefinition of economic and social objectives which is of truly staggering proportions, a liquidation of the privileged groups and vested interests which may well be impossible in many societies, a redistribution of political economic power which may only be achieved through revolutions rather than through an evolutionary change." [10]

That is strong medicine, but he is not the only one prescribing it.

A Third World View

In 1974, President Julius Nyerere of Tanzania spoke to this issue while on a visit to New Zealand. In a lecture given at Christchurch, entitled "Aid and Development from a Recipient's Point of View," he said: "The attack on world poverty is a vital long term concern for the rich. They need to participate in it because of their humanity, and out of self-interest. . . .

"Unfortunately there is no world government which could tax the rich nations for the benefit of the poor nations; there is no international equivalent of social security payments. Instead, we have an acknowledgement of the need for 'international aid.'

"There appears, however, to be some confusion, if not hypocrisy, on this subject. Some people seem to think that any transaction between rich nations and poor nations, which is not settled within a matter of days by a cash transfer, can be classified as 'aid'—quite regardless of the final advantage to one side or the other. I do not agree.

"I believe the term 'aid' should only be used when there is a real transfer of resources to the poor, for the purpose of raising living standards and narrowing the gap between the poor and rich nations.

"By my definition, military assistance would be excluded from the aid figures. It has little relevance to the poverty gap, whatever other justification it may have. Export credits and commercial loans should also be disregarded.

"Nor do I believe that private investment is aid. It is undertaken for the benefit of the investor; local benefit—if any— is incidental. And it is undertaken only in the expectation of a high rate of transferable profit; I am told that foreign investors look for an estimated 20 percent profit before establishing a new enterprise in African nations!

"In the international aid statistics the nearest thing to my definition is 'Official Development Assistance,' and it is worth mentioning that the proportion of the Gross National Product of the major rich nations which was devoted to this actually fell during the 1960s. As these countries themselves increased their wealth so greatly, the amount of money transferred annually did increase slightly.

"Although development aid is a very marginal item for rich countries, it may be important to a poor country. It can do things like village electrification where such an advance is otherwise impossible, but where the electricity will enable the development of village industries, the improvement of water supplies and so on.

"Aid can make a great contribution to development, provided it is given and accepted for what it is—a possible catalyst for local development.

"Poor nations insist that the aid should be given as an expression of partnership, and therefore without political strings being attached to it. Poverty has no ideology. . . . We feel very strongly on this issue; our independence is not for sale." [11]

The Bubble-Up Theory

Development, as it has been practiced for the past two decades, has thus far produced minimum achievements. Mahbub ul Haq says, "When you rip aside the confusing figures on growth rates, you find that for about two-thirds of humanity the increase in per capita income has been less than one dollar a year for the last 20 years." [12]

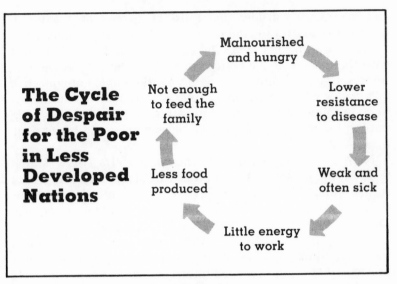

The Cycle of Despair for the Poor in Less Developed Nations

Malnourished and hungry

Lower resistance to disease

Weak and often sick

Little energy to work

Less food produced

Not enough to feed the family

Figure 8

Since both time and experience have proven the trickle-down theory ineffective, let me register in with a theory of my own.

I call it the "bubble-up" theory. I think it has real merit. Development, says Gunnar Myrdal, is the "movement upward of the whole social system." [13] Yet development is not easily defined. It is more a process and direction than it is an event or activity. It cannot be measured by quantity of consumption as we are accustomed to doing in the West.

Most of the world now does not even have a standard of living. It can be called only a "standard of misery." Development must be concerned with qualitative change.

As E. F. Schumacher says in his book, *Small Is Beautiful*, "Development does not start with goods; it starts with people and their education, organization, and discipline. . . . development cannot be an act of creation, . . . cannot be ordered, bought, comprehensively planned . . . it requires a process of evolution."

He goes on to say that "development effort should bypass the big cities and be directly concerned with the creation of an 'agro-industrial structure' in the rural and small town areas." [14] The primary need is for millions of work places and a primary consideration must be to provide maximum work opportunities for the unemployed and underemployed.

What Schumacher is talking about is "bubble-up." You start with the masses at the bottom instead of the elite at the top. Interestingly, in March 1975 the World Bank announced a new policy which bears all the marks of the bubble-up theory. Keep in mind that for nearly twenty years the Bank has been putting its money into industrial development and big agricultural projects.

Now, according to a story in the *Los Angeles Times*, March 9, 1975, the prestigious institution will "double its lending for rural development in the next five years and shift the emphasis of its assistance in poorer countries to small, impoverished farmers, sometimes called the world's 'marginal men.'"

Between 1975 and 1979 the Bank plans to spend $7.2 billion for agriculture and rural development—up sharply over previous years—and some $3 billion of that will be for projects to benefit small farmers. The new style projects will provide a comprehensive program of credits, seeds, fertilizer, water, as well as health service and basic education for the small farmers who cultivate 40 percent of the land in developing countries.

I say bravo for the World Bank!

And bravo for Senator Mark Hatfield who said virtually the same thing in a 1974 address at the James H. Oliphant Forum in New York City. Calling for small farming units to be tied together by lending and marketing cooperatives, the senator from Oregon said: "This emphasis on relatively small operations replacing the present mix of landholding elite and a poor majority of peasants would accomplish several development goals at once: First, it would help stop the flight from rural areas to the even worse conditions of the urban slums prompted by the acquisition of small holdings by the elite and the replacement of the small farmer by technology he cannot afford. In turn, rural development in this fashion would foster rural employment by the maximum use of labor-intensive methods as much as possible.

"Rural employment would begin to create for the rural poor the small measure of prosperity that so enhances population control efforts. Finally, marketing procedures would be simplified, and distribution costs reduced, through the operation of cooperatives, to the benefit of rural producer and urban consumer alike." [15]

Bubble-up means starting where the people are and where the need is. More than 80 percent of the poorest people in developing countries live in rural areas.

In his book, *Crusade Against Hunger*, I. W. Moomaw tells about an interview with evangelist and Christian statesman, John R. Mott. The author talked about being an agricultural missionary, and he quotes from memory Mott's response: "The soul of Asian countries, especially, springs from their villages. Yet it is there that we find the greatest concentration of need and neglect. There could be no greater Christian summons than to work with these people for the reconstruction of life socially, economically, and spiritually. . . . But remember this—whoever engages in this work must feed on difficulties." [16]

The fact that the problems are complex does not mean they are insoluble. The problem is not technology or knowledge, but willingness to act.

Willingness requires a deep motivation. Developed nations have been involved in the lesser-developed world largely from political and economic motives, with a covering of altruism and a feeling of squaring of accounts because of colonial exploitation. But Christian motivation is deeper.

It arises from love, not guilt. It seeks to serve, not exploit. It requires no gratitude, only opportunity. It does not ask, "Am I my brother's keeper?" but "Am I brother to my brother?"

The ultimate goal of development is to provide a better quality of life for all the people on this earth.

Our concern is not necessarily that they should live in luxury, but that they should live at all.

PART THREE

RESPONDING TO HUNGER

Chapter 11
Dialogue: Hard Questions and Harder Answers

I'VE DISCOVERED SOMETHING.

When you listen to a person from the hungry Fourth World tell of his hopes and feelings and hurts—look him in the face, hear his tone of voice, see how he looks at his children—you begin to realize that the issues of hunger and poverty and human need are more real and more complicated than you may have at first thought.

There are lots of simplistic questions being asked these days. Like, "Why don't you just quit having so many babies?" or "Why don't the Indians eat all those sacred cows?" or "Why should we help people who burn down our embassies?"

My mail contains a lot of simple answers. I've wished I could say, "Here, meet this person from the other side of the world. Listen to him for awhile. Try out your answer on him, but hear what he says."

If that kind of dialogue were to go on, what might it sound like? On a recent trip around the hunger belt on three continents, I heard what many people in the less developed nations are saying in response to some of our glib and insensitive talking.

This chapter is a dialogue between two such people. The questions (in italics) come from an all too typical resident of the affluent world. The answers are a composite of answers

I've recorded from people who are always hungry, always sick, always tired, always powerless.

You may think some of it is a bit harsh. Even mean. But let me assure you none of it has been contrived or made up.

This is an account of people shouting and no one really listening.

Why should I even care about you? We have plenty of problems in our own country right now. If we would quit trying to take care of the whole world, maybe we could stop poverty at home, create more jobs, lower our taxes, handle pollution.

All the things you want for your country, your family, we would like to have, too. Why should we accept the view that only *you* have a right to them? If you think you can have those things without our help, my friend, I am afraid you are living in a very narrow, unreal world. You are strong and you will undoubtedly get those things you want. It is much easier for the rich to get more than it is for the poor to get something.

But you have fueled your industrial furnaces with our cheap raw materials. We have contributed so much to your development, and now you don't want to contribute to ours. But the honeymoon will soon be over. The price of oil is just a starter. Other products you need are going to be scarcer and more expensive. Sooner or later, we will get our fair share. We may do it peacefully. I hope we can. But how we do it will largely be up to you.

If you people over there would just work as hard as I do, you could pull yourselves up by your own bootstraps. What's wrong with you?

Don't forget that you had the bootstraps to pull. I don't even have the straps, much less the boots. That's one reason why we need development projects to give jobs to some of us.

Actually, I work longer and harder than people in your Detroit. My day goes from sunrise to sunset—about fourteen hours. You know you will get a check on payday. I may not get any harvest at all. It depends on the rains and the insects.

If I had the bootstraps, you'd better believe I would pull them!

Why don't you grow more food? You have arable land. Besides, you send your bright young men abroad to study agriculture so they can return and help you. But I wonder if they are helping you?

You're right. We do need to grow more food. But let me tell you my problems. During the time when other nations ruled us, our lands were used by outside powers for their own purposes. Where irrigation projects were important to them, we got them. But marginal lands that required capital to make them productive went begging. We're trying now, but it takes money and time.

Then, too, we don't know much about modern farming techniques. Our grandfathers got by with slash-and-burn methods. We can't today, but how do I go about breaking out of a centuries-old cycle? And if I could, I need the right kind of seeds. Most years, the rats eat their share of the stored seed before I can plant it. In famine years, we eat it because that's the only way to stay alive one more year. Can you understand what that means?

Sometimes you criticize us for not having the right tools. You're right—we don't. Sometimes you give us tools through your development programs, but we don't need bulldozers and tractors as much as we need hoes and plows. Sometimes your aid seems to us an insensitive, highly questionable form of involvement in our affairs that all too often leaves us worse off than before you came. A lot of us are sick to death of it.

There's another reason. Our farmers don't have capital to expand their farms and production. That takes money which we just don't have. You may not be rich, but you are able to save up something. I can't. Everything I earn goes into today's food.

Some of my friends have solved the problem of high food costs—they skip several meals a week. But that, too, has its high price. The family gets malnourished, they become sick in mind and spirit, frictions develop. They start striking out . . . but at what? The government, the system? We can't touch that. No, they strike out at each other. Poverty and hunger have caused so many broken homes among my friends.

Please don't give me any of that nonsense about education and nutritional knowledge. Education doesn't give me buying power. Too often, more knowledge about nutrition just makes me angrier because then I know the way out but I can't afford it. Maybe in my next life I'll be able to afford some protein. Perhaps in my next time around I will be able to enjoy once a month what some of you gorge yourselves on every day.

You know, the world is getting painfully crowded. Don't you think you should make a greater effort to stop having so many children? After all, if we are going to help you, we want to be sure we are not just helping to produce excess numbers of children.

It's just that kind of paternal and condescending statement that makes me so mad I can't see straight. Where's your head, anyway? You live in a country where education is easily available and free, yet you seem not to have learned very much. Pardon me, but your question is so horribly general, prejudiced and insensitive that I hardly know how to reply. But I'll try.

My own country is not overcrowded. Oh, I know some are, but why do you make such sweeping generalizations? Some of our urban areas are very crowded and the people there are not happy. (Maybe something like your own urban slums of Chicago, London, New York and Paris?) The people are attracted to the cities here just like anywhere else. But be a little smarter! We still have thousands of square miles that are underpopulated. And if we could get some help to develop these areas, we could reduce the blight of this urban squalor that your foreign journalists love to come to film and write about. But that's another angry subject.

There are some other reasons why we don't "stop having babies," as you would say. Many parents don't know there is any way to stop producing babies except to deny themselves their marital rights. I know of no parents who want to continue bringing into this world sick, malnourished, half-human children. Think about that as you make your broad criticisms.

And another reason is, we love children. Don't you? How

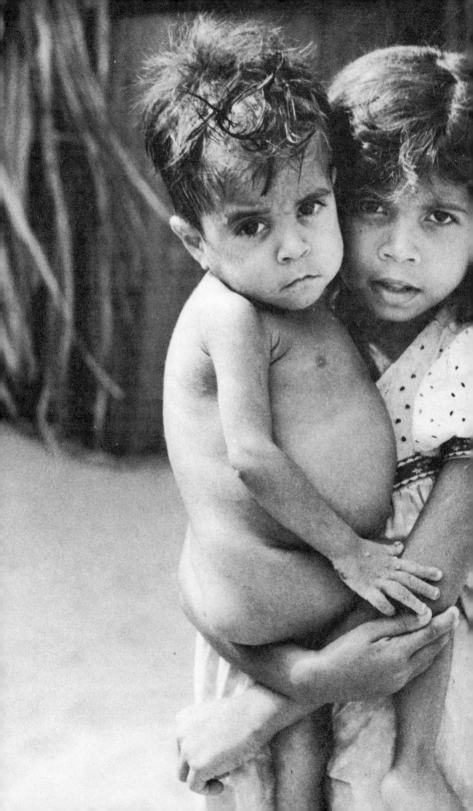

would you like it if I came to your church or club and spoke one evening about the horrors of the American families who had four or five children. Would you like that? And I could document those "horrors" by pointing out that every child in your families pollutes the world fifty times more than the average Indian child; that he would demand up to five times the natural resources which the average African child requires; that he would waste enough food in his lifetime to keep whole villages in Asia alive for months.

Am I carping? Am I being unfair? It seems a fair response to your question. You love your children; we love ours. I would suggest we not look at these little ones as the sole source of our food problem, although of course, their numbers are part of the difficulty.

Yet for many of us, large numbers of children are security in our old age. Did it ever occur to you that in the African bush we don't have Blue Cross, pension plans or social security programs? Our security comes from our children. They care for us—except for those who are so influenced by the West that they no longer care very much. You don't blame us for thinking of the future, do you?

Also, if I have ten children, maybe three or four will live. You've never experienced watching child after child die, have you? It's very hard, but we keep hoping that some will make it. We have deep psychological needs, too, like you. We want to have the joy of human warmth, of the smiles of our children. Don't deny us this privilege. We are proud of our race and of our traditions. Don't exploit us further by suggesting we become fewer while you become more—and richer, constantly putting us more and more in debt.

Somehow I thought the age of colonialism was over. The way you talk makes me wonder if I was wrong.

Why don't you kill all those so-called "sacred" cows that litter up your streets?

Why don't you kill all the dogs and cats that litter your homes? I have heard how much you spend on food for your animals. Why don't you kill them? Does that seem like a rash statement? It does? Then you know how I feel when you tell me to kill an animal that is part of my cultural and religious tradition. I can hardly believe how totally insensitive you are. I guess I need to tell you why the cow is important.

It is a source of milk for our children. Milk isn't plentiful but these cows give some. We plaster the dung on the walls of our houses and when it dries, we burn it for fuel. Wood is scarce and processed fuels are completely out of the question.

We also make the dung into a paste and use it as an antiseptic, cleansing agent in the courtyards of our homes. That might seem strange to you, but it works and we cannot afford commercial sprays and disinfectants. As fertilizer for our crops, this saves us another expense which we can't afford.

You know, of course, we believe the souls of our ancestors live in some of these animals. That is our traditional belief. If you think that is strange, perhaps I could tell you how strange I feel some of your so-called religious beliefs are. But that is another subject.

Please, I ask you, don't come in and suggest we kill all our cows. If you want to learn to be truly sensitive, ask the bigger question: Why the cows? I'll try to explain and then we'll talk about it. But listen to us, hear us, empathize with us. You upset us so greatly by shouting from an ocean away about matters so unfamiliar to you.

Why don't you work harder? I see pictures of masses of people just sitting around all the time. I think you could make it if you would just roll up your sleeves like us and get with it.

If we worked only as hard as you, we would never make it. Our people are not lazy. And I'm not saying your people are. But don't make us work any harder. A lot of us are hungry, malnourished, sick and unable to work like we should. In your country, do you criticize a sick man for not coming to the office or factory? I think not.

Then a lot of us can't find work. That's why you see us sitting around. Seldom do we find work that really pays well. Our economy is struggling. Sometimes we wonder if we are going to make it. You get your raw materials from us at a good price, but when I see some of the finished products in the stores, I can't possibly afford them.

And I, for example, have only the tools and methods my father gave me. I have not been to school, and I do not know of a better way. I really want you to help me. I don't need to learn how to run some big gas-eating machine. Just help me know new ways to grow things, how to store them, how to care for my land. This kind of help I want so badly. Will you please help me?

I really think that one of the reasons you and your people are so poor—and are getting poorer—is because of your strange ways. How can you really expect to become a part of the twentieth century if you still run around half-naked, continuing to believe in so much superstition?

If what you say is a sample of Western thinking today, then we just may never get together. Why should we do everything your way? Do you think the whole world has to be a carbon copy of your culture, your system, your methods? What makes you think we are poor because our traditions are different from yours? I've also heard enough about the rabbit's foot and the black cat crossing your path to know that you aren't completely logical and rational about everything. Are you?

I agree that we do some things in our culture which are not helpful. But those traditions are a part of us. I suppose you think you have found the answer to life just because you have a lot of *things*? No, you don't run around half-naked—except on your beaches—but more than a third of your marriages don't make it. You don't live in grass huts, but you get ulcers and high blood pressure because you live in expensive houses, trying desperately to meet the payments each month.

Sometimes I just wish I had never heard of the West, and that you had never heard of us. I wonder where we would be today? We would probably still have a lot of our own resources. Perhaps our own tribal systems would still be operating along "native lines," as you would say. But we get pretty tired of your telling us how to run our show. Just quit exploiting us . . . quit patronizing us . . . quit pretending you can know what our real needs are.

But we welcome you as a brother if you come to *really* see us, if you are really interested in what our problems are. Skin color is not the real barrier. The barrier exists when you refuse to listen.

Every time we try to help people like you, your fanatic youths burn our embassies or our cultural libraries. Why should we help you when you are so ungrateful? A lot of good, hard-working Americans give tax money so that your people can have a better life. And what do we get for it? No respect. No gratitude. No thanks.

I don't think violence is good. I can't read, but I don't believe young students should burn libraries. That is wrong. But let me tell you a story . . . a story about my eldest son, now twenty-five.

We have always been poor and have always lived here on this humble farm. My son, Raj, was able to go to school. This was the realization of a dream for me. He studied hard. His teachers and friends liked Raj very much. He made good grades.

When he was seventeen he made his first trip to a big city. He was at one of the temples on the first day when a big bus pulled up filled with American tourists. They had cameras, tape recorders, and were dressed so oddly. The men were obviously overfed and the women were very loud.

Raj had never had any contact with foreigners before, but he was afraid of them so he started to walk slowly past the bus. The men pointed their cameras at him and one offered him a rupee to stand by one of the temple statues. It seemed they thought his "strange costume" would make an interesting picture. The group was laughing, and Raj thought they were laughing at him. Burning with rage, Raj ran off, swearing to get even some day.

One day he did. Several weeks later there was a CIA scandal in our country. Raj and some of his friends were filled with anger. Maybe they were encouraged by leftists, I don't know, but late one night they made some firebombs. When the town was asleep, several dozen students went to your cultural center and burned it to the ground.

Like I said, I don't think that is a good thing. But that is my personal story to you. I guess we don't see the average Ameri-

can from your country. I am sure there are many good people
—people who would have been more sensitive to a young boy
dressed "strangely." But we don't see them. And it is hard for
students to understand the goodness of your people. So they
strike out at what they can see—your embassy, your cultural
library.

Please try to understand. Don't just be angry at what some
of our young people do. Try to get to know the reasons behind
their violence.

*Why doesn't your government do something? Why should
we help a government that is so hopelessly corrupt?*

I don't know much about politics. I am a simple man. And
I know there are many corrupt men in our government. Just
like in yours. Too often our government officials are not really
interested in our problems, only in their numbered accounts
in Swiss banks. And I don't blame you for being suspicious.

What kind of government is it if the basic needs of the
people aren't met? There is going to be a revolution one of
these days. Oh, not among those who are dying of starvation.
They can hardly get a bowl of relief rice to their lips. It will
not be they who will storm the palace and the embassies.
They won't throw the Molotov cocktails.

No, the revolution will be started by the reasonably healthy
who want a reasonable life, striking out with great hate and
vengeance at you who live unreasonably. How can you possibly
justify your never-ending greed for goods, for raw products
taken from my country with the ultimate deficit landing on
our heads?

And some of you are Christian. Didn't your Jesus have a
more simple style of living than most of you? And it might be
good for you to remember that he was a West Asian. Maybe
if he came back to live today he would be more on the side of
the exploited, sick, jobless Asian than on yours.

But if you want to help in the best way, don't talk about
nation-building. Consider people-building. What are our needs?
How can you help us to develop in a way that will bring fulfillment and happiness to our lives? Sometimes you will have
to work around our bureaucracies—and maybe yours, as well

—to do this. But you'll find some of our people have feelings like yours and are ready to work with you.

Often it will be better if you do not give through the bureaucracies if the political or social system favors the elite over the poor. By withholding your support, and the support of your country, you may help give rise to revolutionary elements which may, ultimately, bring down the present structures.

I don't know how bad their replacements might be, but knowing the existing corruption and exploitation, I would be willing to risk it.

Well, it seems to me one thing you could do is get an education. Why don't you?

I'd love to, even though I'm fairly old by my country's standards. I'd like to be able to at least sign my name and read simple instructions on packages. Can you suggest where I should go?

Most education in my country is for the elite. And even for those graduates, jobs are not always available. I don't think we really need more universities until we have a lot of village literacy programs. We need simple, practical advice on a level that we nonelites can understand. After all, it is we who make this country go, not the elite who sit in offices. We are the workers, the factory people, the sellers, the merchants. We are proud of our country and want to see it advance. To do this, we also need help.

Please don't be offended at this question. It may sound cruel, but I must ask it. Why should we be responsible for keeping you alive? We can't possibly solve all your problems. If we give you food, that just keeps you alive long enough to have more babies, who in turn will have more babies. It's a vicious cycle and I really wonder if we have all that much responsibility to keep you and your people afloat.

It's hard for me to conceal the anger I feel when you talk that way. It's pretty easy for you to say that. You have all the comforts in the world. You take your job for granted. You have a medical program that takes care of your family. You know about the various methods of birth control—and, more importantly, you can afford them. You have an education. You have money in the bank. In fact, you have all the things that my fellow countrymen and I don't even dare dream about.

You have so much, and still you apparently want more. And I guess one of the ways you can be sure you keep piling up the good things in life is to eliminate us from the picture. Well, let me tell you something. You may not think much of my people and my culture, but I do. We have a lot of pride in who we are. We, also, have worth. What makes you think that you and you alone have the right to live on this planet?

You come from a very young civilization; ours is very old. You have made many beautiful machines—and some not so beautiful. Some of your machines have helped feed the world. But your complicated weapons have also killed many people. Can you understand why I view you with mixed feelings and can't ever quite be sure which is the *real* America? Or maybe it's both. You confuse me.

But I get the feeling you despise us because we don't produce great *things*. You are angry because "all we produce is babies." Well, you simply show your own ignorance when you suggest such a thing. My country has a literary tradition that is centuries old. Our poets and musicians have produced sensitive works that border on genius. Our crafts have made use of our natural resources, and they have been done with great care. We don't plan for the things we make to become obsolete. We plan for them to last.

So you see, I get very upset when you suggest we are people without value—when you feel our population should just sort of "die off."

I honestly don't know how much of our problem is your problem. The truth is, I wish it weren't necessary for us to look to you for all this help. But we have been backed into a corner. We are desperate. This year the rains have failed once again. The trade between my country and yours continues to be heavily in your favor. The corruption in my government prevents so many needed goods from reaching the people they are supposed to help.

These are our frustrations. But we will live through them,

regardless of what you say or do. We have a record of surviving.

I just wonder how you would feel if you were in my place. I hope you will think about it as you look into your full refrigerator tonight.

As I think back on our conversation, I am sure I have sounded terribly ungrateful in some of the things I have said. Believe me, I am not ungrateful. Your generosity—when it has been truly generous—has saved millions of lives.

I admit, though, that I am angry about a lot of things. And I am glad I could talk to you about this anger. Please keep listening to us. We are brothers on this planet. When we suffer and are weak, a little bit of you is also lost. We don't understand how so much inequality can exist, yet it does. We don't understand how you can seem to be sensitive and callous, cruel and generous all at the same time.

I know there are many things about us you don't understand. Your questions indicate that. But I believe dialogue like this can help us understand each other.

I feel you listened to me today. Thank you very much. We still have a lot more to talk about.

But we'll do that next time.

Chapter 12
Response: a Commitment to Care

HOW MUCH IS A HUMAN LIFE WORTH?

That provocative question was posed to his students by a professor of ethics and philosophy at LaGuardia Community College in Long Island City.

Gregory Spence gave the students a series of examples based on the assumption that real belief in putting a $5 value on life would lead to some kind of action. When the premise was stated academically, the students unanimously agreed that a human life was worth at least $5. When action was called for, however, some of the beliefs appeared very shaky.

Then came the crucial premise of the professor's argument: "Can we really say a person has a moral belief if, given many chances to act on that belief, the person fails to act? Don't we call a person a hypocrite who says he believes something but when it comes to action does otherwise?"

The class unanimously agreed that real moral beliefs must be expressed in actions.

Spence concluded: "You have now agreed to two premises: that human lives are worth $5, and that moral beliefs require action. I now accuse you all, and myself, of being hypocrites."

He explained that anyone who really cared about human lives in the last few years would have found some opportunity to give relief money to the starving populations of Bangladesh, Biafra, West Africa, etc.[1]

Now let me ask you a question. How much is that hungry little boy with the sad eyes on the jacket of this book worth? The fact that you have gotten this far into this book without abandoning it says that you are a person who cares. Your concern about our starving world is more than casual.

How are you going to respond to that hungry little boy? He is not an artist's rendition. He is flesh and blood. What would you do if he were sitting in your living room? Does it make any real difference that he is half a world away?

T. S. Eliot has said, "We know too much, and are convinced of too little." [2]

Might that be true of the problem of world hunger? We know so much. Books, television specials, photos and thousands of words in print, the horrors of a starving world on the six o'clock news in living (dying?) color—we have been exposed to so much. But it seems that in spite of this intense, daily exposure to a hurting world we have responded with not much more than a ho-hum.

Maybe Eliot is right.

And perhaps part of the reason is that we aren't really convinced there is anything we can do to make a difference. Everything now is so bureaucratized, so big, so computer-oriented.

Spence says his students tried to get off the hook by objecting that it was not an individual's obligation, but that of governments, to help the starving. He pointed out the parallel in the Nazis' argument that the government, not individuals, was responsible for the mass killings of Jews. Governments, he reminded his students, are composed of people.

We seem to have forgotten the significance of the power of one person. Sometime, somewhere, somehow we were sold a bill of goods—conned again and again into believing that others should make the changes . . . the Pentagon, the president, our church, the school board, the U.N., the amorphous "they." The list is endless.

Everybody . . . anybody . . . but me.

But what about me? What about you? What about the power of one? Revolutions have unseated the mighty because

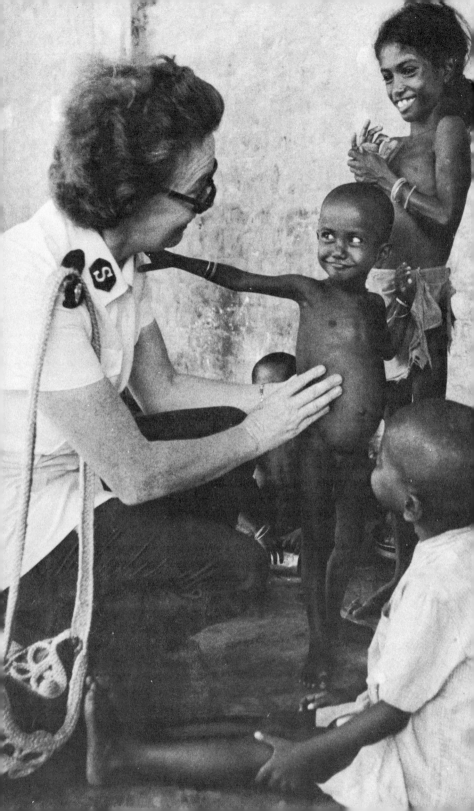

one person had seen enough of the bitter fruit of injustice. Individuals have, through their writings, turned empires on their hinges. One man with a dream made the phrase "civil rights" a household word. And what about that One Solitary Life whose thirty-three years on earth became the pivot point around which human history revolves?

My question to you is this: Do you want to make a difference in our hungry, hurting world? Have you had enough of just reading about it? Are you ready to begin . . . somewhere . . . anywhere?

Paradoxically, let's start with some of the things you probably can't do. After all, realism demands a sensible, manageable involvement.

I know that no single individual can cope with the immense economic, political and logistical issues that complicate our response to the needs of a hungry world. You would have difficulty fully supporting a needy family on your block, much less the millions who live a world away. To tackle India is too much, so let reason and common sense balance out your emotions. Put head and heart together. Head alone will immobilize you. Heart alone will make you ineffective.

I doubt if God wants you to surrender your enjoyment of life for perpetual guilt feelings. Among the joys, food itself is a celebration. Even while he was feeding hungry people, Jesus did not forego an occasional banquet or feast. His cousin John was the ascetic. Jesus loved life. It is probably significant that Jesus told only one man—as far as we know—to sell all he had and give to the poor. He had different messages for his other affluent friends.

As an individual, you can't reverse the many strings-attached, self-serving U.S. policies toward hungry nations. You will need help. But the power of one multiplied by hundreds of thousands will make any congressman sit up and take notice. National leadership responds to the cries—and letters —of a concerned and enlightened electorate.

You can't be expected to live a life filled with guilt because every organization in the country, seemingly, has put your name on its mailing list so that you are constantly bombarded· with pictures of starving babies and emaciated mothers. You have your emotional and financial limits, too.

Neither can you force your view on others. No matter how sensitized you may be, each person has his own level of awareness, his own degree of sensitivity, his own ways in which to respond. Avoid being argumentative and judgmental. To dump your well-thought-out solutions on someone else will probably alienate more than convince.

And there's one more thing you can't do. After having come this far in increasing your own awareness, I don't believe you can continue in isolated, uninvolved affluence while the rest of the world struggles with survival, and still live with your conscience. I am sure those two attitudes are mutually exclusive.

But let's turn it around. What *can* you do? What are some of the creative, meaningful ways in which you can respond to a world in need? Let me say right off that this is an area in which I, too, am struggling. I have not arrived, so I am not suggesting ideas which have necessarily been fully integrated into my own experience.

I'm still working at it.

But I know I am learning to live more sensitively just because I have an awareness that a billion people not more than a few hours away are already mentally and physically retarded for life as the result of a deficient diet. They possess so little, and I know that in many cases it is because I have demanded so much.

You ought to know in the beginning that even daring to think along these lines is dangerous to your status quo. It opens your consciousness to the possibility that the solutions to the problems could affect cultural values and long-held ideas which may seem precious to you. You may not want to take the risk.

But if you decide to go ahead, with the food, resources and money you are able to free up through your new awareness of the problem, you can begin to form a flesh-and-blood relationship with the undernourished two-thirds of the world. You will begin to feel a kinship, and that may be an important preparation for a future in a world of seven billion plus—just twenty-five years away.

Here is how the process of change worked with one person:

I had always assumed that only three elements were needed for agriculture: sun, water and soil. And since these elements are almost omnipresent in the planet, I thought that agricultural potential must also be. . . . But how exceptional America is! We are endowed with *all* the complex requirements for high agricultural productivity, more so than any other nation in the world.

At about the same time I came across the fact that a very large portion of the superb agricultural resources are funneled into the production of meat. I wondered whether this was really the most productive use of our rich agricultural land.

Suddenly I began to see the world's problems with food as my point of reference. . . . Don't [coffee and tea] grow on agricultural land . . . that might otherwise be growing nutritious food? . . . I saw now that a world where only a minor portion of the land is really well suited to agriculture, man is using much of the best land with dubious efficiency . . . much agricultural land which might be growing food is being used instead to "grow" money. . . . I finally concluded instead of studying geography to understand the earth's food-producing potential, I should be examining what man is doing with the food he *presently* produces. . . .

Re-establishing a sense of our direct impact on the earth through food may be the first step toward changing our cultural pattern of waste.[3]

Of waste there is plenty. It is probably the one thing most shocking to our foreign guests. Our throw-away society is strange and unique in the whole world, and the object of consternation to those who cannot afford to throw away anything.

Some who are aware of this waste and reckless use of resources have started "intentional communities." For some, this may be a live option. Here is how it works: A group of like-minded people buys or rents houses within easy walking distance of each other. It's a kind of noncommune commune. They do not live under the same roof, but there is a sharing of virtually everything—lawnmowers, babysitting, food, automobiles. Literally, everything belongs to everyone. Not only does this bring down costs and unnecessary demands on resources (do ten families really need ten lawnmowers?), but, even more significantly, this kind of living situation opens

people to each other—to fuller, healthier personal relationships. Life has a fishbowl quality to it and, obviously, some
cannot adapt to it. The risks are great. But for those who
can make it, so is the payoff.

But even without such a drastic step, there are places where
we can begin. For one thing, we can avoid expensive packaged
foods and items with large amounts of preservatives. Paul
Ehrlich says any food with "a lot of preservatives to maintain
a semblance of freshness has probably already lost much of its
nutritional value." [4] Research has strongly indicated that food
additives may be a major cause of hyperactivity in children.

Again and again research shows that what is natural is often
good for us; what is uncomplicated is usually good for us.
Even before we begin thinking about the needs of a hungry
world, we should at least understand that there is something
terribly right for *us* in this kind of creative living. Often the
more we demand in newer, better and more sophisticated
techniques, better packaging, etc., the worse it is for us as
persons. And the more we tinker with making it "better" for
ourselves, the less time we will have to consider seriously the
needs of others who struggle to survive just one more day.

What great things might be done for the less developed
world if more industrial research went into people-oriented programs instead of product-centered promotion.

I'll probably be bounced off Madison Avenue on my next
trip to New York for what I am about to say next, but here
goes. We must try not to respond to most of the advertising
we see on television. Who will deliver us from the immature,
unethical and insulting advertising that pummels our senses
from dawn to midnight? Hack writers are vandalizing our
poets, our Holy Scriptures, great art forms, our sexual expectations—all in the name of a consumer society—for goods
built not to last.

We know there are few qualitative differences in the soap,
cars, dog food and headache remedies we see peddled. Yet the
ad men work overtime to make our glands salivate, creating an
insatiable desire to consume the next thing that is flashed by
us in living color. Buy it, and you remain content just long
enough—until the next ad or the next visit to a shopping
mall, where the juices start flowing again.

Who's in charge anyway? Most of the time it is certainly not
the consumer. He has been manipulated out of his ability to
make sensible choices. Perhaps one way to scrutinize our
spending habits might be to ask ourselves these questions:
What are the excesses in my life? What do I have too much
of? Do I really need any more?

Now another theme. Population. That's a touchy one. No
one likes to be told how many little feet can patter around in
his own house. But just that is the big question. How many
feet per square foot can this world support?

If you see this problem as critical where you live, then it
would be profitable to investigate the availability of family
planning services in your community. Press for adequate
facilities, if necessary.

Insist on open forum discussions on birth control, abortion,
artificial insemination, genetic control and death control in
your church or club programs. Some of these subjects, unfortunately, seem to be outside the orbit of evangelical Christian concern. In London, the editor of a weekly evangelical
newspaper ran a series of articles on such subjects as abortion,
narcotics, homosexuality, and mental health. The series, timed
to coincide with discussions in the British parliament, provoked an avalanche of mail. Not a few were vitriolic. A Christian's duty, the writers pointed out, was to preach the gospel
and keep himself unspotted from the world till the Coming
Crowning Day. There was to be no truck with the Social
Gospel. The aborted, the stupefied, perverts and mentally dis-
turbed were an intrusion in an orderly Christian perspective, not to be mentioned in pious company except in outright
condemnation.

More baloney.

Gandhi said: "In my judgment the Christian faith does not
lend itself to much preaching or talking. It is best propagated
by living it and applying it. . . . When will you Christians
really crown [Jesus Christ] as the Prince of Peace and pro-
claim him through your deeds as the champion of the poor
and the oppressed?"

But while discussing population control, we must try to
refrain from critical judgment on the apparent lack of it in
Third World countries. Some of the available birth control

methods are difficult to use successfully without Western amenities of privacy, running water, adequate facilities and medical services. These countries are asking for guidance, not judgment.

Now another area. What about our transportation habits? A bondage to freeway living locks many of us into a bumper-to-bumper way of life. A lot of that is unavoidable, but there may be other ways to cut back.

When possible, we should switch to less energy-consuming conveyances such as walking or biking, to gear down on our share of America's energy consumption—about six times the world's per capita average.

President Gerald Ford has reminded Americans that if we drive only 5 percent fewer miles, we could save an almost unbelievable 250,000 barrels of foreign oil per day. That means less pollution, more good exercise for our bodies, less money spent, and just plain more enjoyment.

What about our view of the critical issues that hold today's world in a vise grip? Perhaps the first and most essential thing we can do to protect ourselves from some unpleasant surprises is to stay informed about the state of the world. So many of our high school and even college courses don't talk about the world as it really is. And it shows up later in Pollyanna, unrealistic views of a very gutsy world.

We all have our filters through which we perceive the world. That's O.K. and unavoidable. But let's at least be aware that we have them. What we as Americans do not need at this point in history is a sense that all is well and we have our rights! Because the hungry world is shouting back, No, no, no! Things are not well, and we have rights, too.

Have you thought critically why the young in our society have reacted so violently against the present academic process? I think it may have been because they have an intuitive feeling their courses would not really prepare them for survival in a bankrupt, overcrowded world. Of course, young people are lacking in the experience and wisdom to help them put their lives into cosmic perspective, but it appears their perception of the real issues of life has often been closer to reality than many of their detractors.

For instance, they may have sensed long before we did the futility of every college student's getting an education which fitted him or her only for a "white-collar" job when there are so many dirty-hands jobs in the world.

Now, very personally. The words of Jesus in Matthew 25: 31–46 contain a very disturbing thought. It is this: *Jesus Christ is starving.* It is impossible to avoid any other conclusion when you hear him say, "I was hungry and you fed me . . . . When you did it to these my brothers you were doing it to me!" To feed the hungry is to render a personal service to Christ himself.

As followers of Jesus, most of us enjoy gobbling up the goodies—fellowship with other Christians, air-conditioned places of worship, graded church school materials, potlucks, activities at the church every night of the week, choirs that (most of the time) sing on key, and a pastor to give spiritual guidance and direction. Those are all good and important, but they are the sideshows, not the main event. They are the fringe benefits of faith.

But too many of us have made the extra benefits the chief end, and so our belief hangs near the edge of heresy. After all, heresy is simply truth carried to extremes.

What about the rest of the gospel? That part that talks about the importance of sharing in our Lord's suffering? Is that also an important part of our theology? How much have we felt the pain that God feels when a little skin-and-bones boy in Bangladesh dies from a simple disease just because his body had no more resistance? Are our hearts moved liked the Master's when we see streams of refugees fleeing from their homes in Vietnam, running into social cesspools in inhospitable, overcrowded cities that offer neither security nor food?

Do we, can we, feel the hurt? Are we really convinced that to care for others in their physical affliction is an indispensable part of the Christian life?

We'd better believe it, because without it, we have only half a gospel.

Colin Morris said it well: "When our churches have crumbled and our vestments have rotted and the wind blows through the ruins of our ecclesiastical structures, all that will stand and have eternal significance are creative acts of compassion—the effectual signs of the presence of the Kingdom. Because the Gospel is simple; the judgment is immediate." [5]

Perhaps the real miracle of the feeding of the five thousand was not the fact that they were fed. Could not the real message be that the owner of the few fish and loaves was willing to part with them? That was the miracle. He had the goods and was willing to deliver.

Take a look at the world today. We are certainly talking about more than five thousand people who are hungry, lonely, scared to death. They number in the millions—people who are hungry for love, for a touch, for a meal.

Together with others, you and I have the resources. And like the story, the significant miracle is not just in feeding the hungry in our world today. That can be done. The food is available. The fragile miracle takes place when we *will* to do it. The boy in the story gave the entire contents of his lunch box. Because of his generous gift, more than five thousand hungry people ate.

It is a matter of the will. Not of resources. It is the will. Not of technological capability. It is the will. Do we have the will to get involved?

It's a hard comment, and coming from Lenny Bruce, the so-called sick comedian, some may turn it off. But here is what he says: "I know in my heart, by pure logic, that any man who claims to be a leader of the church is a hustler if he has two suits in a world in which most people have none." [6]

Most of us have come a long way from the simplicity and caring of Jesus, the man for others—the man with *one* robe.

While in Rio de Janeiro recently, I talked with the pastor of an English-speaking congregation in that city. He told me of a conversation he had with an official of his church whom he had approached about increasing the low wages of the Brazilian gardener who tended the church grounds, to help him keep up with inflation. The church official had lived in Brazil for twenty-five years where he had made it big. He belonged to the yacht club and various other elitist clubs in Copacabana, Rio's rich suburb.

Said the pastor: "We really need to pay the gardener more."

Member: "He's already getting ten cruzeiros more than the minimum wage. Are you trying to spoil him?"

Pastor: "No, I just don't think it's right for us to keep him in poverty."

Member: "With an attitude like that you shouldn't be in Brazil."

Pastor: "With an attitude like yours, you shouldn't be in the church of Christ."

The man isn't in the church any longer. He was "religious," but the message of Jesus had never come through.

As I said, I don't know all the answers, and I still haven't applied personally *all* the ones I do know. Frequently I get frustrated. By the size of the problem. By the indifference of many. By my own lack of resolve.

And when I get frustrated, I talk out loud to God. The conversation usually goes something like this:

Lord, what do you want me to do about it?

You want me to keep my head, I know.

You haven't asked me—yet—to sell all I have and give to the poor. Sometimes I wish you would; it would make for an uncomplicated life. But would it really fulfill my commitment?

And what would I do afterwards? Become the object of someone else's charity? That would mean learning the grace of receiving, and I'm not naturally humble.

I suppose I could eat less, but I need to be kept fit so that I can work and plan to help others in far-off Mali (and, incidentally, why didn't the French do more in that area—wasn't it once theirs?).

I suppose I could give more, but India has the sacred cow and the atom bomb and that appalling inconsistency of attitude.

The pictures and stories of starvation pain me deeply, adding agony to my frustration. But I must be careful. What good would an agonizing and possibly unbalanced soul do them?

For their sake, I've got to keep a clear head at all costs. You wouldn't have me otherwise. You and I know too well that fatal affinity between religious emotion and a self-indulgent life, and I don't want to fall into that trap again.

Yes, I am aware that of the world's GNP 7 percent goes on arms, only .3 percent on aid. But isn't this inevitable? You can't expect the Christian ethic where there is no Christian experience.

And another thing. Even those we help are often ungrateful. Never a word of thanks. They sneer at us behind our back, regard our bounty as their right. When some bigger benefactor comes along they tell us to find ourselves another beggar.

And sometimes while I am talking, I am interrupted by remembering these words:

"What is that to thee? Follow thou me."

Then I am ashamed, and I say:

Renew a right spirit within me. Take the dimness of my soul away. Lord, set me free from the power of words. Bring me into the place of thy light.

It is inconceivable even to think that after that kind of dialogue Christians of our nation can pass by on the other side. World conditions shout out for a speedy return to a simpler, less energy-consuming, more reasonable life style. It will probably be forced upon us whether we like it or not. But, I hope we will make some of the necessary changes before that. Not just because it is expedient, but because it is the right thing to do.

In an address to a church gathering, Senator Mark Hatfield outlined four suggestions for Christians who really want to respond to the needs of our hungry world:

1. "Every congregation could establish a specific budget amount directed to meeting the needs of starving people in some particular point of the world.

2. "Christians can be asked to give a specific tithe just for the purpose of relieving hunger; further, we should consider a graduated tithe, which increases in its percentage according to the amount of one's income.

3. "We should renew the Christian discipline of fasting as a means for teaching us how to identify with those who hunger, and to deepen our life of prayer for those who suffer.

4. "We must all analyze, in prayer before God, our own

habits of food consumption. Specifically, we can drastically
alter our consumption of meat, and the money we save we
can give to alleviate world hunger. Some Christians may decide that part of their witness means being a vegetarian.
Families can decide how to limit their consumption of beef,
perhaps to only certain days, or as times of special celebration,
or just on certain days of the week."

Churches are proposing covenants to be adopted voluntarily
by their members. I have seen one such covenant from Hope
Presbyterian Church in Richfield, Minnesota, a suburb of
Minneapolis. It reads:

> As a citizen of a very rich nation, out of Christian concern for
> my hungry neighbors around the world and aware of the grow-
> ing world food shortage, I commit myself to the following
> actions:
> 1. I shall economize on my consumption of high cost protein
> by eliminating meat from my diet one day a week.
> 2. I will limit my use of commercial fertilizer to food produc-
> tion, not use it on my lawn.
> 3. I will keep myself informed about the problems of domestic
> and world hunger through every means available to me and will
> communicate my conviction about this problem to my senator,
> my congressman, other political leaders and my friends.
> 4. I will follow (with my doctor's permission) the Christian
> discipline of fasting as a means for teaching me how to identify
> with those who hunger and to deepen my life of prayer for those
> who suffer.
> 5. I will contribute (through what I save through faithful
> stewardship of natural resources) a portion of my annual in-
> come to the church or other responsible agencies (such as
> World Vision) for the purpose of feeding hungry people and
> sharing the good news of the Gospel of Christ.

Thousands of people are getting involved in significant
ways. A small Lutheran church in the northwest has made a
decision to borrow $100,000 against the church property for
use in emergency aid. The Episcopal Diocese of Southern Ohio
designated a minimum of $150,000 from its funds for world
hunger.

The Church of the Brethren, reactivating an approach used
during World War II, now gives food production certificates

to persons and groups who through reducing their own consumption of various resources, commit funds to agricultural and other development programs at the village level overseas.

A clergyman and his family in California regularly give 2 percent of their gross income—above the tithe to their church —to development projects.

The Mennonite Central Committee has encouraged its constituency to reduce their food consumption and expenditures by 10 percent and contribute this to meet the food needs of others.

Haverford College in Pennsylvania is contributing the funds it normally would have spent next year on fertilizer for the campus lawns.

World Vision through its Project FAST is asking people to go on a "planned famine" for thirty hours, getting others to sponsor their fast with money which will be contributed to hunger programs.

And the list could go on and on. The ideas can be as varied and as creative as the people involved.

Since 40 percent of Americans are reported to be overweight anyway, the idea of cutting back and eating less should have its own personal attraction.

Mrs. Helen Sheard, home economist for the Hawaiian Electric Company, offers these suggestions for eating less and not feeling hungry afterwards:

1. Limit yourself to one serving. Absolutely no seconds. And no midnight snacks.

2. Take small mouthfuls. Chew slowly. Relish the taste.

3. Get in some dinner-table conversation, an all-too-scarce commodity in these days of rush, rush, rush.

4. Don't gulp and run.

You'll be surprised, she says, at how satisfied you can feel after a meal of less than heroic proportions.

When it's all sorted out, it is still the individual who helps the individual. In World Vision, we are constantly reminding people that just because they can't do everything, they shouldn't refrain from doing something. It doesn't have to be a lot. Food on a plate will nourish a child for a day, but a contribution that will encourage community development will help nourish him for life. You don't have to give a railroad car full of wheat. No one expects you to be responsible for equipping an entire medical clinic—unless you have the means to do so.

Individual response will make the ultimate difference.

For the Christian, the commands to respond are unavoidable. Not because of what this book may say, but because of what another book says. A book that has spoken clearly to the issues of hungry people and unjust societies for a very long time. A book that strongly suggests that God is on the side of the oppressed.

The Holy Scriptures.

But now that you have read this book, go back and reread the New Testament. Perhaps you'll see what it says with new eyes and a freshly sensitized conscience. What you read will probably go something like this:

Giving to the needy should never be connected with image-making (Matt. 6:1); there is absolutely no license in the Lord's Prayer to ask for daily food for yourself—it's "our daily bread" (Matt. 6:10); if you insist on clinging to a highly self-oriented life style, your own sense of well-being will diminish (Matt. 10:39); Christ's incentive and reward system for sharing with the needy breaks down to the smallest unit— a cup of cold water (Matt. 10:42); man-made systems of honoring God may sometimes be ignored in the face of human need (Matt. 12:1); when churchmen refused to consider Christ's compassionate acts as adequate credentials and requested sky-writing, he walked out on them (Matt. 16:1–4).

Christ never conditions his love. We do. Jesus doesn't tell us, "When the government of Bangladesh cleans up its corrupt bureaucracy, then get involved." He doesn't say, "When the Indians, or Indonesians, or Africans get their populations under control, then lend a hand."

The reason he doesn't is because it is Jesus who is starving. Jesus has tattered robes. Jesus is cold.

Love won't wait.

One way to expose yourself and your church, club or civic group to the problems and solutions is through films. Here is a brief list of agencies where you may obtain good films:

Audio-Visual Center
Indiana University
Bloomington, Indiana 47401

Carousel Films, Inc.
1501 Broadway
New York, N.Y. 10036

Church World Service
475 Riverside Drive
New York, N.Y. 10027

UNICEF Films
Association Films, Inc.
600 Grand Avenue
Ridgefield, N.J. 07657

American Freedom from Hunger Foundation
1717 H Street, N.W., Suite 437
Washington, D.C. 20006

World Relief Commission
National Association of Evangelicals
P.O. Box 28
Wheaton, Illinois 60187

World Vision International
919 W. Huntington Drive
Monrovia, Calif. 91016

We've talked about a lot of things in this chapter. The summary that follows may help put some of those thoughts together. This list of ways to get involved may also provide a springboard for individual, group or community action.

—Develop a series of educational experiences for your community that emphasizes the pressing need for food aid in the hurting countries of our world—places like India, Bangladesh, Pakistan, Ethiopia, Honduras, the Philippines, Upper Volta.

—As churches and as individuals, organize days of fasting. Give the money saved to relief agencies to help people who fast all the time—involuntarily.

—Be as responsible and conservative as possible in planning meals for your family.

—When you have a party or entertain guests, offer a simpler menu and explain why.

—Have a famine meal one time each week. Eat, for example, a few soda crackers, a bowl of broth and a glass of water. Use that time to discuss as a family the problems of our hungry world.

—Adopt a "skimp a meal" plan during the week. This idea, used by the Arcadia Presbyterian Church, Arcadia, California, was suggested by a layman in the church. Recipes are provided for nourishing but skimpy meals, and families are encouraged to set aside the money which would normally have been spent and give it to relief programs.

—Come to a fuller understanding that the gospel is concerned with two kinds of bread: bread for the soul and bread for the body. To deny hungry people either of these is to distort the truth of the Christian message.

—Experiment with changes in your diet. Try eating on a welfare allowance (16 cents per meal) for a week or so. See how it feels.

—Use cookbooks with recipes for well-balanced diets that cut down on waste and make the most of high protein, meatless meals.

—Take a stab at raising your own garden. It will be a lot of work, but chances are you'll develop a whole new appreciation for the sun and the soil.

—Consider planting community gardens on vacant city lots or unused land in your city.

—Evaluate school lunches in your community. See if there is excessive waste. Suggest ways to improve the program.

—Encourage the introduction of nutrition education into your school's curriculum.

—Have nutrition programs presented to groups of which you are a member.

—Feed pets more table scraps instead of high protein commercial pet foods.

—Decrease (or eliminate) your use of commercial fertilizers on home lawns.

—Decrease consumption of foods produced by high grain intake (such as top-grade beef) and increase the amount of direct protein through a diet of whole grain and soybean products.

—Ask for grass-fed calf at your meat market. It's available in many places and will be increasingly so as people demand it.

—Ask hard questions of relief organizations. Questions like: How much do you spend for overhead and fund-raising? How much actually gets to the person in need? How do you determine whom you will help? Are you doing development for self-reliance as well as immediate relief?

—Ask yourself what is perhaps the hardest question of all: Is my life style supporting a famine somewhere in the world today?

—Finally, keep sensitive to the hurts of the world. Don't allow overexposure to dull your conscience, your emotions or your capacity to respond.

At an international congress held not long ago, the question was raised of the plight of Jews in the Soviet Union who are not permitted to leave the country and are suffering other forms of persecution for their faith. At the conference was Simon Wiesenthal, director of the Jewish Documentation Center in Vienna, one of the prime purposes of which is to locate and bring to justice Nazi war criminals.

Wiesenthal reported that one Jew had called his hotel at two o'clock in the morning.

"Why are you calling me at this hour?" he demanded irritably.

"Because," said the caller, "you were sleeping."

The world bleeds and starves.

It is no time to be asleep.

Chapter 13
Questions: Guideposts to Understanding

ARE YOU STILL LEFT WITH QUESTIONS?

Good.

I haven't even tried to answer all the questions which could be raised about hunger, its causes, and our response to it. One reason is that I don't know all the answers.

Another is there may not be any answers for some of the questions. Maybe not ever. Or maybe not yet.

But that shouldn't keep us from asking the questions and searching, if not for final answers, at least for a direction in which to move. I'd like to suggest some that need to be grappled with. You may have some answers. Perhaps you could pose some of these questions to lawmakers and churchmen and press them for a response. We must continue to challenge ourselves and our leaders to face the hard questions and seek the often difficult answers.

I am not afraid that some of the answers may be beyond us.

I am only fearful that we will stop asking questions.

Our Responsibility

The concepts of caring for those in need, of being responsible for each other, of sharing are found in most of the world's great religious and ethical systems. In North America, our Judaeo-Christian heritage and a well-developed humanitarianism still encourage us to be concerned about others, whether across the street or across the world. The growing interdependence of the world, however, makes our concern also a matter of self-interest. We must care about what is happening in those places which are the sources of so many of our raw materials and the markets for so much of our exports.

1. Yet when there are hungry people in our own country, should we concentrate more efforts at home before helping those elsewhere? Is there any justification for making a national boundary the limit of our caring?

2. At present, U.S. foreign economic aid is less than .5 percent of our gross national product, and we rank fourteenth among the sixteen major developed nations in our per person aid to less developed nations. Should the U.S. contribution to meeting world need—food needs in particular—be limited to a percentage of what other countries do? Or should we do all we can?

3. Since we possess much of the world's wealth and technical knowledge, what should be our attitude about sharing this wealth and knowledge with others? Should it carry a price tag? Should we give it away freely? Should we help only those who agree with us politically? How about only those who show a willingness to take steps toward self-help.

4. Are we well fed primarily because we've worked hard? Because God has "blessed" us with abundance? Are "they" hungry because "they" haven't worked hard? Or because God hasn't provided? What do you think about this comment by Robert Frost: "What makes a good nation in the beginning is a good piece of geography"?

5. What should we teach our children, at home as well as in school, about world need and our response to it? To what extent are we willing to expose ourselves and our children to the issues and to learn more?

Population Growth

Here is where so many people start.

And stop.

The world's population is growing rapidly, no question about that. The growth is unevenly distributed and the resources in some parts of the earth are severely strained. But what are the real implications of that growth? Is "the pill" really the answer to the world's hunger problem?

1. Since Americans consume up to five times the resources of typical persons in the Third World, this makes our effective population five times what it actually is in numbers. Is this as important an implication as numbers themselves?

2. The strain of feeding an increasing population is compounded by its unequal distribution. Would a partial solution be to control migration to already overcrowded urban areas through deliberate decentralization of industries (or a merging of the agricultural and industrial sectors in some manner)? Would you favor legislation which restricted the population of a certain area or city? What about forced migrations to lesser populated areas within a country?

3. Are restrictions on immigration a fair way to limit population growth? Should communities limit growth through zoning ordinances? Do such actions tend to discriminate against the poor and the unskilled?

4. Assuming that most governments agree that a global population strategy is desirable, how can the U.S. best support it? By our own example? Through increased support of U.N. population and development programs? Through more research in fertility, contraception and the relation of family size to economic development?

5. Can understanding the different reasons for having children help us creatively deal with the population explosion?

6. Would you favor requiring population limitation policies as part of all development aid programs? Would this be unwarranted interference in the domestic affairs of another nation? How would you feel if other nations insisted on such policies as a requirement for helping us?

7. Given present growth trends, should Americans limit their families to two children? Would that make any difference to the rest of the world? To the U.S.A. of the future? If family limitation seems desirable, what will this mean to our views on sterilization, abortion, and birth control?

Food Distribution and Food Aid

Producing food is only one aspect of the problem. Distribution is another factor. Nations which lack an internal transportation infrastructure will have a hard time placing food where it is needed. In many places, bartering is still the principal method of trade. Marketing systems may be nonexistent, outmoded or inequitable. In some countries, as much as 30 percent of the stored grain is eaten by rats and insects. Sending food from one country to another (food aid, trade) is slow, expensive, and limited in quantity and variety.

1. Is there a basic human right to eat? If so, what are we to say to a world where some have more than they need while many have little or nothing?

2. Of all the exported food in the world, the United States exports 44 percent of the wheat, 57 percent of the animal feed grain, and more than 90 percent of all soybeans entering the world market. What some people get to eat—indeed, if they eat at all—will depend on U.S. policies on food trade and aid. Do we have a responsibility to share all we can with less developed nations? Do you agree with the U.S. secretary of agriculture that food is a "political weapon"? Would you be willing to pay higher prices at home if that is the cost of sharing food with a hungry world?

3. Should lack of gratitude on the part of recipient governments affect our giving of food aid?

4. Since we can't give food aid forever, is giving such aid simply postponing inevitable misery for those who are starving?

5. How would you feel if you were the one who was starving and people with food said they "couldn't afford" to send you some?

The Use of Resources

One of the major concerns today is our waste of natural resources. Many people feel we must keep and preserve much of the natural environment in its present state. This creates a conflict with those who say that more energy, food, and

basic goods must be produced whatever is the cost to the environment. Certainly resource use is not evenly distributed. Twenty percent of the world's population, living in the largely affluent, Western "Christian" nations, control or consume well over half of the world's wealth and resources.

1. Does the high resource consumption level of Western nations give them a special responsibility to help feed the world's hungry? Some experts say that as standards of living rise, people tend to have fewer children. If we managed our use of resources better and made a more equitable distribution of them, might this eliminate the need for strict measures of population control?

2. Does the biblical directive to "be fruitful and multiply, and fill the earth and subdue it" not demand that we have some understanding of the ability of the basic environment to support life? Has this directive been fulfilled already?

3. What is the best way to meet world food needs—more production or less consumption combined with more sharing? Or both?

4. In a world where many people have yet to discover the plow, should we be encouraging them to use tractors? Is high-level technology the approach to increased production or is simpler and more appropriate technology preferable?

5. If we are, as an American president once said, "the best-clothed, best-fed, best-housed people in the world," what right do we have to demand still more resources? If we have so much, why do you think we are seemingly reluctant to expand our foreign economic aid programs?

For Local Churches to Consider

There are over three hundred forty thousand local church congregations in the U.S. and Canada and these constitute a significant potential source for resources and public pressure. The individual church member can multiply his or her impact by working together with other members on issues such as hunger.

1. For church members, does not the Bible exhort us to care first for those who share our faith? Is this being done? If not, how can we start? Is there a priority for caring, or are

we to care, help and share with all the needy we can? Does
Jesus' story of the Good Samaritan offer any guidance (Luke
10:29–37)?

2. Do you know which people in your church or local community are hungry or malnourished?

3. In 1974, Americans spent over $900 million on build-
ings to be used for religious purposes. Should we reflect and
rethink our use of such money at a time when many people
don't even have a roof over their heads?

4. Do you know what percentage of the budget of your
church is used for ministries directed at helping those in need?
Should this figure be increased, decreased, or is it about right?

5. Can churches be maximally effective if they limit their
efforts to education and motivation of members concerning
world food problems?

6. Are American church members so identified with technology, consumerism and "Madison Avenue hard-sell" that
they cannot live any other way?

Governments, Systems and Structures

As individuals, we cannot effectively send food overseas to
feed the hungry. This can be done to a limited degree by private agencies, but in significant quantities it must be the task
of governments. Government policies, therefore, will determine how much is shipped, when, and to whom. Food that
enters international trade is controlled by private businesses
and governments as part of a complex system of agreements,
procedures, transportation systems and policy decisions.

Food production and distribution within a nation are greatly
affected by government policies, private business systems, and
the political structures that direct a country. Any significant
modification in food availability is dependent upon the actions
of governments, systems and structures.

1. Elected officials say they are influenced by letters received from constituents. When was the last time you wrote
to your elected representatives in government to express your
views on its policies? What would you say concerning hunger
and food aid?

2. A U.S. senator has revealed that U.S. corporations in-

vested (1959–69) about $5.8 billion in developing countries, and took out $15.1 billion in profits. In other words, the poorer nations sent $9.3 billion to support the United States. Is this defensible in the name of making profits? If corporations reduced their investments in developing nations, would that not have serious economic impact on those nations, perhaps causing more unemployment and increasing poverty? How would you propose tackling this problem?

3. Someone has said that in helping developing nations, the affluent world must move beyond charity to social justice —but one man's justice may be another man's injustice. Can you suggest an outline of governmental policies that could guide international trade, food aid, and technical assistance?

4. Is it really possible for an individual or a group to have an impact on government decisions and policies? If not, does this mean you should stop trying? Are there other ways to influence governments? Can you think of ways, apart from governments and businesses, to help developing nations?

5. If you work for a business or corporation (especially one with overseas operations), how can you help make its influence overseas a positive one for the recipient peoples and nations?

6. What do you think about placing issues, as well as candidates' names, on election ballots so that people can express their views?

Life Styles and Values

The world is a series of interdependent systems. When North Americans consume more, our factories must produce more which means that, in turn, they must import more raw materials from developing countries to support our consumer economy. It is our consumption level and style of living that largely determines what must be produced. This means that in a world of limited resources when some have more, others must have less.

1. With less energy, higher food prices, general shortages, and inflation or recession, our individual styles of life will be affected sooner or later. It has been said that most people change their life styles only when they are forced to do so.

What would force you to change yours? Would you rather intentionally decide what you will do?

2. Someone has said that if the rich keep considering their wealth as a right, the poor will consider their vengeance as justice. Is wealth a right? Does earning wealth give a right to keep it all?

3. In what we personally use and consume, how much is enough?

4. Could you, as an individual, or together with your family, continue to live adequately on your present income if you decided to give a greater proportion of future wage-salary increases toward meeting world hunger needs?

5. If you modified your way of life and discovered that you were spending less money, what would you do with what you saved?

6. If we do not modify our values about such things as population growth, consumption and wealth, what kind of world will our children live in? Our grandchildren? Do you think they would like that kind of world?

7. If we contribute to meet the needs of others, should we do so only from our surplus or at some personal sacrifice?

8. Try to imagine what it would feel like to live as a person in a less developed country (see Robert Heilbroner's example in chapter 1). How does this affect the way you think about your life and your possessions?

Let's Make a Start

As you can see, these are not easy questions. I don't have all the answers; I don't think anyone does. But I believe that these questions and others like them must be asked of ourselves and of those who direct the governments and systems of our hurting, hungry world.

But don't let the "question and answer" routine degenerate into nothing more than a philosophical, academic exercise. Remember the numbing, sickening, crushing hunger and poverty that is the daily life of so many fellow human beings.

Gandhi said, "God himself dare not appear to a hungry man except in the form of bread."

The Bible is emphatic on the responsibility of those who

have toward those who have not. Attempts at evading a personal response are useless. Asks the Apostle John: "But if a man has enough to live on, and yet when he sees his brother in need shuts up his heart against him, how can it be said that the divine love abides in him?" (1 John 3:17, NEB).

The Apostle Paul is no less firm: "Command those who are rich in this present world not to be arrogant nor to put their hope in wealth, which is so uncertain, but to put their hope in God, who richly provides us with everything for our enjoyment. Command them to do good, to be rich in good deeds, and to be generous and willing to share" (1 Tim. 6:17, New International Version).

If that were to become the criterion for our trade, aid and international assistance programs, the results could be pretty revolutionary.

There you have it.

Information. Comments of peasants, presidents, development experts. Scientific projections. God's plan and order for things.

Now here you and I are, about to decide what it is we will do. I'm trying to make a start.

Care to join me?

And by the way—what do *you* say to a hungry world?

For Further Reading: A Selected Bibliography

There are many books, articles, pamphlets, reports and films that present some aspect of hunger and human need. The sources that follow are a few that are generally available and are nontechnical.

AMERICAN FREEDOM FROM HUNGER FOUNDATION. *A Select Bibliography on Hunger and the Associated Problems of World Development.* Washington, 1969. Lists books, films and resource organizations on hunger, malnutrition, poverty, development and agriculture. Available from AFFH, 1717 H St. N.W., Washington, D.C. 20006.

BHAGWATI, JAGDISH. "Revolution in Agriculture." In *The Economics of Underdeveloped Countries.* World University Library. New York: McGraw-Hill, 1966. A well-written introduction to the facts and figures of poverty in the world, with good charts, tables and photographs.

BORGSTROM, GEORG. *Hungry Planet: The Modern World at the Edge of Famine.* 2nd rev. ed. New York: Macmillan, 1972. From the perspective of an agricultural scientist.

BROWN, LESTER R. with ECKHOLM, ERIK P. *By Bread Alone.* New York: Praeger Publishers, 1974. Recent and readable summary of almost every aspect of the world hunger situation. Extensive bibliography.

EHRLICH, PAUL R. and EHRLICH, ANNE H. *Population, Resources, Environment.* Stanford University, Issues in Human Ecology. San Francisco: W. N. Freeman & Co., 1970. By the author of

The Population Bomb, The End of Affluence, and other writings on the implications of population growth.

ELLER, VERNARD. *The Simple Life: The Christian Stance Toward Possessions.* Grand Rapids: Eerdmans, 1973. Reflections on a biblical basis of life style.

GHEDDO, PIERO. *Why is the Third World Poor?* Maryknoll, N.Y.: Orbis Books, 1973. Uses more European and Third World sources. Good chapter on Christian responsibility.

HARDIN, CLIFFORD M., ed. *Overcoming World Hunger.* Englewood Cliffs, N.J.: Prentice-Hall, Spectrum Books, 1969. Edited by a former secretary of agriculture, the book consists of four long essays by experts which give a comprehensive overview of the problems and possibilities entailed in expanding food production and feeding the world's hungry people.

HEILBRONER, ROBERT L. *An Inquiry Into the Human Prospect.* New York: Norton, 1974. Reflections of basic global issues for the future.

——————. *The Great Ascent: The Struggle for Economic Development in Our Time.* New York: Harper & Row, 1963.

LAPPÉ, FRANCES MOORE. *Diet for a Small Planet.* New York: Ballantine, 1971. Readable discussion of global nutrition needs. With recipes.

——————. "Fantasies of Famine." *Harper's,* New York, February 1975. Hard look at U.S. food consumption.

McNAMARA, ROBERT. *One Hundred Countries, Two Billion People: The Dimensions of Development.* New York: Praeger Publications, 1973. Compilation of speeches as president of the World Bank. Topics include development, population, malnutrition, unemployment, aid, trade, industrial expansion, the environment and social equity.

MEADOWS, D. L., and MEADOWS, D. H. *The Limits to Growth.* New York: Universe Books, 1972. A report for the Club of Rome's project on the predicament of mankind. A computer-based study of world resource limitations. Controversial. Includes some data, tables and graphs.

MILBAUER, BARBARA and LEINWAND, GERALD. *Hunger.* New York: Simon & Schuster (Pocketbooks), 1971. Describes the "problem and challenge" of the hunger and poverty of 25 million Americans.

MORRIS, COLIN. *Include Me Out! Confessions of an Ecclesiastical Coward.* London: Epworth Press, 1968. A mission executive contrasts the reality of human need with the seeming "unreality" of some ecclesiastical debates.

MYRDAL, GUNNAR. *The Challenge of World Poverty, a World Anti-Poverty Program in Outline.* New York: Random House, 1970. An extensive discussion of world development, emphasizing the limitations of current economic theories, the need for radical reforms in underdeveloped countries, the responsibility of the developed countries, and the politics of development.

OWENS, EDGAR and SHAW, ROBERT. *Development Reconsidered.* Lexington, Mass.: D. C. Heath & Co., 1972.

PRICE, DANIEL O., ed. *The 99th Hour: The Population Crisis in the U.S.* Chapel Hill: University of North Carolina Press, 1967.

ROUNTREE, ESTELLE and HALVERSTADT, HUGH. *Sometimes They Cry.* New York: Friendship Press, 1970. Selected readings from scholars, development professionals and the poor and hungry themselves. Also contains charts and tables, poetry and pictures, questions for classroom discussion, suggested activities and lists of resource materials. Preaddressed postcards are bound into the book to facilitate writing for suggested materials.

SCHUMACHER, E. F. *Small is Beautiful: Economics As If People Mattered.* New York: Harper & Row, 1973. An unconventional, thought-provoking approach to development.

STAMP, ELIZABETH. *The Hungry World.* Rev. ed. England: Oxfam, 1972. Available from Oxfam America, 1028 Connecticut Ave., N.W., Room 922, Washington, D.C. 20036. A basic introduction to hunger, its causes and consequences; the problem to be solved and the work now being done. Especially suitable for high school students.

STOESZ, EDGAR. *Beyond Good Intentions.* Akron, Pa.: Mennonite Central Committee, 1972. A discussion of development at a practical field level by a Mennonite development worker.

WARD, BARBARA. *The Rich Nations and the Poor Nations.* New York: Norton & Co., 1962. General review of global development, contrasting the rich and poor nations and focusing on four "revolutions" that have significant global impact.

WIRT, SHERWOOD. *The Social Conscience of the Evangelical.* New York: Harper & Row, 1968. Discusses various social problems from evangelical Christian perspective.

WRIGHT, RICHARD T. "Hunger, Malnutrition and Famine: The World Food Problem." In *Our Society in Turmoil,* edited by Gary R. Collins. Carol Stream, Ill.: Creation House, 1970. Basic overview.

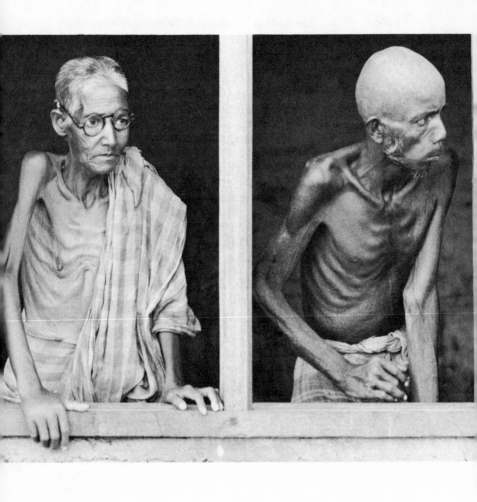

Notes

Preface

1. *Newsweek,* November 11, 1974.
2. Gunnar Mydral, *The Challenge of World Poverty* (New York: Random House, 1970), p. 339.
3. "Aid and Development from a Recipient's Point of View," lecture delivered at New Zealand Institute of International Affairs, Christchurch, March 18, 1974, quoted in *Africa,* May 1974, p. 66.
4. Estelle Rountree and Hugh Halverstadt, *Sometimes They Cry* (New York: Friendship Press), 1970.
5. Elizabeth Browning, "The Cry of the Children," *The Complete Poetical Works of Elizabeth Barrett Browning,* Cambridge Edition (New York: Houghton Mifflin Co., 1900), pp. 156–58.
6. Colin Morris, *Include Me Out! Confessions of an Ecclesiastical Coward* (London: Epworth Press, 1968), pp. 39–41.
7. Rev. Theodore Hesburgh, "How You Can Help Ease World Famine," *Los Angeles Herald Examiner,* April 18, 1974, p. A–6.
8. "The Dual Challenge of Health and Hunger—A Global Crisis," 1968.

Introduction

1. Acts 17:26, Phillips.
2. Guy Carson, ed., "Ze the Train Robber, Hunger in Northeast Brazil," *Nutrition and Development* (OXFAM-Canada, n.d.), p. 36.
3. Job 22:7, LB.
4. Job 33:13–28.
5. Matthew 25:44, 45, LB.
6. Colin Morris, *Include Me Out!,* pp. 7–8.
7. Dietrich Bonhoeffer, *Ethics,* paperback edition (New York: Macmillan, 1955), p. 137.

PART I. CONTEXTS OF HUNGER

Chapter 1: Poverty

1. Robert McNamara, *One Hundred Countries, Two Billion People* (New York: Praeger Publishers, 1973), p. 30.
2. C. E. Jackson, "Poverty," *Christian Herald,* January 1968.
3. E. J. Kahn, *The American People: A Noted Journalist Explores the Findings of the 1970 Census* (New York: Weybright and Talley, 1974).
4. Robert Heilbroner, *The Great Ascent: The Struggle for Economic Development in Our Time* (New York: Harper & Row, 1963), p. 59.
5. Alfred Marshall, *Principles of Economics* (New York: Macmillan, 1890).
6. Carolina Maria de Jesus, *Child of the Dark* (New York: E. P. Dutton, 1962).
7. McNamara, *One Hundred Countries, Two Billion People,* pp. 104–5.
8. Quoted in *The Radical Bible* (Maryknoll, N.Y.: Orbis Books, 1972), pp. 100–101.
9. Mahbub ul Haq, "The Crisis in Development Strategies," *Anticipation* 12 (September 1972):7
10. McNamara, *One Hundred Countries, Two Billion People,* p. 28.
11. Barbara Ward, *The Rich Nations and the Poor Nations* (New York: Norton & Co., 1962), p. 38.
12. Barbara Ward, *The Angry Seventies, Second Development Decade —A Call to the Church* (Rome: Pontifical Commission on Justice and Peace, 1971).

Chapter 2: Ignorance

1. William E. Smith, *We Must Run While They Walk: A Portrait of Africa's Julius Nyerere* (New York: Random House, 1971), p. 4.
2. E. F. Schumacher, *Small Is Beautiful: Economics As If People Mattered* (New York: Harper & Row, 1973), pp. 185–6.
3. Smith, *We Must Run While They Walk.*
4. Marjorie Dye, et al., *Literacy—The Essential Skill,' A Handbook for Literacy Workers* (New York: Committee on World Literacy and Literature, 1964).
5. M. N. Smart, "Literacy via the Press," *Africa,* February, 1974.
6. Heilbroner, *The Great Ascent,* pp. 23–27 (summarized).
7. Myrdal, *The Challenge of World Poverty,* p. 169.

Chapter 3: Climate

1. Tom Alexander, "Ominous Changes in the World's Weather," *Fortune,* February 1974.
2. *Time,* Nov. 11, 1974.
3. Robert Heilbroner, *An Inquiry into the Human Prospect* (New York: Norton, 1974), p. 52.
4. Ibid., pp. 54–55.
5. Quoted in "Monsoon Begins; India Hoping to End Drought," *Los Angeles Times,* June 27, 1974, p. 28.
6. Isaiah 35:1, 7, KJV.

Chapter 4: Dispossession
1. *The Link,* September-October 1974. Published by Americans for Middle East Understanding, New York.
2. Ibid.

Chapter 5: Urbanization
1. Alvin Toffler, *Future Shock* (New York: Random House, 1970), p. 23.
2. Ibid., p. 37.
3. Heilbroner, *An Inquiry into the Human Prospect,* p. 37.
4. Paul Ehrlich and Anne Ehrlich, *Population, Resources, Environment* (San Francisco: W. N. Freeman, 1970), p. 128.
5. Paul Ehrlich, *The Population Bomb* (New York: Ballantine Books, 1968), p. 38.
6. Ehrlich and Ehrlich, *Population, Resources, Environment,* p. 296.
7. October 27, 1969 in New York, quoted in F. C. Terzo, *Urbanization in the Developing Countries* (New York: Ford Foundation), p. 7.

Chapter 6: "The System"
1. The story of Juan Diaz has been excerpted, with permission, from Thomas Fenton, "Coffee, the Rules of the Game, and You," rev. ed. pamphlet published by The Christophers, 12 East 48th St., New York, N.Y. 10017.
2. Ibid.
3. *The Radical Bible,* p. 19.
4. Mark 14:7, RSV.
5. *The Radical Bible,* p. 63.
6. Edgar Snow, *Journey to the Beginning* (New York: Random House, 1958).
7. Isaiah 1:17, 13–15, KJV.
8. I. Rosier, *El Pueblo No Cree Mas en Promesas,* Carlos Lohle (Buenos Aires: Soc. Anon. Ind. y Com, 1971), p. 94.
9. *Ceres,* U.N. Food and Agriculture Organization Review, September-October 1968.
10. *Los Angeles Times,* May 5, 1974.

PART II. PERSPECTIVES ON HUNGER

Chapter 7: Population
1. D. H. Meadows, et al., *The Limits to Growth* (New York: Universe Books, 1972), pp. 27–28.
2. "Man's Population Predicament," *Population Bulletin* (Population Reference Bureau, Washington, D.C.) 27, no. 2 (April 1971):5.
3. Meadows, *The Limits to Growth,* p. 23.
4. Philip Hauser, ed., *The Population Dilemma* (New York: Prentice-Hall, 1969), p. 18.
5. Ibid., p. 33.
6. Michael S. Teitelbaum, "Population and Development: Is a Consensus Possible?" *Foreign Affairs* 52, no. 4, July 1974.
7. Ehrlich, *The Population Bomb,* p. 28.
8. Teitelbaum, "Population and Development."
9. Ibid.

10. Lester R. Brown, *In the Human Interest: A Strategy to Stabilize the World Population* (New York: W. W. Norton, 1974).

11. Josue de Castro, *The Geography of Hunger* (Boston: Little, Brown and Co., 1952), pp. 160–2.

12. Pierre Pradervand, "The Neo-Malthusian Myth," *Africa Report*, July-August 1974, p. 34.

13. Harold Shane, "Education for Tomorrow's World," *The Futurist*, June 1973, p. 104.

14. Robert and Leona Reinow, "Moment in the Sun," cited in Ehrlich, *The Population Bomb*, p. 149.

15. Stewart Udall in *The 99th Hour*, Daniel O. Price, ed. (Chapel Hill: University of North Carolina Press, 1967).

16. *Christian Century*, October 9, 1974, p. 935.

17. McNamara, *One Hundred Countries, Two Billion People*, pp. 40–41.

18. Estelle Rountree and Hugh Halverstadt, *Sometimes They Cry* (New York: Friendship Press, 1970).

19. Lester Brown, *In the Human Interest*, p. 157.

20. Mark Hatfield, speech delivered to Conservative Baptist Association of America Convention, June 18, 1974, quoted in *The Church Herald*, July 26, 1974, p. 13.

21. Ehrlich, *The Population Bomb*, p. 134.

Chapter 8: Food Production

1. Abbreviated from an article by Joseph Lelyveld in *The New York Times*, August 28, 1974.

2. Quoted in the *Wall Street Journal*, October 7, 1974.

3. Roger Revelle, "Can the Earth Feed the Growing Multitudes?" *UNESCO Courier*, July-August 1974.

4. Philip W. Quigg, "World Environment Newsletter," *Saturday Review/World*, October 9, 1973, p. 39.

5. Graham T. T. Molitor, "The Coming World Struggle for Food," *The Futurist*, August 1974, p. 177.

6. "Running Out of Food?" *Newsweek*, November 11, 1974, p. 67.

7. I. Rosier, *El Pueblo*, p. 94.

8. "Running Out of Food," p. 67.

9. Lester Brown, "Scarce Food: Here to Stay," *The Washington Post*, July 15, 1973, quoted in *Current*, September 1973, p. 59.

10. Quoted in *New York Times*, August 21, 1974.

Chapter 9: Food Consumption

1. From a UPI news report published in the *Charleston Evening Post*, Charleston, S.C., Dec. 12, 1974, p. 8A.

2. *Consumer Reports*, September 1974.

3. Frances M. Lappé, *Diet for a Small Planet* (New York: Ballantine Books, 1971), p. 3.

4. Deut. 24:19, KJV.

5. Luke 12:13–21; Luke 16:19–21, NEB.

6. Vernard Eller, *The Simple Life: The Christian Stance Toward Possessions* (Grand Rapids, Mich.: Wm. B. Eerdmans, 1973), p. 20.

7. Reay Tannahill, *Food in History* (New York: Stein & Day, 1973), pp. 311–13.

8. Frances M. Lappé, "Fantasies of Famine," *Harper's,* February 1975.

9. Georg Borgstrom, *The Food and People Dilemma* (Belmont, Calif.: Duxbury Press, 1973).

10. *Consumer Reports,* September 1974.

11. Ibid.

12. Lappé, *Diet for a Small Planet,* p. 9.

13. Molitor, "The Coming World Struggle for Food," p. 172.

14. "Running Out of Food?" p. 58.

15. Georg Borgstrom, "The Dual Challenge of Health and Hunger— A Global Crisis," Population Reference Bureau "Selection" No. 31, January 1970.

16. The story of the Barick family is adapted from the *National Observer,* September 21, 1974.

17. *Time,* November 11, 1974.

18. Ibid.

19. de Jesus, *Child of the Dark,* p. 45.

Chapter 10: Development

1. Joe Kimmins, *Development—It's Why We're Walking,* pamphlet issued by Freedom from Hunger Foundation, 1717 H Street, N.W., Washington, D.C. 20006.

2. McNamara, *One Hundred Countries, Two Billion People,* p. 8.

3. Tibor Mende, "The Development Crisis, The Real Questions," *Cooperation Canada,* January-February 1973.

4. Ibid., p. 107.

5. Peter T. White, "Tanzania Marches to Its Own Drum," *National Geographic,* April 1975.

6. Quoted in Thomas Fenton, "Coffee, The Rules of the Game, and You."

7. Quoted in Gunnar Myrdal, *The Challenge of World Poverty,* p. 349.

8. Michael Hudson, *Super Imperialism: The Economic Strategy of American Empire* (New York: Holt, Rinehart & Winston, 1972), p. 132.

9. *U.S. News and World Report,* December 17, 1973.

10. Haq, "The Crisis in Development Strategies," p. 4.

11. Julius Nyerere, "Our Independence Is Not for Sale," *Africa,* May 1974.

12. Haq, "The Crisis in Development Strategies," p. 3.

13. Myrdal, *The Challenge of World Poverty,* p. 267.

14. Schumacher, *Small Is Beautiful,* p. 159.

15. *Congressional Record,* December 4, 1974, vol. 120, no. 168.

16. I. W. Moomaw, *Crusade Against Hunger* (New York: Harper & Row, 1966), p. 27.

PART III. RESPONDING TO HUNGER

Chapter 12: Response

1. *The New York Times,* December 4, 1974.

2. T. S. Eliot, "A Dialogue on Dramatic Poetry," *Selected Essays 1917–1932* (New York: Harcourt Brace, 1932), pp. 31–45).

3. Lappé, *Diet for a Small Planet,* pp. xii–xiii.

4. Paul Ehrlich and Anne Ehrlich, *The End of Affluence* (New York: Ballantine Books, 1974), p. 213.

5. Morris, *Include Me Out!*, p. 41.
6. Quoted in Morris, ibid.